The Economics of Political Instability

A Westview Replica Edition

The concept of Westview Replica Editions is a response to the continuing crisis in academic and informational publishing. Library budgets for books have been severely curtailed. Ever larger portions of general library budgets are being diverted from the purchase of books and used for data banks, computers, micromedia, and other methods of information retrieval. Interlibrary loan structures further reduce the edition sizes required to satisfy the needs of the scholarly community. Economic pressures (particularly inflation and high interest rates) on the university presses and the few private scholarly publishing companies have severely limited the capacity of the industry to properly serve the academic and research communities. As a result, many manuscripts dealing with important subjects, often representing the highest level of scholarship, are no longer economically viable publishing projects--or, if accepted for publication, are typically subject to lead times ranging from one to three years.

Westview Replica Editions are our practical solution to the problem. We accept a manuscript in camera-ready form, typed according to our specifications, and move it immediately into the production process. As always, the selection criteria include the importance of the subject, the work's contribution to scholarship, and its insight, originality of thought, and excellence of exposition. The responsibility for editing and proofreading lies with the author or sponsoring institution. We prepare chapter headings and display pages, file for copyright, and obtain Library of Congress Cataloging in Publication Data. A detailed manual contains simple instructions for preparing the final typescript, and our editorial staff is always available to answer questions.

The end result is a book printed on acid-free paper and bound in sturdy library-quality soft covers. We manufacture these books ourselves using equipment that does not require a lengthy make-ready process and that allows us to publish first editions of 300 to 600 copies and to reprint even smaller quantities as needed. Thus, we can produce Replica Editions quickly and can keep even very specialized books in print as long as there is a demand for them.

About the Book and Author

The Economics of Political Instability:
The Nigerian-Biafran War
E. Wayne Nafziger

Integrating the political scientist's view of political instability with the economist's analysis of inequality, deprivation, and competition, this book examines the economic determinants and consequences of the 1967-1970 Nigerian-Biafran war. Dr. Nafziger critiques the "ethnic," "Praetorian," and "Marxist" approaches to domestic conflict, maintaining that insufficient attention has been given to the processes by which colonialism and post-colonial dependency, by intensifying regional and class conflict, increase the probability of internal political strife. His detailed examination of the civil war in Nigeria and a comparative case study of Pakistan demonstrate the effects of a variety of economic factors on domestic political violence--among them international dependence, economic development, regional differences, ethnic competition, income disparities, class antagonisms, agrarian discontent, worker strikes, and unemployment. Presenting new paradigms and hypotheses for scholars studying political instability in the Third World, the book also includes extensive economic data from Nigerian government sources.

Dr. Nafziger, a professor of economics at Kansas State University, is the author of many books and articles on Africa and development.

To Brian and Kevin
May they contribute to a more just and stable world.

The Economics of Political Instability

The Nigerian-Biafran War

E. Wayne Nafziger

Westview Press / Boulder, Colorado

A Westview Replica Edition

Published in 1983 in the United States of America by
Westview Press, Inc.
5500 Central Avenue
Boulder, Colorado 80301
Frederick A. Praeger, President and Publisher

Library of Congress Cataloging in Publication Data
Nafziger, E. Wayne
The economics of political instability.
(A Westview Replica Edition)
Bibliography: p.223 Index: p.237
1. Nigeria--Economic conditions--1960- . 2. Nigeria--Politics and government--1960-1975. 3. Nigeria--History--Civil War, 1967-1970. 4. Political stability--Nigeria--History. I. HC1055.N33 330.9669'05 82-20044
ISBN 0-86531-932-4

Printed and bound in the United States of America

10 9 8 7 6 5 4 3 2 1

Contents

Tables and Figures

Tables

Figures

Acknowledgments

I did the research for this book at the Economic Development Institute, University of Nigeria, Enugu (1964-65), Ahmadu Bello University, Zaria (1969, 1970), and the University of Ibadan (1976) with funds from the University of Denver Graduate School of International Studies, the Social Science Foundation, the American Philosophical Society, and Kansas State University (KSU). Douglas Rimmer, John Fage, and A.F. Robertson arranged my 1976 sabbatical affiliation as Honorary Research Fellow at the University of Birmingham's Centre of West African Studies, and Visiting Scholar at the University of Cambridge's African Studies Centre.

Colleagues attending my lectures at the African Institute of the Soviet Academy of Sciences (Moscow), a U.S. Department of State Conference on Nigeria, and a KSU history seminar, in 1978-79, contributed to the study. I also benefited from the comments and criticisms of Gregory Dennis, William Richter, Robin Cohen, Michael Suleiman, Aruna Michie, Robin Higham, Ted Robert Gurr, A.H.M. Kirk-Green, Robert Melson, Richard Sklar, and Crawford Young.

Milton Manuel, John Due, David Norman, Vernon Larson, and William Stamey supported my research and writing. The Fulbright Foundation arranged a visit to Pakistan in early 1971. Susie Winkler and Debbie Rowland typed, and Lowell Brandner and Karen McCulloh edited the final manuscript. I tested many ideas with my wife, Elfrieda. She, Brian, and Kevin tolerated inconveniences, and assumed responsibilities to leave me more time for research. I am grateful to all who helped, but I am solely responsible for any weaknesses.

I received permission to reprint Figure 1.3 from the *Times*, 1 December 1977. Portions of "Biafra and Bangladesh: The Political Economy of Secessionist Conflict," written jointly with William Richter, in the *Journal of Peace Research*, XIII, No. 2 (1976), 91-109, were reprinted with the publisher and co-author's permissions. Tables 2.4, 2.5, 2.6, and the appendix to chapter 2 were reprinted from *African Capitalism: A Case Study in Nigerian Entrepreneurship*, by E. Wayne Nafziger, with the permission of the publishers, Hoover Institution Press, Copyright © 1977.

E. Wayne Nafziger
Kansas State University

Introduction: An Economic Approach to Internal Political Instability

> The problems of violence still remain very obscure.
>
> Hannah Arendt, *On Violence*, 1969.

> The term "ethnic" is one of the vaguest known to sociology. We use it here merely to designate a state of fact, going in no sense into the question of explaining the fact.
>
> Vilfredo Pareto, *The Mind and Society: A Treatise on General Sociology*, 1923.

This book applies an economist's analysis of inequality, deprivation, and competition to the study of political instability. Its major focus is domestic political violence in Nigeria, including the two coups d'état of 1966, the Biafran secession of 1967, and the civil war of 1967-70. It attempts to answer two major questions: (1) What were the economic factors that contributed to the Nigerian civil war? (2) What were the economic impacts of that war?

In the final chapter, I use the economic approach to examine the roots of the civil war in Pakistan (March-December 1971), in which East Pakistan won independence as the Republic of Bangladesh.

Pakistan and Nigeria are the two most populous countries that have fought secessionist civil wars since 1960. The analysis of their experiences should provide a starting point for scholars seeking to generalize about Afro-Asian internal political instability.

To understand political instability, researchers using an economic perspective ask some of the following questions:

What have been the impacts of colonialism on (1) communal economic competition, (2) uneven rates of modernization, (3) regional educational differences, and (4) the post-colonial economic elite?

How much does economic dependence on developed countries limit the ability of a third-world polity to cope with political crises?

What impacts do class formation and conflict, economic inequality and deprivation, labor and student unrest, worker strikes, the discontent of the educated classes, and seniority, recruitment, and promotion patterns in the army have on the potential for internal war?

What are the origins of regional and communal economic conflicts that give rise to political disintegration?

What impact might an abrupt change in regional economic performance, such as the rapid expansion of crude-oil output in Eastern Nigeria in the early 1960s, have on the costs and benefits of secession?

That economic factors, including the international economic context, need to be considered implies that several prevailing approaches are not adequate. In the most frequently used approach (the "ethnic model" of internal political violence), language, race, tribe, religion, national origin, or some other cultural sense of identity is considered the primary factor contributing to conflict. Huntington's "Praetorian" model indicates that political decay and instability depend on the level of political participation relative to political institutionalization. For Gurr, relative deprivation, the "perceived discrepancy between men's value expectations and their value capabilities," increases the potential for political violence.[1] Contemporary Marxists, although emphasizing such economic factors as class conflict and imperialist economic domination, neglect the economic roots of regional and communal conflict.[2] My economic approach differs from Dudley's application of game theory, from Post and Vickers's ethnic model, and from Kirk-Greene's theory of fear, all used to explain the Nigerian-Biafran war.[3] But the following assessment of their models is a base for understanding the need for an approach that emphasizes economic factors, without adopting Marxist economic determinism.

APPROACHES TO DOMESTIC POLITICAL INSTABILITY

Ethnic Models

For Rabushka and Shepsle, ethnic groups are products of "primordial sentiments," based on "permanent and separate histories, separate social institutions, customs and practices, and separate leaders." The distinguishing feature "of the plural society . . . is the practice of politics almost exclusively along ethnic lines." The primary task in such societies "is the subordination of 'primordial sentiments' to the requirements of civil politics." Individual tastes, values, and preferences, whose origins are not probed, are aggregated into collective choices on the basis of a political decision function, e.g., dictatorship, majority rule, or unanimity. Conflict between communities arises from the incompatibility of their collective choices (or "ethnic preference functions"). The political entrepreneur or politician aggregates preferences, while manipulating social cleavages and exploiting or suppressing conflict in politically salient ways.

Rabushka and Shepsle state that plural societies tend to move through historical stages from ethnic cooperation before independence to competition after independence. Leaders left out of the ruling coalition appeal to ethnic chauvinism, exacerbating communal hostility and competition, which leads to political violence and the eventual breakdown of democratic procedures.

Although Rabushka and Shepsle question its feasibility in light of anti-colonial sentiments of most citizens of imperialist societies, "colonial or foreign rule represents . . . one solution for the problem of ethnic conflict that so often disturbs the peace in plural societies. Since independence provides the prize of decision-making authority over which communal groups inevitably fight, continued colonial rule precludes the crystallization of interethnic hostility.[4]

Although Rabushka and Shepsle present many quantitatively elaborate theoretical tools, the tools do not fit into a comprehensive conceptual scheme. A number of their basic concepts are unclear or inadequate, and their reasoning is often circular. Despite their seeking a "theoretical model of democratic instability," they conclude " . . . neither to move cautiously towards the formation of a few tentative hypotheses, to allude to problems of measurement, nor to get lost in a maze of methodological discussion." A crucial concept, democratic society, is not defined, nor are its attributes distinguished from an undemocratic, plural society.

Their finding that conflict in the plural society is based on ethnic competition is a tautology, because the distinguishing feature of plural societies is the practice of ethnic politics. I discuss why political entrepreneurs and leaders consider ethnicity salient for political mobilization rather than other forms of social stratification, such as class, economic group, or occupation in chapter 4 (Nigeria) and chapter 9 (Pakistan). The controversy is not over ethnic conflict, but its explanation. Rabushka and Shepsle do not analyze the origins of ethnicity, which is regarded as a primordial sentiment. In contrast, my "political economy" approach views ethnic identity as being influenced by, among other things, a wide range of economic conditions.

In setting stages from pre-independence cooperation to post-independence competition, Rabushka and Shepsle assume that colonial rule dampened ethnic conflict, that colonial power ceased to influence communal hostility after independence, and communal conflict increased substantially after independence. Actually, British and French colonial rule created or exacerbated differences of caste, region, and community among people they colonized. The British tended to establish separate institutions for different communities in Nigeria and the Indian sub-continent (which included present-day India, Pakistan, and Bangladesh). British hegemony was exercised in Northern Nigeria, India, Malaya, and Uganda under various forms of "indirect rule," an arrangement beneficial to the colonial power and the indigenous rulers of the affected areas. Protecting loyal communities, such as the Muslims in India and the Northern traditional aristocracy in Nigeria, impeded assimilation and integration. In India, conflict and competition between Hindu and Muslim led ultimately to partition and the creation of Pakistan. The Indian army was recruited among usually loyal ethnic groups regarded as "martial races," including the Pathan and Punjabi Muslims for what became West Pakistan, but excluding Bengalis in what became East Pakistan. Ethnic imbalance in the army, a colonial legacy, contributed to animosity between East and West Pakistan after independence. When the French were the mandatory power (1920-43), they drew the boundary line between Lebanon and Syria to favor their Christian allies in Mt. Lebanon, supported reserving the posts of president and army commander to the Maronite Christians, and established sectarian social and political institutions, which maintained Christian majorities in the parliament, cabinet, and civil service.

After the independence of the Indian sub-continent and Nigeria, British policy of military and economic assistance favored the ethnic and regional groups that remained in harmony with British interests. In Lebanon, the United States and other western powers provided military and economic assistance to support rightists (predominantly Maronite Christians) who favored integration with international capitalism, and to pressure leftists (disproportionally Muslim and Druze) and (in the 1970s) Palestinians. Class antagonisms in newly emerging countries, which Rabushka and Shepsle neglect, were also a product of policies and relationships of the colonial era, and post-colonial economic and military support for cooperating elites.

According to Nordlinger, successful conflict-regulating practices worked out by conflicting groups in societies with deep ethnic divisions include stable governing coalitions, allocation according to proportionality, mutual veto, purposive depoliticization, compromise, and concession. Without any of these six practices, democratic majoritarianism or building a national identity is not a suitable way to regulate severe conflicts. To regulate conflict, elites must have some common motives, such as avoiding external threat, economic loss, bloodshed, and suffering within their own segments, or acquiring or retaining political power.

The emergence of conciliatory attitudes among elites is enhanced by their political security and predominance. Among contemporary nonwestern societies, socioeconomic modernization reduces the likelihood of conflict-regulating outcomes, because it further exacerbates intense conflicts, promotes rejection of regulatory practices by the masses, and facilitates a violent response.[5]

Looking at Afro-Asian polities, Nordlinger, like Rabushka and Shepsle, neglects historical factors, including colonialism, which contribute to differences in political culture and economic interest at the elite level. A historical glimpse also would assist in identifying regulatory processes or conflict exacerbators that have persisted over time. Neither does Nordlinger discuss the differential impact of military assistance, economic aid, and foreign investment upon class and communal groups after independence, all factors that frequently contribute to instability.

Nordlinger devotes little attention to the way economic and class differences give rise to conflict. For him, in deeply divided societies, as Nigeria in 1964-65, class identities are rarely of equal salience to ethnic loyalties, when the two compete. When cleavages coincide, in his view, mild conflicts can be transformed into intense conflicts. In Eastern Nigeria, status as a refugee or factory worker reinforced an Ibo identity, while Northern identity was supported by being a worker or trader competing with an Easterner, or a ruling bureaucrat.

Although elites may be responsive to nonelite wishes and demands, Nordlinger thinks that only elites can make a direct and positive contribution to the development and implementation of conflict-regulating practices, because nonelites are too numerous, scattered, fragmented, weak, and unskilled to work out and operate such mechanisms. Since elite predominance helps regulate conflict, the major positive role of nonelites is to allow their leaders to work out conflict-regulating practices and accept them.

My view, however, is that elites, by maintaining and enhancing their power and benefits, often by pursuing economic policies that favor their benefactors from developed capitalist countries, contribute to a worsening conflict with workers and peasants. In Nigeria, attempts by elites to be politically secure at the regional and federal levels, and to provide and expand perquisites, privileges, and patronage for clients, exacerbated political instability. Regional economic elites in Nigeria were major contributors to, not resolvers of, the conflict. In Lebanon in 1975-76, civil authority broke down partly because the traditional Muslim confessional-feudal leadership (*za'im*) no longer represented the Muslim masses and could not control them. Finally, Nordlinger correctly indicates that modernization can increase expectations, social mobilization, and political participation. Still anxieties and fears that exacerbate communal conflict among lower classes put pressure on regional and ethnic elites, which intensifies conflict.

Glazer and Moynihan's 1963 study of blacks, Puerto Ricans, Jews, Italians, and Irish of New York City suggests that ethnic communities not only survive in a highly modernized society, but that they also continue to be a focus for the mobilization of the pursuit of group or individual interests.[6] In a 1975 volume, Glazer and Moynihan argue that ethnicity is the most effective basis for asserting interests in society. But they did not explain why ethnic identity is more salient than other forms of attachments. Bell, a contributor to their volume, indicates that ethnicity is more salient because of its affective ties and common identifications--language, food, music, and names--while other social roles are more abstract and impersonal. Since a class tie, "with its overtones of social differentiation . . . carries with it . . . a lowered social ranking and esteem and a sense of inferiority [it] reduces the ability of a class identification to be an effective source of cohesion." Class attachments and economic position are thus weaker and less persistent than ethnic ties as primary factors contributing to social division and conflict.[7]

A weakness of focusing on ethnicity is that it tends to reduce the emphasis on class antagonisms, economic discontent, and power disparities. The preoccupation of western intellectuals and journalists with conflicts between Christians and Muslims in Nigeria and Lebanon, between regions in Pakistan, or among Yorubas, Ibos, and Hausas in Nigeria deemphasizes antagonisms between workers, on the one hand, and government and capitalists, on the other. And, as Dahl contends, ethnic identification is strongest where members are predominantly of one class, such as the proletariat.[8] Although Glazer and Moynihan complain that the category "worker" or "white collar employee" is too broad or diffuse to be politically useful, one can also question whether a highly aggregated group like white Anglo-Saxon Americans, Scots, or Yorubas share enough interests for these designations to be useful categories for discussion.

For Anderson, von der Mehden, and Young, ethnic identity is less a "primordial" phenomenon than an awareness formed in the process of modern social competition and political mobilization. The salience of multiple levels of identities--extended family, subgroup, clan, ethnic or linguistic community, nation-state, or world region--varies, depending on the nature of social interaction and conflict. Thus, for example, in Zaïre in the 1950s and early 1960s, Mongo self-awareness grew with the competition for education, government jobs, and political office, but declined after President Mobutu Sese Seko seized power in 1965, regrouped provinces, and eliminated competitive electoral politics.[9] On the other hand, Ibo identity in Nigeria, enhanced by the competition for benefits from the nationalist movement and decolonization from the 1940s through the early 1960s, increased in the mid and late 1960s with the competition for government jobs, the election crises, the 1966 coups, the politicization of the army, the violence against Ibos in the North, the return of the Ibo to his ethnic homeland, the interregional contention for oil revenues, and the Biafran secession and civil war.

Melson and Wolpe, who examined Nigeria in the 1960s, also challenge the premise that new roles created with economic development and social change undercut "tribalism" and communalism. Instead, modernization reinforces communal conflict and creates conditions that lead to new communal groups and ethnic identities. They credit Nigeria's relatively rapid economic growth for "sowing the seeds" of the nation's communal conflict in the late 1960s.[10] Actually, comparative cross-national data, subject to wide error, do not clearly indicate that Nigeria's economic growth was above average for developing countries in the 1960s.[11] Furthermore, Hibbs's survey of several quantitative studies indicates, if anything, a positive relationship between economic development and domestic political stability.[12] In fact, rapid economic growth should help political leaders satisfy the demands of many interest groups. Thus, an alternative hypothesis to Melson and Wolpe's is that political frustrations and communal mobilization increased as the gap between social aspirations and economic development widened in Nigeria in the early 1960s.[13]

Melson and Wolpe also contend that differential rates of development between communal groups and attempts to narrow the differences exacerbate communal conflict.[14] Southern Nigeria had more experience in parliamentary government, higher literacy, and higher economic development than Northern Nigeria. Northerners resented the disproportionate representation of southerners in skilled positions in the army and civil service, and the immigration of southern entrepreneurs and technicians to the North. Policies of regional discrimination and protection in the North to reduce sub-national differences, and responses to the policies in the south, contributed to the bitter enmity that broke up the Nigerian federation (see chapter 4). Thus Melson and Wolpe's contention, which holds true in the Nigerian case, can serve as a hypothesis for cross-national testing.

Young, like other students of communalism, regards ethnicity, language, culture, religion, and caste as crucial determinants of political alignment and conflict. But in refining an explanatory framework developed in collaboration with Anderson and von der Mehden, Young views communal identity, not as congealed into a firmly fixed position, but as subject to continual change and readjustment from such social transformations as urbanization, increased communication, literacy, and education. He recognizes the ways colonial policy creates and shapes ethnic identity, how communal strength is affected by foreign military and political support and intervention, how ethnic configuration varies with changes in political structure and social conflict, and how ethnic interaction depends on the relationship of international factors to the country. Although he focuses on ethnic identification, he suggests that "cultural pluralism has nothing to do with the general causes of insurrection." Once political violence takes place, however, ethnicity acts as a lens through which individuals and groups try to understand the composition of the insurgents and the nature of social competition.

In discussing the relationship between social stratification and communal cleavages, Young indicates that unequal social opportunities between ethnic communities result in an overlap between ethnicity and class. But the salient identity in explaining political conflict is ethnicity, not class. Thus, his two chapters on Nigeria fail to mention how class identification contributes to political violence, for example in the general strike by workers, the long-standing grievances by Western cocoa farmers concerning the wide spread between world and producer prices, and the low morale among junior army officers (chapter 3), which contributed to the overthrow of the 1960-66 civilian regime. Young maintains that the "politics of communal distribution, as in . . . first republic Nigeria, leaves little place for class-oriented ideologies." And he does not discuss such other crucial economic factors as the expansion of Eastern Nigeria's crude-oil industry, with its implications for the levels of living, foreign exchange position, government finance, and the international political power of an independent region, on Biafran secession, or the parallel effects of East Pakistan's strong prospective international balance-of-payments position on the viability of Bangladesh secession.[15]

The "Praetorian" Model

Huntington considers "political underdevelopment . . . [in] the modernizing countries of Asia, Africa, and Latin America" one of the urgent problems in international politics. At the roots of the underdevelopment and instability are high levels of popular mobilization and mass participation in politics (an "excess of democracy") in relation to the institutional capacity to absorb new participants or "social forces." An example of such forces is a previously quiescent ethnic, religious, regional, economic, or status group who begin to participate in politics, usually after urbanization, industrialization, literacy, education, or other manifestations of modernization. A given group that promotes members' interests in conflict with the interests of other groups is a social force. The heterogeneity of ethnic groups (primordial social forces) contributes to political instability, as in the Nigerian insurgency of the mid-1960s.

Huntington's goal (political order) is achieved by maintaining "the authority, effectiveness, and legitimacy of government." When a group maintains order, resolves disputes, selects authoritative leaders, and thus promotes community among social forces, it is a political institution. Political institutionalization is associated with "the capacity to create public interests," defined in terms of "the concrete interests of the governing institutions," and not with natural law, justice, right reason, the will of the majority, a specific class, or the result of the competitive political process.

The public interest of the U.S.S.R., for example, is approximated by the statement: "What's good for the Presidium is good for the Soviet Union." Furthermore, "Praetorian oligarchies may last centuries (while) mass praetorian systems usually (last) only a few years."

Political institutions can be more effective when built under authoritarian military regimes like those of General Ayub Khan in Pakistan and Generals Pak Chung Hee and Kim Chung Pil in South Korea. According to Huntington, the development of political order can be planned and controlled more systematically where state power is concentrated and political participation is limited. In contrast to his view, I argue in chapter 9 that a Praetorian oligarchy, like that of Ayub Khan, contributes to political decay.

A politically underdeveloped society is characterized by a "government with a low level of institutionalization, . . . a weak . . . (and) bad government." Although achieving modernity breeds stability, the process of modernization breeds instability. Effective governments tend to be found in advanced industrial countries--totalitarian or democratic--insulated to political decay and revolution, "the extreme case of the explosion of political participation" relative to political institutionalization.[16]

For Huntington, the state is above the conflicts between parochial interests within society. At times, however, control of the state may be the object of conflict, as when Royalists fought Cromwell's Parliamentary party in the 1642-52 English civil war, and when rightists and leftists clashed in the 1975-76 Lebanese civil war. The state also may be party to the conflict and engage in politically destabilizing activity, as by the Lebanese state militias' attacks (aided by rightist Christian parties) on leftists and Palestinians in the early 1970s, and the 1972 declaration of martial law by President Marcos to overturn the Philippine Supreme Court's decision unfavorable to U.S. property rights.

In the Praetorian model, political order is endangered by threats to government authority and effectiveness, from discontented groups participating in rioting, mob violence, guerrilla insurgencies, and military coups d'état. Political order can best be attained by a consort of elites developing a strong centralized political party, to mobilize the orderly entrance of new "social forces" into politics. The modernization of political institutions does not include developing institutions to disperse power, nor those developed and used by dissidents.

For Huntington, social reform as a response to political dissent is more likely than the alternative response, repression, to result in political decay. Yet evidence from the use of state power in Nigeria and Pakistan, discussed here, contradicts Huntington's analysis. Instead of political instability, regime overthrow, and power transfers by dissenters leading to political decay, they may result in a broader choice for new political institutions and political suzerainty by more "modernizing" classes. Finally, if the disorder from a threat to the stability of the governing elites or centralized political party is accompanied by wider popular participation and self-reliance,[17] the disorder may be preferred to political stability.

When Huntington suggests that the "mitigation of class conflict" in the United States is relevant to other polities, he fails to view class antagonism and labor specialization in an international context. The dominant role of the U.S. in the international capitalist system gives its population disproportional representation in skilled and remunerative positions within the international division of labor. Thus the brunt of exploitation and unrest resulting from class antagonism under capitalism is experienced in developing countries, where unskilled workers and peasants are present in disproportional numbers, not in the United States, where workers are relatively privileged. Huntington also neglects conflict between industrial workers and government, as he assumes that the workers, who are favored by government policy, are almost members of the elite.[18] Chapters 3 and 9 demonstrate the error of that assumption, at least when it is applied to Nigeria or Pakistan.

The "Relative Deprivation" Model

Relative deprivation, a variable linked to the socio-psychological literature on the "frustration-anger-aggression syndrome," in Gurr's view, is the actors' perceptions of discrepancy between goods and conditions they expect and those they can get and keep. Relative deprivation induces social discontent, and sometimes anger, which provides motivation for potential collective violence. The probability of political violence is inversely related to the institutional mechanisms that permit nonviolent hostility to be expressed and is directly related to common experiences and beliefs that sanction violence, and the extent to which groups give normative support, protection from retribution, and cues for violence to the deprived. Political violence refers to all actual and threatened collective attacks within a political community against the political regime, its actors or its policies.

Like Huntington's, Gurr's definition does not consider the state as a possible party to the conflict. Rather than violent interaction between the state and dissidents, riots, guerrilla wars, civil wars, and revolutions are treated as attacks by dissidents on the political regime and its actors. The impact of foreign support for dissidents on the likelihood of internal war is discussed, but not foreign reinforcement for ruling groups engaged in politically destabilizing activity, as in Nigeria and Pakistan before their secessionist conflicts. Political violence is distinguished from other forms of collective violence by "the resort to illicit violence." The role of the state is to regulate and resolve political violence by "policing."[19]

Gurr, with Duvall, later uses a simultaneous equation model with values based on data from 114 nation-states to indicate the way relative deprivation, much of which is economic, influences the magnitude of domestic political violence.[20] That research design improves the precision of estimation and the generality of findings, but several specific problems remain: (1) the quantitative indicators used to express relative economic deprivation are inadequate; (2) it is difficult to measure the magnitude of internal political violence; (3) the causal relationship between composite indicators is often unclear; and (4) cross-national data on regional, communal, and class disparities are rarely available, especially in comparable forms. These weaknesses are discussed in chapter 10.

A Marxist Model

In Baran's explanation of economic backwardness and political instability, the chance for an indigenously derived capitalist revolution in less developed countries was retarded by western economic and political suzerainty, especially in the colonial period. Capitalism entered not through the growth of small competitive firms, but rather by transfer from abroad of advanced monopolistic business. The comprador bourgeoisie, who lacked the strength to spearhead the thoroughgoing institutional change needed for major capital accumulation, was compelled to seek allies among other classes. In certain instances, the bourgeoisie tried to ally with moderate leaders of workers and peasants to form a progressive coalition with a "New Deal" orientation (such as the Congress Party government under Nehru in India). At the outset the popular movement was essentially democratic, anti-feudal, and anti-imperialist, and supported domestic capitalism. The native capitalist middle classes, however, were either unwilling or unable to provide leadership for a sustained economic development to ameliorate the poverty and subjugation of the masses. In time, the local bourgeoisie, frightened by the threat of labor radicalism and populist upheaval and their possible implications for the expropriation of capital and abolition of property ownership, were impelled into an alliance with the landed interests, and those governments supporting the foreign bourgeoisie that could provide economic and military assistance to stave off impending disaster.

Differences within this "counter-revolutionary" coalition are much less than its common interest in preventing socialism. The coalition is incapable of significantly raising the rate capital is accumulated through such measures as a progressive tax system to eliminate nonessential consumption, channeling landed aristocracy savings into productive investment, and undertaking substantial public investment in sectors where private capital does not venture, where monopolistic controls block expansion, or where social overhead projects are necessary. This conservative alliance thrusts the popular forces even farther along the road of radicalism and revolt, leading to further polarization. Such an alliance increasingly encounters peasant uprisings, violent strikes, guerrilla warfare, and other forms of political violence led by the lower classes, which usually culminate in "sweeping away the holdover institutions of a defunct age," the expropriation of land and capital, and the establishment of a new regime based on the "ethos of collective effort, the creed of the predominance of the interests of society over the interests of selected few."[21]

Although Baran's approach helps explain the difficulties that reformed capitalism encounters in attempts to provide economic development to the masses in less developed countries, his theory is limited in explaining political violence there. While some indigenous agents, managers, merchants, industrialists, bureaucrats, and politicians benefit considerably from foreign capital, technology, and manpower, some native capitalists' interests compete with foreign businesses. Such indigenous capitalists, with their allies, typically provide leadership for independence.[22] They then may grow in strength as the colonial economic nexus gradually declines. Economic policy under a coalition of national capitalists and politico-bureaucratic classes may be oriented toward an erosion of foreign capital power. Furthermore, divisions within the indigenous bourgeoisie between allies and competitors of foreign businessmen can be a source of political instability.

Neither does Baran pay attention to conflicts between regional and communal elites that contribute to domestic political violence. This is not to suggest that class conflict is absent in domestic war in developing societies, but regional and ethnic factors, which Baran neglects or denies as salient, also are important. In this study, I examine both class and communal conflicts.

APPROACHES TO THE NIGERIAN CIVIL WAR

Game Theory

Dudley's insightful study of political instability in Nigeria investigates (1) the January 1966 overthrow of the parlimentary government, (2) the subsequent transfer of power from Major C.K. Nzeogwu, the only mutineer not quelled, to the general officer commanding the Nigerian Army (G.O.C.), Major General J.T. Aguiyi-Ironsi, (3) factors contributing to the disillusionment with the Ironsi regime and its eventual overthrow, (4) the growing rift between the federal and Eastern regional military governments after the July 1966 coup, (5) the events leading to Biafran secession and the civil war, and (6) the broad movements of the war that led to the federal victory. Dudley's conceptual scheme applies game theory to the maneuverings to form coalitions among Nigeria's three major regional elite groups (supported by political parties in the civilian era) with bases in the North, East, and West. In his view, political actors in Nigeria perceive politics as a "zero-sum" game, in which the winner takes all. Furthermore, the failure of the political elite to adhere to the established rules of the political "game" was one of the major contributors to political disorder. But he largely abandons his highly formalized model--with concepts of least-cost winning coalition, vote-cost relationship, political transaction exchanges, corruption coefficients, dialectical constitutive and regulative rules, violence as a lagged function of corruption, and action sets of political support and rewards--when discussing events of the 1960s in Nigeria, perhaps because the model is inadequate for analyzing the complex political crisis that he recounts so well.

Dudley does not ignore the way Nigerian dependence on the international economy and international policy affects the broad movements of the war. Like the official federal Nigerian view, Dudley blames the French government, the African governments recognizing Biafra, the church aid organizations, the relief agencies, and the mercenaries not only for prolonging the war, but also for contributing to more deaths on both sides. But he fails to consider the effect of international dependency on the economic and political weaknesses of the parliamentary regime, 1960-66. Unlike many political analysts Dudley is cognizant of the impact of rapidly expanding crude-petroleum output in Eastern Nigeria on its aspirations for secession, but he does not mention labor unrest, class conflict, or the 1964 general strike, possibly because he does not perceive this discontent as being based on real deprivation. He points out that unskilled urban workers already earn almost three times the average per capita income.[23] Finally, even though it is true that poisoned relationships under the Ironsi government contributed to the massacres of Ibos in the North in 1966, Dudley, like the official Nigerian government position of the late 1960s, underestimates the wide support for anti-Ibo measures in the North, and overemphasizes the link between the January 1966 conspirators and the Ironsi government, and the government's link with the movement for Biafran secession.

Ethnic Pluralism

Post and Vickers state that "tribalism", the "primordial" loyalty, a total commitment transcending that to any other group, was the root of regional conflict in Nigeria. Its "Structural Frame" (constitutional and institutional matrix), in which each of the three major ethnic communities, Hausa-Fulani, Ibo, and Yoruba, was identified with a region and a political party, intensified ethnic disparities and self-awareness, control by communal elites of the share of the rewards of the regions, competition by elites for fruits of the center, and alienation of regional minorities. Most Nigerian politicians in the early 1960s merely wanted to continue and stabilize a system to distribute rewards to the regional elites. But by 1964, so much of the population had been mobilized into political participation that the system of rewards failed to "pay off" enough people to be viable.

These authors' account of shifting fortunes and alliances of the major parties and regional elites of the Nigerian parliamentary government, and the detailed narrative and diagnosis of the elections of 1964 and 1965 may be the best yet published. But their analysis of political events is not enhanced by a series of "models" of a Conglomerate (ethnically plural) Society, with a Structural Frame run by Structural Elites (the military and bureaucracy) and a Political Hierarchy (political elites and those mobilized to participate in politics) whose power is buttressed by a System of Rewards (all their capitalization). In statements such as "The Structural Frame, which located the major control capacities, both political and administrative, in the regions, thus had operated, in conjunction with the System of Rewards, to polarize the conflict into one between North and East," the models substitute for explanations. They permit a brief examination of the colonial basis for ethnic and regional divisions but they do not explain the issues of "neo-colonialism" and international economic dependency raised by the 1964 southern-based political alliance.[24]

Since the study was completed, Post, the senior author, has converted to the view that only Marxism can provide an integrated approach to an explanation of the political system. From his newly found viewpoint, "this study is focused . . . on the superstructural level of institutions and consciousness, and therefore tends to be epiphenomenal in character." Perhaps his new approach would avoid the problem they mention of excluding the behavior of the masses, the analysis of socioeconomic class, and the importance of international economic factors. They defend the exclusion on the grounds that political activity in the 1960s was "determined by an ideology of 'tribalism' rather than class consciousness," and international factors "were not immediately active."[25]

But the factors they exclude are at the center of my analysis in which the ideology of "tribalism" is explained in relation to such economic factors as class formation, class antagonism, economic inequalities, and international economic linkages.

The Theory of Fear

Kirk-Greene's five major causes, of the 1966-70 conflict were: the threat by a regionally based political party to the security of the ruling elites in other regions, the primacy of politics in the formulation of national economic decisions, subordination of the "necessary politico-economic demands of the nation-state" to "loyalty to the dominant ethnic . . . or cultural . . . group", self-perpetuating elites who used patronage to control the politically mobilized stratum below them, and the lack of political unification between Northern and Southern Nigeria during the first half of the twentieth century. Ultimately the war emanated from fear of: constitutional imbalance, uneven distribution, threat to traditional values, regional inequalities in educational and employment opportunities, and discrimination and penal measures by the political leadership to coerce and convert. Since the greatest source of this fear (*Angst*) was concentrated "regionalism" of the political culture, General Gowon's creating twelve states to replace the four regions in May 1967 (just before Biafran secession) had more potential for suppressing the fear than any other prescription.[26]

Perhaps putting loyalty to the ethnic community above national sentiments produces fewer inter-communal strains and conflicts than do excessive demands for nation building and subordinating sub-national interests to alien interests of the center. In Nigeria, communalism among the Hausa-Fulani, who were underrepresented in business, government service, the professions, and the schools, was exacerbated by the nationalist movement of the late 1940s and early 1950s, and by abolishing the regions and imposing a unitary administration in May 1966. Pakistan's effort to promote Muslim nationalism through an official language, Urdu, written in the Perso-Arabic script, and its ban on songs by Rabindranath Tagore, an esteemed Hindu Bengali man of letters, and on Hindu Bengali festivals, only strengthened Bengali cultural nationalism. Ironically, since the independence of Bangladesh in 1971, the Chakma tribal people have intensified their resistance to Bengali symbols and identification. Attempts to establish Hindi as the sole official language in India led to riots among southerners, especially Tamils, who feared losses in competition for government jobs.

Kirk-Greene's five sources of conflict obviously are not primary variables, but they call for further explanation. "Older . . . socio-cultural antagonisms" and "traditional antipathies" are not merely "carried over" into the sphere of contemporary politics, but ethnic identities and animosities are formed, mobilized, and politicized in the context of competition for the benefits of self-government and modernization. Kirk-Greene also fails to recognize the inherent contradiction built into Nigeria's "zero-sum political game" in the middle 1960s--the fact that the quest for greater security by one regional elite undercut the security of the others.

The charge of the "primacy of politics" in economic decisions, a familiar one in Nigeria, lacks meaning without designating the difference between an economic and a political decision. Because different weights are placed on the benefits of different recipients in economic decisions, considerations of income distribution imply political judgments. Moreover, Kirk-Greene has no explanation for why regional and local interests ("politics") prevail in making national economic decisions.

Finally, it is not clear why fear is the ultimate variable contributing to Nigerian disintegration. Instead it may be that the psychological variable, fear, arises from more objective variables one can measure and analyze, such as conflicts of economic interests between classes or communities, uneven distribution, high economic costs, and low economic integration. Fear by Northerners of economic competition from Ibo petty businessmen, by Yorubas of Ibo competition in the federal civil service, and by Ibo army officers in 1965 of slow promotion[27] had tangible economic bases, as subsequent chapters indicate.

An "African" Approach

Okpaku, editor of *Nigeria: Dilemma of Nationhood*, says it is an African analysis of the Nigerian-Biafran war. Since the "proclamations" of most western scholars and journalists are simple-minded and characterized by "uniform, boldfaced, arrogant ignorance," partly as a result of their "inability or unwillingness to understand the depth of the African mind," the "best of African minds must give their best to the analysis of African problems as they are the only people competent enough and with sufficient commitment to provide solutions to African problems" and with the ability to offer "a more meaningful insight into the crisis."

Although Okpaku's diatribes against the ethnocentrism of American and European Africanists are superficial, the very able collaborators he chooses add substantially to understanding the Nigerian conflict despite their spectrum of views lacking unity and integration.[28]

Ekeh's analysis of the civil war in terms of the intense "primordial" commitments of different ethnic groups is implicitly contradicted by the subsequent contributor, Nnoli, who finds the "genesis" of the hostilities "in economics," arguing that "to say that tribalism [i.e., ethnicity] is the cause is to leave unexplained the cause of tribalism itself." Amoda states that political support of the Nigerian nationalist leaders lay primarily in the peasantry and working classes, while Lawal labels these leaders as a "British-educated 'bourgeois' elite," who were not interested "in the revolutionary overthrow of the colonial system," but in replacing the British exploiters.

Omatete argues that, despite the substantial expense, "in young, unstable countries [like Nigeria], where a national image is just being forged, the intelligence system has to have information on citizens . . ., for such countries are vulnerable to danger from within." His view would not be accepted by Lawal, who sees the state as an instrument of the ruling economic class who exploit the masses. Nor would Okpaku accept that view while arguing for the establishment and protection of civil rights, leading to a postwar state where Nigerians are "taught the limitations on the powers of the government, the public official, the soldier, the policeman, and the man next door. . . . [A] citizen should know that he cannot be searched indiscriminately by anyone, [and] that he cannot be insulted or struck by any policeman or soldier."[29]

Amoda deals skillfully with the divisions of the Nigerian nationalist movement, the origins of Nigerian political parties, and the association of each with a particular ethnic community, but he tends to overemphasize the clash in values between North and south, neglecting somewhat the intense competition between the two areas for the benefits of modernization. Useful in understanding the tripartite political struggle among the three majority groups are Ekeh's distinctions among regional majorities (Eastern Ibos, Northern Hausa-Fulanis, and Western Yorubas), the minorities in the regions, and the marginals (such as Western Ibos and Northern Yorubas, with ethnic affiliations with one of the majority groups but placed in a different region). His distinctions also help explain why secessionist tendencies were concentrated among majorities, why minorities and marginals tended to identify with a strong central government, and the impact of the twelve-state structure decreed in May 1967 on strengthening minorities and marginals relative to majorities. But his preoccupation with whether commitments to Nigeria and Biafra were narrow primordial or broader civic identities seems hairsplitting when nationalism is viewed as a phenomenon that can be associated with a nation-state or ethnic, cultural, regional, or language community.[30]

Nnoli's analysis of external economic and political intervention, and international linkages contributing to instability is useful. But when considering "socialism . . . the answer to the problems of tribalism," his selective examples of communal strife and animosity fail to mention nationality problems of Yugoslavia and the Soviet Union. Neither the nature of the socialism he advocates nor the way it would reduce "tribalism" is clear.

Nziramasanga points out the lack of autonomy of African countries which must depend on foreign powers for training, equipment, and sometimes budgets for their armed forces. But his recommendation that the "institution of the tribe" needs to be subordinated to "a well-ordered execution of priorities" in a nation-state with "strong central authority" fails to recognize that nationalism is probably hampered by attempts to repress communal nationalism.

Diejomaoh's analysis is one of the best on regional economic factors related to the conflict, but it does not discuss the *intra*-regional conflicts and such economic factors as class and occupational groups that contributed to disintegration. And it overestimates the economic advantages to the regions from Nigerian federation.[31]

A Political Approach

Nigerian Politics and Military Rule: Prelude to the Civil War, edited by Panter-Brick, has the best political description of events leading to the war. Lloyd's essay on the ethnic background recognizes that hostility derives, not from ethnic differences, but from competition between groups for wealth and power. The essay explains communal hostility in terms of uneven economic and educational development, migration from overpopulated to underpopulated areas, differences in criteria for appointment and position, competition for positions in the modern sector of the economy, and the struggle for political domination, not merely "primordial" factors of "tribe," language, religion, and race.

Panter-Brick's skillful recounting of events between the first coup of January 1966 and the Biafran secession in May 1967, indicates how Ironsi's commitment to a unitary form of government threatened the interests especially of the Northern traditional authorities, educated class, and armed personnel, and led to Ironsi's downfall, and how Gowon was able to consolidate support of the federation except for the Eastern Region for a state of emergency and the creation of twelve states, 27 May 1967, despite a prior polarization between forces backing a looser confederation and those backing a stronger central government with more states. Luckham explains the fragmentation of the army's authority system after the January 1966 coup as a product of the interplay of the small size of the officer corps (especially after the high rate of attrition among senior officers during 1966), the poor discipline resulting from the distorted age and promotional structure determined by the rapid indigenization of the officer corps, cleavages deriving from cliques among peers of the same age and rank, and communal differentiation and political tension resulting from the transfer of power between regions when soldiers ascended to power. Dent discusses the attitudes of the military government toward politicians, its initial failure to appreciate the necessity to fulfill the political function, and the lack of cooperation among political figures until bitter experience under General Ironsi, the supreme commander of the military government in January-July 1966, convinced the subsequent Head of State General Gowon to provide representation of some of the politicians of the first republic.

Dudley explains political disorders in Western Nigeria in 1965 in terms of a struggle between North and East for coalition partners, examines Yoruba disillusionment with the Ironsi military government of the first half of 1966, and analyzes the complex divisions among Yorubas in 1966-67 between federalists and confederalists. Whiteman discusses the factors contributing to a gradual movement toward secession in the East rather than an immediate secession after the 29 July 1966 coup, the role of Eastern minorities opposing Biafran secession and pressing for new states, the strengthening of Ibo communal identity after World War II, the reaction of the East and the rest of the federation to the massacre of Easterners in September-October 1966, and psychological factors that intensified sentiments among the Eastern masses in 1966-67. Panter-Brick and Dawson focus on division within the Northern delegation at the ad hoc constitutional committee meetings in September-October 1966 between those advocating more states and those pressing for confederation, the reason why the delegation eventually consented to the demand for more states, the financial difficulties of Northern states during the war, and the imbalance in availability of manpower among the states.[32]

Lloyd fails to emphasize either the struggle for benefits from petroleum or the regional allocation of revenue as factors exacerbating ethnic hostility. He indicates discontent among younger graduates regarding decreases in openings and promotions in the 1960s. And Luckham mentions a similar frustration by junior army officers, but no one mentions blue-collar workers' discontent with employers and government, which culminated in a general strike in 1964 that substantially weakened the civilian government.

Except for Lloyd's short discussion of regional differences between indirect and direct colonial rule, and uneven regional development, how Nigeria's post-independence political weaknesses arose from the political and economic legacy of colonialism is mostly ignored. Finally, there is almost no emphasis upon the intricate transnational political and economic linkages as factors contributing to the civil war.

THE POLITICAL ECONOMY APPROACH

Early in this chapter, I argue that economic analysis is necessary to understand the origin of domestic political instability. The major differences between the approach of the non-Marxists I reviewed and my "political economy" approach, then, is my emphasis on such economic factors as uneven economic modernization during the colonial period, transnational economic linkages, economic class discrepancies, changes in the relative incomes of class and occupational groups, communal economic competition, regional educational differences, and effects of differential regional economic development on the costs and benefits of political integration.

Baran's Marxist approach emphasizing economic factors differs from my approach in at least two ways. First, my analysis of internal war includes economic conflict between regional and communal elites. Second, rather than limiting my discussion of class conflict to relationships between owners of the dominant mode of production, capital, and the working class, I examine the discontent of relatively deprived classes and economic groups who are not contesting the ownership or control of capital.

After a historical sketch that includes the colonial legacy, my analysis of the Nigerian civil war focuses on the following three variables: (1) transnational economic linkages, (2) class conflict and economic discontent, and (3) regional and communal competition and conflict. (The same three variables are used to analyze the Pakistani civil war in chapter 9.)

Colonial rule affects the rules and institutions for trade and investment, foreign economic ties, elite and class relationships, and the different levels of economic development among various regions and communities after independence. This colonial legacy, together with a sketch of regional conflict and political enmities after independence, is the focus of chapter 1 on Nigeria and a brief portion of the comparative material in chapter 9 on Pakistan.

Only Young, of the non-Marxists reviewed here, analyzes transnational factors contributing to domestic political violence. I discuss Nigeria's transnational linkages in chapter 2, and Pakistan's in chapter 9. The economic and political dependence of less developed countries (LDCs), like Nigeria and Pakistan, on the capitalist developed countries (DCs) hampers the LDCs' internal political integration. DCs, like the United States, Canada, Western Europe, and Japan, use military and political strength, superior resources, and transnational economic ties with LDCs to keep them dependent. Countries like Nigeria and Pakistan became highly dependent on Britain, the United States, and western capitalist countries for trade, aid, investment, technology, political support, and military assistance, training, and equipment.

Economic, political, and military power enables the DCs to transform conflicts of economic interests between DCs and LDCs into harmonies of interests between elites of both countries. In Nigeria and Pakistan, large portions of the political elite and local bourgeoisie relied on and profited from economic and military assistance and political support from western countries for position, success, and even survival. Economic and political interests of local elites depending on activities of foreigners are constraints on foreign policies and internal socioeconomic policies. Domestic elites, because of their dependence, protect foreign interests, often at the expense of local economic interests. During crises, indigenous elites often acted in harmony with outside economic interests, even when military force and aggressive diplomacy were absent.

Readers will recognize similarities between my approach and Frank's "dependency" theory.[33] Unlike Frank, however, I do *not* argue that dependence causes economic underdevelopment. Instead my analysis concentrates on the way dependence of developing countries helps explain their internal political instability.

The common interest between elites in DCs and LDCs corresponds to disharmony of interest in the poor country, which results in political discontent and the potential for political violence. The following types of conflicts of interest exist in LDCs: those between (1) the elites and masses, (2) upper and lower elites, (3) "comprador" and national elites, and (4) different groups of regional or communal elites. The first and second (class conflicts), the focus of chapter 3, are based on property ownership, education, position in the bureaucracy, and occupational group interests. The third conflict, in the background of the transnational relations in chapter 2 and a section in chapter 9, is between "compradors," i.e., elites who cooperate with or are intermediaries for foreign interests, and elites who compete with these interests.[34]

A wide range of economic conditions affect (4) regional and communal identity and conflict, discussed in chapter 4. These conditions include economic competition for the benefits of employment and business activity, the rise of ethnic consciousness in response to a lack of economic benefits from nationalism or modernization, and the emphasis on cultural identification by governing elites--to divert attention from class antagonisms and economic discontent. The elites accentuate the pre-colonial and colonial identification with ethnic, regional, and speech communities. The elites use these sentiments to transfer potential hostility from class discrepancies within their communities to the rulers and subjects of others.

Although the political economy approach, like the Marxist approach, includes transnational political and economic factors to explain internal war, the two approaches differ in several other respects. Baran recognizes the conflicts between elites and masses, and some other Marxists, the different interests between elites who cooperate and those who compete with foreign interests. But virtually no Marxist acknowledges the conflicts between regional and communal elites emphasized by scholars assuming the "ethnic" model. On the other hand, although these scholars--Rabushka, Shepsle, Nordlinger, Glazer, and Moynihan--provide evidence of ethnic politics, they fail to investigate the underlying bases for communal conflict.

Thus, in the political economy model, the probability of domestic political violence is partly a function of internal economic factors--regional economic rivalries, conflicts among elite groups, class conflict, economic inequality, and domestic economic policy--all of which depend, to a degree, on international variables. And the explanations of the relationships rely in part upon economic analyses of data pertaining to such variables as wage and employment rates, the labor market, agricultural prices, development planning, interregional trade and migration, economic structural change and growth, regional revenue allocation, industrial concentration rates, and patterns of foreign trade, aid, investment, and transfer of technology.

THE ORGANIZATION OF THE BOOK

The discussion of economic factors contributing to the Nigerian civil war includes: chapter 1--a historical sketch; 2--transnational linkages; 3--class conflict and economic discontent; and 4--regional and communal competition and conflict.

Chapters 5-7 analyze the effect of the coups of 1966 and the civil war of 1967-70 on economic activity. Chapter 5 focuses on the war's effect on aggregate variables--output, prices, wages, employment, and the international balance of payments. Chapter 6 looks at the major economic sectors affected by the war: oil, manufacturing, transportation, domestic trade, and agriculture, with primary emphasis on the federal Nigerian economy. Chapter 7 examines the Biafran economy.

Chapter 8 considers the longer run economic impact of the war, while chapter 9 explains the secessionist conflict in Pakistan in 1971, providing further support for a political economy approach to internal conflict in LDSs.

NOTES

1. Alvin Rabushka and Kenneth A. Shepsle, *Politics in Plural Societies: A Theory of Democratic Instability* (Columbus, Ohio: Charles E. Merrill Publishing Co., 1972), pp. 8-10; Samuel P. Huntington, *Political Order in Changing Societies* (New Haven, Conn.: Yale University Press, 1968); and Ted Robert Gurr, *Why Men Rebel* (Princeton, N.J.: Princeton University Press, 1970), p. 13.

2. Paul A. Baran, "On the Political Economy of Backwardness," *The Manchester School*, XX (January 1952), 66-84, and *The Political Economy of Growth* (New York: Monthly Review Press, 1957).

Earlier Marxist writings on national, communal, and regional identity and conflict include Karl Marx, *The Jewish Question* and *The Capacity of Today's Jews and Christians to Become Free*, written in German in 1843, now available as Karl Marx, *A World Without Jews*, Dagobert D. Runes, ed. (New York: The Wisdom Library, 1959); Karl Marx and Friederich Engels, *Ireland and the Irish Question: A Collection of Writings* (New York: International Publishers, 1972), written in German in the nineteenth century; Rosa Luxemburg, *The National Question: Selected Writings* (New York: Monthly Review Press, 1976), written in Polish in 1908-09; Joseph V. Stalin, *Marxism and the National Question*, in Stalin, *Works, 1907-1913*, II (Moscow: Foreign Languages Publishing House, 1953), first published in Russian in 1913; and various works by Vladimir Il'ich Lenin, 1913-25, including "Critical Remarks on the National Question," in Lenin, *Collected Works*, XX (London: Lawrence and Wishart, 1964), 17-51; and "The Ukraine," in ibid., XXV, 91-2. Robin Cohen called these earlier writings to my attention.

3. B.J. Dudley, *Instability and Political Order: Politics and Crisis in Nigeria* (Ibadan: Ibadan University Press, 1973); Kenneth Post and Michael Vickers, *Structure and Conflict in Nigeria,*

1960-1966 (Madison, Wis.: University of Wisconsin Press, 1973); and A.H.M. Kirk-Greene, *The Genesis of the Nigerian Civil War and the Theory of Fear* (Uppsala: The Scandinavian Institute of African Studies, 1975).

4. Rabushka and Shepsle, *Politics in Plural Societies*, pp. 8, 20, 213.

5 Eric A. Nordlinger, *Conflict Regulation in Divided Societies*, Occasional Papers in International Affairs, No. 29 (Cambridge, Mass.: Harvard University, Center for International Affairs, 1972).

6. Nathan Glazer and Daniel Patrick Moynihan, *Beyond the Melting Pot: The Negroes, Puerto Ricans, Jews, Italians, and Irish of New York City* (Cambridge, Mass.: M.I.T. Press, 1963).

7. Glazer and Moynihan, "Introduction," pp. 1-26, and Daniel Bell, "Ethnicity and Social Change," pp. 157, 169, in *Ethnicity: Theory and Experience*, Glazer and Moynihan, eds. (Cambridge, Mass.: Harvard University Press, 1975).

8. Robert A. Dahl, *Who Governs? Democracy and Power in an American City* (New Haven, Conn.: Yale University Press, 1961), pp. 34-6.

9. Charles W. Anderson, Fred R. von der Mehden, and Crawford Young, *Issues of Political Development* (Englewood Cliffs, N.J.: Prentice-Hall, Inc., 1974), pp. 22, 28-78.

10. Robert Melson and Howard Wolpe, "Modernization and the Politics of Communalism: A Theoretical Perspective," *American Political Science Review*, LXIV, No. 4 (December 1970), 1112,13.

11. World Bank, *World Bank Atlas: Population, Per Capita Product and Growth Rates* (Washington, D.C.: 1973), p. 5; and Everett E. Hagen, *The Economics of Development* (Homewood, Ill.: Richard D. Irwin, 1968), pp. 25-7.

12. Douglas A. Hibbs, Jr., *Mass Political Violence: A Cross-national Causal Analysis* (New York: John Wiley, 1973), pp. 24-5, 188.

13. See Huntington, *Political Order*, pp. 53-5, on the "gap hypothesis."

14. Melson and Wolpe, *American Political Science Review*, LXIV, No. 4, 1115-8.

15. Crawford Young, *The Politics of Cultural Pluralism* (Madison, Wis.: The University of Wisconsin Press, 1976), pp. 22, 213, 518.

16. Huntington, *Political Order*, pp. 3, 26, 28, 198, 308, 403; Donal Cruise O'Brien, "Modernization, Order, and the Erosion of a Democratic Ideal: American Political Science, 1960-1970," *The Journal of Development Studies*, VIII, No. 4 (July 1972), 359; and Terry Nardin, "Violence and the State: A Critique of Empirical Political Theory," Sage Professional Papers in Comparative Politics Series Number 01-020 (Beverly Hills, Calif.: Sage Publications, 1971), p. 27.

17. Huntington, *Political Order*, p. 373; Nardin, "Violence and the State," pp. 12-13, 26-7; and Richard L. Sklar, "Review of *Political Order*," *American Sociological Review*, XXXIV, No. 4 (August 1969), 571-3.

18. Huntington, *Political Order*, pp. 138, 287.

19. Gurr, *Why Men Rebel*, and "Psychological Factors in Civil

Strife," *World Politics*, XX (January 1968), 245-78; and Nardin, "Violence and the State," pp. 23-4.

20. Ted Robert Gurr and Raymond Duvall, "Civil Conflict in the 1960s: A Reciprocal Theoretical System with Parameter Estimates," *Comparative Political Studies*, VI, No. 2 (July 1973), 135-69.

21. Baran, *The Manchester School*, XX, 66-84, and *The Political Economy of Growth*.

22. For example, the Ivorian cocoa farmers who opposed the formation of French cocoa plantations were major supporters of Felix Houphouet-Boigny's *Parti démocratique de la Côte d'Ivoire* in the 1950s.

23. Dudley, *Instability and Political Order*, and "The Politics of Adebo," *Quarterly Journal of Administration*, VI, No. 3 (January 1972), 133. In chapter 4, I indicate Dudley's error in trying to compare average wages to per capita income.

24. Post and Vickers, *Structure and Conflict*, p. 185.

25. Ibid., pp. 6, 10.

26. Kirk-Greene, *The Genesis of the Nigerian Civil War*, p. 19. See chapters 1 and 4 for further discussions of regionalism in Nigeria.

27. See Ibid., pp. 14, 19.

28. No one could disagree with Okpaku's disillusionment with those "Western scholars, some of whom may have spent a week or two in a suburban hotel as far from Nigeria as Cairo, and others, who may have flown over Africa sometime during World War II and by so doing qualified as 'experts' on all aspects of African life from rural culture through sexual behavior and industrial development to literature and philosophy." [Joseph Okpaku, ed., *Nigeria: Dilemma of Nationhood--An African Analysis of the Biafran Conflict*, (Westport, Conn.: Greenwood Publishing Co., 1972), p. 3.] But the broader attack on the qualifications of whites who study Africa, a parallel to attacks on men who research women's history, or Germans or Swedes who analyze American society, is palpable nonsense.

True, the differing social location of insiders may help them perceive some truths outsiders overlook. [R.K. Merton, "Insiders and Outsiders: A Chapter in the Sociology of Knowledge," *The American Journal of Sociology*, LXXVIII, No. 1 (July 1972), 9-47.] In the case of African studies, outsiders have been prone to analyze African history and society from the standpoint of the colonial government or western economic interests, understating African nationalism, resistance, and institutional strength. [Guy C.Z. Mhone, "The Case Against Africanists," *Issue* (a quarterly journal of opinion published by the African Studies Association), II, No. 2 (Summer 1972), 8-13.] On the other hand, insiders, taking the "African side of history," frequently adopt the perspective of African political elites, and may accept their policy goals without asking whether they are appropriate for the underprivileged portions of the population. Perhaps the most serious failure of white Africanists in the U.S. has been their neglect or rejection of the substantial body of scholarship on Africa in the late nineteenth and early twentieth centuries, contributed primarily by Afro-Americans. [John Henrik Clarke, "The African Heritage Studies Association (ASHA): Some Notes on the Conflict with the African Studies Association (ASA) and the Fight to Reclaim African History," *Issue*, VI, Nos. 2 & 3 (Summer/Fall 1976), 5-11, and Elliott P. Skinner, "African Studies, 1955-1975: An Afro-American Perspective," ibid., pp. 57-67.]

29. Peter P. Ekeh, "Citizenship and Political Conflict: A Sociological Interpretation of the Nigerian Crisis," in *Nigeria: Dilemma*, Okpaku, ed., pp. 71-80; Okwudiba Nnoli, "The Nigeria-Biafra Conflict--A Political Analysis," ibid., p. 124; Moyibi Amoda, "Background to the Conflict: A Summary of Nigeria's Political History from 1941 to 1964," ibid., pp. 14-75; Ogbemi Ola Omatete, "The Security of the Nigerian Nation," ibid., p. 299; Jimoh Lawal, "Nigeria--Class Struggle and the National Question," ibid., pp. 258-86; and Okpaku, "Nigeria Today: The Dilemma of Peace," ibid., p. 377.

30. Karl W. Deutsch, *Nationalism and Social Communication: An Inquiry into the Foundation of Nationality* (New York: John Wiley & Sons, 1953), pp. 21-4.

31. N. Nziramasanga, "Secession, Federalism, and African Unity," in *Nigeria: Dilemma*, Okpaku, ed., pp. 229-57; and Victor P. Diejomaoh, "The Economics of the Nigerian Conflict," ibid., pp. 318-65.

32. P.C. Lloyd, "The Ethnic Background to the Nigerian Crisis," in *Nigerian Politics and Military Rule: Prelude to the Civil War*, S.K. Panter-Brick, ed. (London: The Athlone Press, 1970), pp. 1-13; S.K. Panter-Brick, "From Military Coup to Civil War, January 1966 to May 1967," ibid., pp. 14-57; Robin Luckham, "The Nigerian Military: Disintegration or Integration?" ibid., pp. 58-77; M.J. Dent, "The Military and the Politicians," ibid., pp. 78-93; B.J. Dudley, "Western Nigeria and the Nigerian Crisis," ibid., pp. 94-110; K. Whiteman, "Enugu: The Psychology of Secession, 29 July 1966 to 30 May 1967," ibid., pp. 111-27; and S. K. Panter-Brick and P.F. Dawson, "The Creation of New States in the North," ibid., pp. 128-38.

33. Andre Gunder Frank, *Capitalism and Underdevelopment in Latin America: Historical Studies of Chile and Brazil* (New York: Monthly Review Press, 1967), and *Latin America: Underdevelopment or Revolution* (New York: Modern Reader, 1969).

34. This approach is a modification of Johan Galtung, "A Structural Theory of Imperialism," *Journal of Peace Research*, VIII, No. 2 (1971), 83-4, for whom a harmony of interests between elites in the rich and poor countries corresponds to conflicts of interests between the elites and masses in the poor state. Wallerstein's distinction between peripheral and semi-peripheral states, though useful in some contexts, adds little to the explanation of Nigerian or Pakistani political violence. See Immanuel Wallerstein, *The Modern World-System: Capitalist Agriculture and the Origins of the European World-Economy in the Sixteenth Century* (New York: Academic Press, 1974), and *The Capitalist World-Economy* (Cambridge: Cambridge University Press, 1979).

Part 1

Economic Factors Contributing to the War

1
A Historical Sketch, 1900–1967

> It is evident that decolonization is not, cannot ever be, a honey-smooth process.
>
> Paul Henissart, *Wolves in the City: The Death of French Algeria*, 1973.

> Nigeria is not a nation. It is a mere geographic expression.
>
> Chief Obafemi Awolowo, *Path to Nigerian Freedom*, 1947.

> The so-called common "Nigerian nationality"--which is a complete misnomer, as there is no such thing as a Nigerian nation anyway--is a veneer or facade consciously or unconsciously put up by some Nigerians to cover up what many of their fellow men see quite plainly as rabid nationalism.
>
> Obafemi Awolowo, *The People's Republic*, 1968.

This chapter is not a comprehensive history. Nor does it analyze systematically the effect of British hegemony and colonialism on Nigeria's political instability since independence. This is a historian's task. Instead, the purpose of the chapter is to provide the historical background necessary for discussing international economic linkages, class antagonisms, economic discontent, and communal conflict that lay at the root of the Nigerian civil war.

A number of scholars partially link the Nigerian coups and civil war to policies during British colonial rule. Perhaps the most authoritative analysis of the colonial period is by Nicolson, a British scholar and former administrator in Nigeria. For him, the main roots of the Nigerian-Biafran war grew during the British colonial period. Specifically, he argues:

> [Sir Frederick] Lugard's most crucial and characteristic decisions [as high commissioner for Northern Nigeria, 1900-06] worked against future amalgamation [of Nigeria], and his later decisions as amalgamator [when governor-general of Nigeria, 1912-18] were aimed at the destruction of his predecessors'

> achievements in establishing a rational and modern system of administration. In the North, there was his choice of conquest rather than peaceful penetration, followed by the decision to keep the institution of Fulani rule, while replacing each ruler by a creature of his own; there was the decision to impose direct taxation; the decision to keep out of the North the influence of missionaries, lawyers, traders, and civil administrators from other territories; the decision not to establish a capital in a commercial centre; there was a whole series of decisions to avoid contact and co-operation with the South, and to concentrate all power in one pair of hands. All this was not so much civil administrative behaviour as the kind of military behaviour in civil situations in which the term "militarism" can fairly be applied.

> In 1918-48, British administration in Nigeria

> was administration on a shoestring. There was no more than 5s [less than $1.50] per head of population, for all the current needs of central government, for many of the purposes of local government, and for heavy interest charges on loan capital, mostly used to improve the transportation services on which the whole prospect of prosperity and increasing revenues depended. . . . [During] the upheaval of a second World War. . . . the over-stretched administrative machinery came very near to collapse.[1]

The first two sections of this chapter, which emphasize economic factors, indicate additional legacies of British imperialism and colonialism that contributed to political instability in post-colonial Nigeria. One part of the analysis of the colonial legacy focuses on: (1) the uneven impact of colonialism on social change and modernization among various regions and communities, and (2) policies in the terminal colonial era that helped establish a post-independence elite favorable to British interests. Another part of the analysis looks at the relationship among nationalism, communalism, and elite interests. The third section discusses regional interests and political enmities after independence.

EARLY BRITISH IMPERIALISM

Imperialism here is the extension of economic and political power by one state over another, resulting not only from formal conquest and empire, but also from informal controls.

The European struggle to establish forts and trading-posts on the West African shores between about 1640 and about 1750 was part of the wider competition for trade and empire in the Atlantic. The British, like other newcomers to the slave trade, found they could compete with the Dutch in West Africa only by forming national trading companies. The first effective English one was the Company of the Royal Adventurers, chartered in 1660 and succeeded in 1672 by the Royal African Company. Only a monopoly company could afford to build and maintain the forts considered essential to protect slaves bought from African merchants, and to hold stocks of slaves and trade goods. In the early eighteenth century England and France destroyed the Dutch hold on West African trade, and by the end of the French Revolutionary and Napoleonic Wars (1793-1815), England had become the dominant commercial power in West Africa. Britain's profits from overseas trade helped finance her industrial development, which in turn stimulated further expansion of her foreign trade and shipping.[2]

The slave trade was one of the major causes of the devastating internecine strife in Southern Nigeria during the three centuries or so before it was abolished. Although Britain made the slave trade illegal for her subjects in 1806, it increased as other westerners filled the vacuum, until slave trading came to an end in the mid 1840s. In the nineteenth century, Britain was more interested in opening markets for her manufactured goods than in slave commerce, which was not as conducive to expanding such legitimate trade in West Africa as palm oil and ivory. To make the oil and ivory trade secure required that she usurp the power of coastal chiefs in what became Nigeria.[3]

The need for formal protection and eventually colonization of Nigeria resulted not only from the necessity to safeguard the expanding trade interests in the Nigerian hinterland but also to forestall potential formal claims by other colonial powers like France and Germany, with imperial designs in the region.

By 1850, British trading interests were concentrating in Lagos and the Niger River delta. British administration in Nigeria formally began in 1861, when Lagos became a crown colony, a step taken in response to such factors as: the activities of slave traders, the disruption of trade by Yoruba civil wars, and fears that the French would take over Lagos.[4]

By the mid-nineteenth century, the British naval fleet patrolled West African waters, while British traders, explorers, and missionaries penetrated its interior. In 1885, the Berlin Conference clarified European powers' spheres of influence so Britain had a clear hand in formally proclaiming the Niger delta area the Oil Rivers Protectorate.[5] In 1886, the Niger Company, a monopoly welded from the major British companies trading in the Niger River area, was granted a royal charter to exercise the political authority necessary to facilitate trade in south-central Nigeria. By 1903, the British had subdued upper Northern Nigeria, which had been a part of the Fulani empire since Usman dan Fodio's successful *jihad* (Muslim holy war) against the Hausa states in the early nineteenth century.

In 1900 the British government took over from the Niger Company, and proclaimed the Protectorates of Northern Nigeria and Southern Nigeria. By 1906, most of present-day Nigeria was under British control.

THE COLONIAL LEGACY

The world-wide political and military hegemony of Britain for decades before World War I enabled her to hold a commanding position in the international capitalist system as major conqueror, colonizer, banker, trader, investor, and industrialist. Colonies[6] like Nigeria became a part of the system as economic satellites specializing in raw materials, minerals, and food important for the industrial development of the leading capitalist countries.

Britain tried to encourage tropical export crops in Nigeria, and to stimulate its demand for English manufactured goods. Building a railroad network between the 1890s and World War II and accelerating the growth of road construction after the 1920s, together with introducing an easily portable, universally accepted medium of exchange, helped develop export trade in tin, cotton, cocoa, groundnuts, and palm oil.[7] Britain procured and maintained its economic suzerainty in the colonies through military power and alliances, together with the collaboration of indigenous rulers.

Colonialism, by interfering with internal political and economic development, especially by affecting the shape of national boundaries, social structure, and resource allocation within them, contributed to post-colonial instability. By providing the overriding opportunity structure within which competition was to operate, colonial rule influenced the development of nationalism and communalism.

The Differential Impact of Colonialism

Britain's piecemeal penetration of Nigeria contributed to unevenness in social change and modernization among various regions and communities. Several groups in Nigeria had centuries of economic contact with the west before British administration was formally established in 1900. For more than two centuries, coastal groups, particularly in the Niger delta region, had been involved in trade, e.g., that of slaves in the seventeenth to eighteenth centuries, and of palm oil and other products beginning in the latter part of the nineteenth century. Commerce in the far North from the Middle Ages to the colonial period, was oriented toward the Mediterranean areas of Morocco and Tripoli, and across the Sudan. This trade dropped markedly during the colonial period.

Although British colonialism helped facilitate a feeling of identity by creating internal peace, maintaining law and order, imposing a common government, developing an internal transportation and communication network, establishing a uniform monetary system, investing in education, and unifying the African government service, the impact of colonial rule differed substantially from region to region. The coastal areas of Southern Nigeria, where British intrusion was longer and more intense, had more experience in parliamentary government, a great political consciousness, higher literacy, and more developed capitalist institutions than inland regions.

Northern and Southern Nigeria were administered as separate territories, even to the extent of having frontier controls until 1914. Despite their amalgamation in 1914, the two protectorates were never effectively united, the administrative individuality of the formerly separate territories was maintained, and Lagos even preserved a unique legal status. Governor-General Frederick Lugard established a policy of "indirect rule" in the North, where day-to-day administrative responsibility was maintained by compliant Fulani emirs. The policy had to be significantly modified in the South, because of the limited power of traditional chiefs in the southwest, their absence in most of the southeast, and the lack of well-defined procedures for tax assessment and revenue collection. In Northern Nigeria, indirect rule was mutually advantageous; the British economized on officers and used a well-developed tax collection system and the existing well-organized emirate states. At the same time, the Fulani rulers under the British achieved a secure hegemony by eliminating important sources of both internal and external opposition. Maintaining these rulers hampered the development of nationalism and a strong native bourgeoisie.[8]

Southern Nigeria had more experience than the North in the central government. Between 1923 and 1946, Africans were elected to four reserved seats in the Legislative Council--three from Lagos township and one from Calabar--by an electorate consisting of wealthier members of the communities. In addition, the British governor appointed seven to ten Africans from the interior areas of the Southern provinces to the Council. But not until 1946 was there indigenous representation from the North.[9]

Sir Frederick Lugard, head of the Nigerian colonial administration from 1912 through 1918, stated that self-government for the Nigerian masses was to be achieved by educating their own traditional authorities, who conceivably could represent the people, rather than by introducing an alien system of rule by British-educated and politically minded progressives. Lugard's policy of excluding educated Africans from the "native authorities," i.e., local government system, and preventing their contact with the masses, was more thoroughgoing in the North. There were only a few educated elite among Northern authorities even in the 1930s. In the same decade, the policy of excluding educated Africans from the traditional authorities was clearly rejected in the South, partly in response to the burst of organizational activity by the growing number of educated persons, who desired to participate in the affairs of their home villages or districts. The educated groups, who had become convinced they were destined to serve forever as clerks and subalterns in a perpetual British administrative structure, believed that the chiefs were unwitting or reluctant tools of the government, and not representative of the people.[10]

In 1939, the Southern Protectorate was divided into western and eastern provinces. By the end of World War II, the administrative devolution was great enough to give the three major areas, the North, the West, and the East, substantial individuality, which was strengthened by the Richards Constitution of 1946, the subsequent designation of three regions in the Constitution of 1951, and the movement toward greater autonomy in a federation under the revised Constitution of 1954.[11]

The British Approach in the Terminal Colonial Era

World War I diminished the dominant position of Britain in the international economy and the United States took its place.

Although World War II and its aftermath accelerated decolonization, Britain continued to import raw materials, and to export and invest overseas. Some degree of "political stability" (a concept that included maintaining an economy open to trade with, and investment from, capitalist countries) was ensured in English-speaking Africa by western military and economic strength, Commonwealth trade-and-aid arrangements, and cooperation with indigenous elites.

After 1948 the British were more prepared to meet what they considered the reasonable demands of the Nigerian nationalist movement, a step that eased the colonial burden and helped to shape a post-independence elite favorable to British interests. In return for their cooperation, aspiring Nigerians, primarily in the south, obtained access to power, privileges, and patronage of the British before the end of the colonial period--especially in the civil service and government agencies. In the North the traditional ruling aristocracy continued to enjoy the support of the colonial regime.

Two examples illustrate the way the British supported the political elite they helped to create. First, the Harragin Salaries Commission of 1951 (consisting of British officials) established a basis for Nigerian senior civil servants to retain many of the privileges the colonial administrators had enjoyed, such as high salaries, automobiles, educational allowances, and lengthy vacations. Second, the colonial government acquiesed to demands by national leaders, especially in the West and East, seeking a power base in the regions. The British grant of self-government before independence to the Western and Eastern Regions in 1956 and the Northern Region in 1959 reduced the eventual strength of the federal government. In the clamor for political and economic power, the benefits most national leaders acquired by cooperating with the British made them more compliant and excluded radical anti-British spokesmen.[12]

Nationalism, Communalism, and Elite Interests

British rule exacerbated differences of class, region, and community in Nigeria. The colonial government did not need deliberately to divide to rule. Foreign rule itself is sufficient to cause divisions and conflict. Since hostility cannot be directed to the powerful foreign oppressor, it is transferred to an indigenous scapegoat.[13]

In Nigeria, especially before World War II, the British supported the development of separate institutions and identities for different ethnic and religious communities, a system of "native administration" to reflect communal loyalty and federate fragmented elements of clans, and an educational system aimed at cultivating a "love of tribe." In the early 1920s, Governor Hugh Clifford clearly emphasized that the idea of a Nigerian nation was both inconceivable and dangerous. Even the nationalist leaders before 1934 tended to think of nationalism in terms of regional or ethnic community.[14]

Although the official language in Nigeria is English, there are more than 200 linguistic groupings, which correspond roughly to ethnic communities. The three largest communities, Hausa-Fulani,

Ibo, and Yoruba (see table 1.1), dominated the politics of the Northern, Eastern, and Western Regions, respectively, and became rivals in the struggle for power in the federal government.

TABLE 1.1
Populations of Major Ethnic Communities in Nigeria, 1963 Census

Ethnic community	Population (thousands)
Hausa	11,653
Yoruba	11,321
Ibo	9,246
Fulani	4,784
Kanuri	2,259
Ibibio	2,006
Tiv	1,394
Ijaw	1,089
Edo	955
Annang	675
Other Nigerians	10,176
Other Africans	55
Non-Africans	47
Unspecified	10
Total	55,670

Source: Nigeria, Office of Statistics, *Population Census of Nigeria 1963*, III, *Combined National Figures* (Lagos, 1968), 10-11.

The nationalist movement, spearheaded by a new elite, was promoted mainly by persons who expected to gain economically and politically. The movement first became multi-ethnic between 1930 and 1944 in the South, when the real incomes of many participants in Nigeria's money economy decreased from a falling trend in the net barter terms of trade (the ratio between the indices of average export and import prices). The world depression during the same period and the disruption of war had adversely affected Britain's investment, imports, and government spending in Nigeria.[15]

Additionally, as the colonial government assumed complete control of the economy during World War II, it issued trade licenses only to established firms, which froze the superior competitive position of foreign firms. Besides that, peasants received lower than world prices from marketing boards, workers faced wage ceilings, traders encountered price controls, consumers sustained shortages of import goods, and troops experienced racial discrimination.

Labor organizational activity grew during the war in reaction to several policies of the colonial government: (1) the Colonial Development and Welfare Act of 1940 encouraging the establishment of trade unions in the colonies, (2) the defense regulation of October 1942 making strikes and lockouts illegal for the duration of the war, and (3) denying African workers the cost-of-living allowances that European civil servants received. In addition, the government increased wages only modestly, while the cost of living rose 74 percent from September 1939 through October 1943. In June-July 1945, 43,000 workers, most of whom were performing services indispensable to the country's economic and administrative life, went on strike for more than 40 days. Aspiring Nigerian entrepreneurs, deprived of new economic opportunities, and trade union leaders, politicized by the strike's success, channeled their grievances into nationalist agitation. Educated persons, whose primary economic opportunities were limited to private business and professional activity, demanded more participation in the colonial government.[16]

Traditionally, except for some aristocratic groups among the Hausa, Fulani, and Kanuri, ethnic identity was weak among Nigerians.[17] However, the struggle to obtain the benefits of modernization strengthened ethnic nationalism, especially around the mid-twentieth century. The heightening of Yoruba nationalism in the West after 1948 was partly in response to the Nigerian national movement in the 1940s, led by the Ibos, an overpopulated Eastern ethnic community with many emigrants to other parts of Nigeria.[18] Hausa-Fulani nationalism was aroused about the same time in response to rival leadership in the drive for independence, and the threat of southern economic supremacy. The elite accentuated precolonial and colonial identification with traditional political and cultural entities, sentiments they used to transfer potential hostility from class discrepancies (within their own ethnic groups) to other ethnic communities.

Since 1949, when the Nigerian new elites were first consulted by the British in a constitutional review, peoples of Nigeria have engaged in a continual regional, communal, and class struggle for a share in the economic benefits of decolonization and independence, and the accompanying modernization. The two coups d'état of 1966 and the civil war of 1967-70 were the most virulent of the struggles.

Between the first regional elections of 1951 and the overthrow of parliamentary rule in 1966, the elite consisted primarily of high-ranking politicians, indigenous rulers, senior civil servants, leading businessmen, and professionals. Most of them came to prominence after World War II, when the British handed positions, patronage, perquisites, and economic benefits to Nigerians so they were favorably placed to rule after independence in 1960.

In the south[19] the older leaders of the nationalist movement were joined by a rising educated elite of influential politicians, civil servants, lawyers, doctors, teachers, and businessmen, and a few far-sighted chiefs. The emirs, the hereditary Fulani rulers in the far North, retained power in Northern Nigeria.[20] The lines of local administrative and party organization were virtually coextensive. Accordingly, the emirs were supported by district and village heads, judges, and Native Authority employees, together

FIGURE 1.1
Nigeria, 1963-67

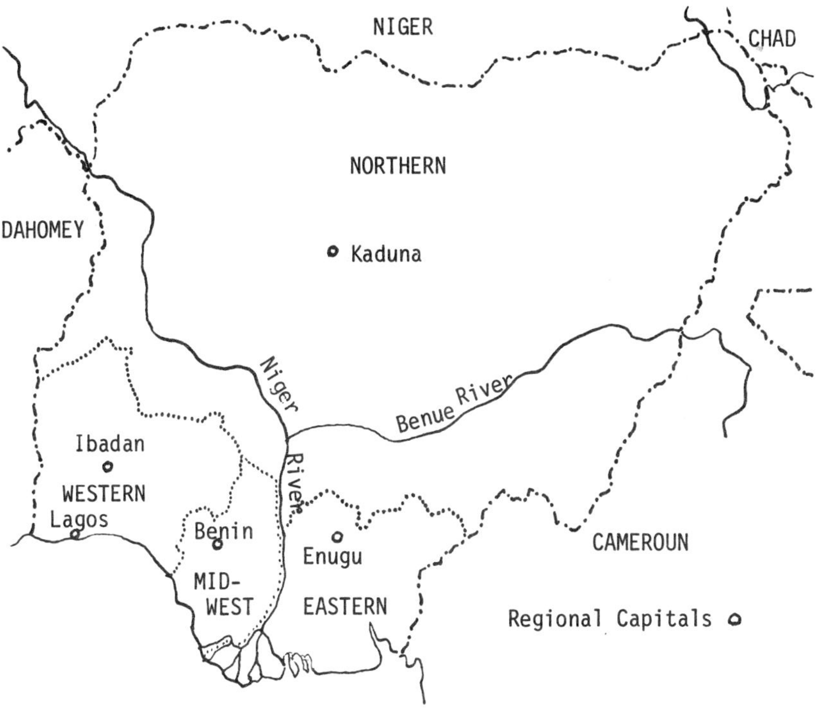

with a few new men, such as former headmaster Alhaji Sir Abubakar Tafawa Balewa, federal prime minister from 1956 to 1966.[21]

During 1951-60, each of the three major political parties, the Northern Peoples' Congress (N.P.C.), the National Council of Nigeria and the Cameroons (N.C.N.C.), and the Action Group (A.G.), all played leading roles in unifying and locally mobilizing the socioeconomic elite, and each achieved security and hegemony in one region only, the Northern, Eastern, and Western, respectively. Elites from majority parties in the regional assemblies who also cooperated with the ruling federal coalition dispensed a wide range of political rewards and sanctions, thus retaining their own positions and power, and keeping the masses subordinated. Positions and employment in government service and public corporations, licenses for market stalls, permits for agricultural export production, land rights to establish enterprises, roads, electricity, running water, and scholarships were allocated by the governing elite to its supporters. Each major party was backed by a bank, which assisted in the transfer of substantial public funds to the party.[22] As Dudley indicates, "politics in Nigeria, like

FIGURE 1.2
Nigeria, 1967-76

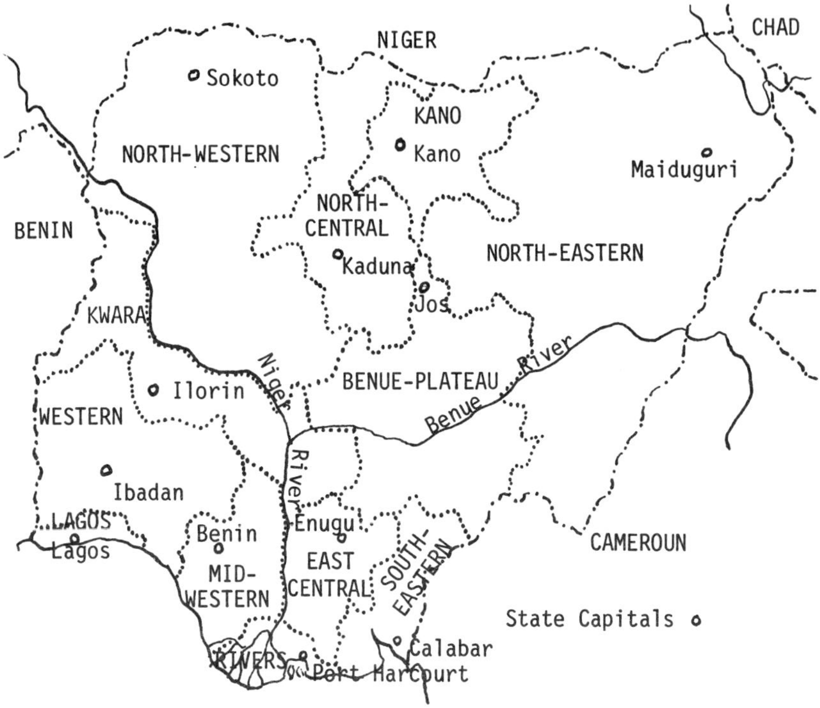

some other states, is not about *alternative policies* but about the *control over men and resources*."[23]

At all levels--local and regional after 1951, and federal after 1954--political leaders could use a range of controls, extending over local councils, district administration, police and courts, to subdue any dissident minority, especially in the far North, where clientage was the major social adhesive of the emirate system. Political superiors offered protection, patronage, and economic security in exchange for loyalty and obedience of inferiors. In the far North, clientage represented the major channel for upward mobility toward and within the ruling circle. Attaching to a patron provided virtually the only defense for those outside the elite against arbitrary taxes, injurious treatment in court proceedings, or discrimination in the allocation of public services.[24]

The elite attracted clients and socially inferior groups not only in the far North, where the Muslim religion legitimized the traditional hierarchy, but even in Iboland, where power had been widely dispersed before the twentieth century.[25] Although the

FIGURE 3.1
Nigeria, 1976-

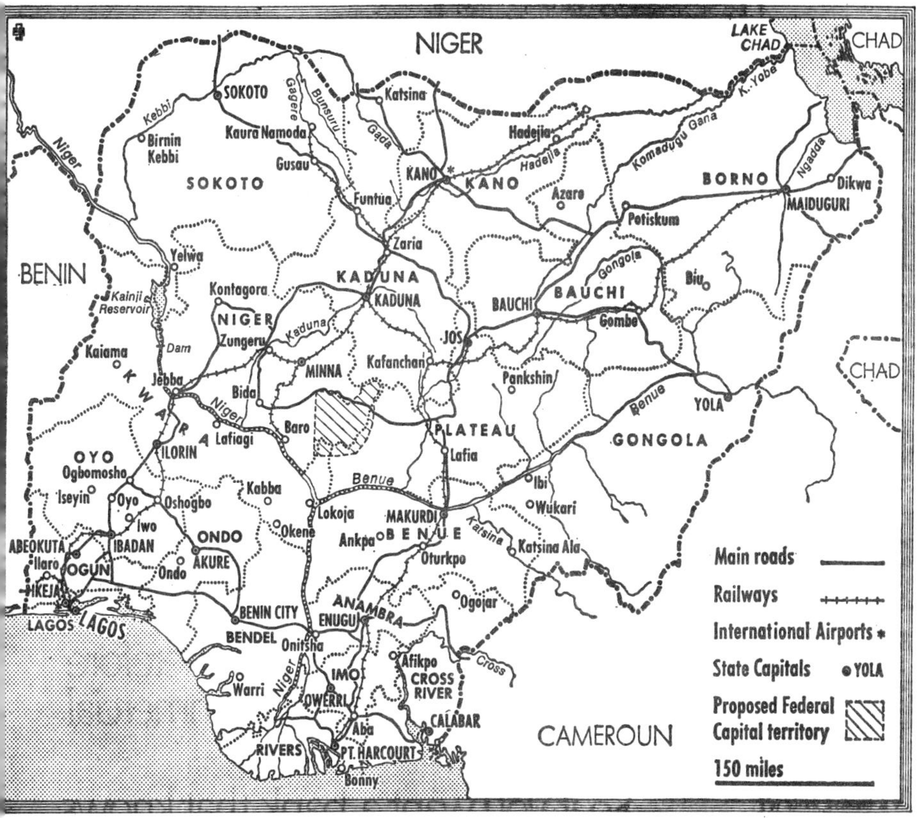

"Nigeria," *The Times* (Supplement), (1 December 1977), p.VIII.
By permission.

elites of the three regions preferred to close ranks to share the fruits of office and to prevent challenges to their positions, by independence, policies to enhance the security of one regional elite threatened the security of others.

From about 1950 to 1963, class consciousness and mobilization among the lower classes was minimal, especially in the North, where the prevailing political ideology legitimized authority and inequality. Although the N.C.N.C., the prime vehicle for the nationalist movement at its establishment in 1944, started as a pan-regional organization with some radical and trade union support, by the time the first elections were held in 1951, its strength remained only in the south. As noted below, the A.G., which in 1959 became the first major party to try to mobilize support on a pan-regional and class basis, was undercut by the ruling, regionally oriented parties. From time to time labor parties were formed, but they won virtually no seats because of the small size of the wage-earning class and the cross pressures between communal and class-oriented parties.[26]

REGIONAL INTERESTS AND POLITICAL ENMITIES

One of the first threats to the security of regional elites occurred during 1949-53 when the Northern ruling class opposed any plan for Nigerian independence where southerners--not sympathetic to maintaining society based on the authority of the traditional aristocracy--were dominant. The British support of Northern resistance, together with southern impatience for early independence, led to an agreement in the 1950s to leave the Northern Region intact with a majority of representatives in the federal legislature. As indicated below, however, the quest for security by the Northern aristocracy--which required supremacy at the federal level--became a danger to the parties in the other regions.

After 1951, the smaller ethnic groups became aware of the danger of perpetual subjection to one of the three largest communities, Hausa-Fulani, Ibo, or Yoruba. In 1958, the Willink Commission, appointed by the Constitutional Conference, found against the creation of states, thus ensuring that the Northern Region, with more than half the federation's population, would retain supremacy. The Commission's findings were supported by the major parties based in the East and West because they opposed the creation of new states in their regions. Dissension from the findings also would have delayed independence, and jeopardized agreements between the North and south. No one wanted to prolong colonial rule, or to be blamed for holding up self-rule.[27]

The Period of Civilian Government

After independence, the political elite increasingly perceived the availability of economic perquisites and benefits as a "zero-sum game," where gains by those politically mobilized in one region were at the expense of another region. The first major party to be effectively undermined in its region of primary strength was the Action Group, the Western ruling party and federal opposition party until 1962.

Some members of the A.G. under its leader, Chief Obafemi Awolowo, planned to reorient its support to a broader constituency, comprising individuals and classes from all regions (including the far North) who felt excluded from the distribution of patronage and positions, and who might be attracted by a program of egalitarian socialism. The shift in strategy by the A.G. came after its campaign for seats, and agitation for the creation of new states, in minority areas in the North and East during the late 1950s. These actions bitterly antagonized the ruling coalition--especially the Northern Peoples' Congress (N.P.C.), the instrument of the powerful aristocracy whose staying power depended on its dominance in an undivided North exercising hegemony at the center.

Chief Samuel Ladoke Akintola, premier of the Western Region, led a minority that broke from the A.G. and was primarily supported by rural businessmen, large landlords, and cocoa plantation owners who hoped to protect their regional economic interests. Even many of those who remained with the Action Group were dissatisfied with its pan-regional, anti-capitalist strategy. The faction led by Akintola instigated a disturbance in the Western assembly, which provided an excuse for the federal ruling coalition (N.P.C. and N.C.N.C.) to declare a state of emergency in 1962, and to suspend the A.G. government of the Western Region for six months.

During the next two years the ruling alliance used several politico-legal measures to crush the A.G., to depose its leader, and to facilitate the rise of a more compliant party in the West. The report of an inquiry into the misappropriation of public funds by A.G. officers, and a ten-year prison sentence for Awolowo (and imprisonment of his colleagues) for treason in an alleged coup d'état attempt, effectively emasculated the radical wing of the A.G. Constitutional moves were initiated that eventually severed the Mid-West from the Western Region in 1963. After the regional assembly suspension was lifted, Akintola's wing of the A.G. formed the nucleus of a new coalition, which in 1964 became the Nigerian National Democratic Party (N.N.D.P.), the majority party in the West and a member of the ruling coalition at the center.[28]

A crisis resulted when partial returns from the 1962 Nigerian census indicated that the majority of the population was in the south rather than the North. The census was politically important because it was the basis upon which parliamentary representation was proportioned. The Northern Peoples' Congress became alarmed that the Eastern-based N.C.N.C. might become dominant in the Western and forthcoming Mid-West regions, and win the south and a majority of the parliamentary seats.

Accusations from the North concerning the inflation of census figures, especially in the East, led to the census being suppressed. A Northern-inspired re-count in 1963, not surprisingly, gave the North a majority that closely approximated the previous official (1952-53) census (see table 1.2). Despite protests from the East, the N.N.D.P. supported its Northern ally in the federal parliament, the 1963 figures were accepted, and a challenge to Northern supremacy was averted.

The 1964 federal election threatened to undermine the security of the Ibo dominant class--i.e., civil servants, businessmen, and

TABLE 1.2
Population of Nigeria by Regions, 1952-53 and 1963 Censuses (in millions)

Region	1952-53 Census	1963 Census
Northern	16.8	29.8
Eastern	7.2	12.4
Western	4.6	10.3
Mid-West	1.5[a]	2.5
Lagos territory	0.3	0.7
Total	30.4	55.7

[a]Before 1963, the Mid-West was a part of the Western Region. The distribution of population between the Western and Mid-West Regions is based on 1963 boundaries.

Note: The four regions and federal territory were divided into twelve states in May 1967, and redivided into nineteen states in February 1976. See table 8.1 for the distribution of population in the 1963 and 1972 censuses, according to the twelve states, 1967-76.

Source: Nigeria Office of Statistics, *Annual Abstract of Statistics, 1964* (Lagos, 1964), p. 12.

professionals--behind the N.C.N.C. The N.C.N.C. joined the Action Group and the Northern Progressive Front to form the United Progressive Grand Alliance (U.P.G.A.) opposed to the N.P.C.-N.N.D.P. coalition, the Nigerian National Alliance (N.N.A.).

Although the U.P.G.A. started the campaign with confidence, it lost virtually the entire North before balloting took place, because its supporters were left off voters' lists, its leaders' speeches were frequently forbidden and obstructed, its candidates and spokesmen were violently harassed, and some were arrested while making nominations. The N.C.N.C., well aware of the fragility of federal opposition parties--such as the A.G. in 1962--feared that losing membership in the coalition federal government might lead to losing their regional base to the ruling parties appealing to minorities and dissident or opportunistic politicians.

Eventually the U.P.G.A. staged an election boycott, anticipating that President Nnamdi Azikiwe, an Ibo sympathetic to the N.C.N.C., would use the boycott as a pretense to postpone the elections and install a caretaker prime minister--presumably favorable to the U.P.G.A.--supported by the army, which was led by a disproportionate number of Ibo officers.

However, the army and the police supported Prime Minister Balewa and the winning N.N.A. coalition. Major General Welby-Everard, an Englishman soon to be retired as general officer commanding the Nigerian Army (G.O.C.), had no inclination to act contrary to the legal advice from the chief justice of the Supreme Court who supported the prime minister.[29] Major General J.T. Aguiyi-Ironsi, the highest-ranking Nigerian officer, was an Ibo, but his promotion to G.O.C. was possible with British personnel departing the next month, and he had no wish to jeopardize it.

Balewa's consultation with top officers in the armed forces helped ensure their loyalty, as they were still largely free of communalism, and the civilian government retained a certain legitimacy. Although the East threatened secession, the federation was kept together temporarily by an agreement between Balewa and Azikiwe: elections in boycotted areas were to be scheduled later, but everywhere else the results were to be recognized, and the N.C.N.C. was to become a member of a broadly based national government with the N.N.A. Nevertheless, the N.C.N.C. retained only two ministers, both former members of the closely-knit "Ikoyi clique," consisting of the leading figures from previous N.P.C.-N.C.N.C. coalitions, one of whom (Chief Festus Okotie-Eboh) was closer to the N.P.C. than his own party. Furthermore, the N.C.N.C. knew that their presence in the coalition government was no longer essential, and that they could be disposed of when convenient.

In its first regional election test (October 1965), the N.N.D.P., the ruling party in the West, won 73 of 94 seats, with U.P.G.A. winning only 17. Nominations and balloting were blatantly rigged by the Western Nigeria Electoral Commission, responsible to the Western Regional Public Service Commission, open to influence by the N.N.D.P. government. The Western or federal government influenced the perpetuation of the following election irregularities: (1) a ban on meetings and processions for a month before the election; (2) a limit on campaigning; (3) massive presence of police and troops; (4) arrests of U.P.G.A. supporters; (5) the absence of local electoral officers to accept nominations by U.P.G.A. candidates; (6) use of thugs to prevent U.P.G.A. candidates from making nominations; (7) multiple voting and ballot-box "stuffing" for the N.N.D.P.; (8) riots, sporadic fighting, and firing by police and troops on crowds on election day; (9) detention of U.P.G.A. leaders announcing the formation of an interim government before taking power in the region; and (10) announcing election results at the regional capital rather than locally.

Within a month of the election, U.P.G.A. supporters and other dissidents responded to the election fraud (and the political manipulation of cocoa prices--see chapter 3) by spontaneous riots, ambushes, arson, and armed rebellion against members of the regional government and their sympathizers. By December 1965, the Western Region was near anarchy.[30]

The Period of Military Government

The 15 January 1966 military intervention in politics, in which Prime Minister Balewa, Federal Finance Minister Festus Okotie-Eboh, Northern Premier Ahmadu Bello, Western Premier S.L. Akintola, and nine army officers were killed, was predominantly spearheaded by young Ibo majors. Some evidence indicates that the rebellion was instigated to forestall drastic measures by the federal government to quash opposition elements in the West (and other parts of the south), which were expected after a 14 January meeting of several leading politicians from the ruling alliance and a few army officers.

As early as December 1965, rumors freely circulated: (1) that the N.N.A. intended to remove officers not identified with the party, such as G.O.C. Ironsi and other southerners; (2) that the federal government planned to foment a disturbance as a basis for declaring a state of emergency in the East and creating a new region there to undermine the N.C.N.C.'s support; and (3) that the premiers of the North and West proposed to use the army to strike against U.P.G.A. supporters in the West.[31]

The principal architect of the coup, Major Chukwuma Nzeogwu, surrendered on 17 January to another Ibo, Ironsi, who as G.O.C. became head of the new federal military government. Despite the ethnic composition of the mutineers and victims leading some to suspect the coup was an attempt to establish Ibo suzerainty, initial reactions were not unfavorable, partly because of disillusionment with the disorder (three months of uncertainty and near anarchy in the West), favoritism, and corruption accompanying civilian rule.

The 15 January conspirators thought they could eliminate a corrupt political order, establish a radical socialist regime, and destroy Northern political dominance by deposing the political elite, enforcing honesty, and proclaiming new policies. Efforts by the army mutineers and the Ironsi government can be interpreted, in part, as an attempt to insure the security of the southern regions and, more specifically, the Ibo community, by removing the firm hold of Northern emirs and administrators on the federal government.

The stresses resulting from the regional and communal competition for a share of the economic pie had been transmitted to the army, and had politicized its officer corps. Perhaps the conspirators perceived that their positions and promotions were endangered by policies of regional quotas for lower ranks, and regional balance for officer recruits, which enhanced the share of the educationally backward North. Additionally, some radical southern soldiers resented the way the ruling coalition used the army for political purposes in the Western party struggle in 1962, in the riots of the Tivs (a dissident lower Northern community) in 1964, in the election crisis during 1964-65, and to repress opponents in the rigged Western election of October 1965. A government's legitimacy among its citizens is threatened when it resorts to force, rather than authority, to maintain order.

Within a few months, potential opposition elements, especially in the North, became convinced that Ironsi was using the powerful political and economic levers at the center primarily on behalf of the Ibo and other southern communities.[32] The Ironsi government 24 May promulgated Decrees 33 and 34, which replaced the regional federation with a unitary administration, imposed a unified civil service, banned parties and communal organizations of a political character, and implied a possible continuance of the regime for three years. Timing of these decrees was inept, because they prejudged several study groups commissioned in the previous three and one-half months.

The Nwokedi Commission was studying the unification of Nigeria's administrative machinery and public services, and the Constitutional Review Study Group was considering the relative merits of unitary and federal forms of government.[33] And the decrees were introduced at a time of fear of Ibo hegemony, present since the coup, but exacerbated by the dependence of Ironsi on advice from fellow Ibos, and his failure to punish the mutineers. The unification of the executive class of the civil service, together with the earlier repudiation by the Northern military governor of the policy of "Northernization" of the private and government sectors, aroused anxieties in the North about losing jobs to better-educated southern Nigerians.

University students, who stood to lose virtually guaranteed high-level positions in the regional government, and civil servants in the North held protest demonstrations against Decrees 33 and 34. Their protests gave impetus to the unrest of such marginal urban groups in the upper North as the unemployed, daily-paid laborers, and petty traders and contractors, threatened by Ibo competition. These groups, who established a symbiotic relationship with the Native Authorities and former N.P.C. politicians, spearheaded the 29-30 May riots in which hundreds of Ibos were killed and much of the property was destroyed.[34]

The dominant economic interests behind Ironsi, the Ibos in the federal administration and the joint-stock companies in Lagos and the East, made few overtures to win the support of the non-Ibo elites in the south, and even some Ibos in the East were disenchanted. The new regime managed to antagonize radical Nigerians in the armed forces, and in the West and Middle Belt who were opposed to the previous civilian government. It even alienated the influential politicians and aristocracy of the far North, while doing little to undercut their base in the Native Authority councils and administration, districts, and villages, and their power to incite the peasants and urban unemployed.[35]

Before 1966, the Northern ruling group had been able to control some of the Middle Belt communities through such negative measures as economic sanctions and political reprisals and through such positive inducements as regional preferences in employment in the modern sector, which especially benefited their educated classes.

Ironsi's government might have offered political concessions to the Middle Belt that would have weakened their tenuous ties to the far North. Instead Ironsi temporarily united the elites of the far North and Middle Belt by threatening the long-standing practice on Northernization of employment, a policy in the interest of both sections.

General Ironsi and a number of other Ibo officers were killed 28-29 July 1966, in a rebellion or counter coup launched in a charged atmosphere of rumors circulating rampantly of an Ibo plan to annihilate key Northerners. Disorders in the army continued for a few days until Lieutenant Colonel Yakubu Gowon, an Angas (a small Middle Belt community), emerged as the head of state. Only he, the senior Northern officer in the army, appeared capable of receiving the support of both the rebelling troops (predominantly from the Middle Belt) and the federal civil servants. After some early doubts concerning the viability of a unified Nigeria, one of Gowon's first acts was to return the country to the federal structure that existed before the May decree. Gowon was more representative of the soldiers and educated classes of the Middle Belt than of far Northern politicians.

The rift between the Eastern and federal military governments, which eventually widened into a civil war, began immediately after the second coup. The East recognized the Gowon government as only an interim regime, on the grounds that Gowon was not the highest-ranking army officer, and on the basis of an understanding by the Eastern government that he was to retain power only until the military had the opportunity to decide on the country's future. Also the violence directed against persons of Eastern origin in the North in May and September-October 1966, and their flight to their ethnic homelands, diminished the economic advantage of the East's continuing in the federation, and strengthened secession forces. Finally, the failure of the coup in the East, the departure of Northern soldiers from that region, and the repatriation of Eastern soldiers in August 1966, meant that its military governor, Lieutenant Colonel Odumegwu Ojukwu, had effective control of all troops there, and of the Nigerian police force in the region.

The legacies of the coups affecting national stability were the decimation of national military leadership and mistrust among military personnel of different ethnic origins. Political and army leaders of the three major ethnic groups no longer felt safe in areas with army battalions dominated by other communities. Yet despite the agreement in early August 1966 between Gowon and the regional military governors, which ordered all soldiers to return to "their respective regions of origin," the federal government kept Northern troops in Lagos and the West.[36]

Although Gowon summoned a meeting of the regional military governors and other members of the Supreme Military Council for September 1966 to review the country's political structure, the Council did not convene until January 1967, in Aburi, Ghana, largely due to the fear of Ojukwu, the military governor of the Eastern Region, that he would be in danger elsewhere in Nigeria. Stremlau's statement about the Aburi talks is accurate. "Anyone who has read [either the federal or Eastern text of] the highly controversial Aburi transcript cannot deny that Gowon was immediately put on the defensive by his adversary from the East who, through careful preparation and quick wit, extracted a series of apparent concessions that could be construed as leaving Nigeria without a central government."[37]

By February 1967, Ojukwu declared that further acts of the federal government would be regarded as illegal by the East, since he contended that the East was ignored and by-passed in the agreements at Aburi. The East, which had previously held Northern produce sent to Port Harcourt for export, and railway rolling stock, 1 April 1967 seized a portion of the federal revenues collected within the region, citing alleged delays in payment of their share of the pool and of salaries to Eastern refugees in federal employment. The Gowon government retaliated by suspending certain services and imposing increased restrictions on converting international currency in the Eastern Region.

Further action by the East within the next three weeks, seizing an aircraft of Nigeria Airways, purchasing £6 million sterling, taking over all federal statutory bodies, authorizing its marketing board to enter into direct contracts with foreign buyers, abolishing appeals to the federal Supreme Court, and calling all Easterners serving in the federal police and navy to return, led to additional economic sanctions, including a limited embargo, against the East.[38]

The Eastern Region's Consultative Assembly 26 May 1967 began a meeting that gave Ojukwu a mandate for secession late on 27 May. Earlier that same day, anticipating the mandate, Gowon proclaimed a state of emergency, and decreed the creation of twelve states from the previous four regions and federal territory.[39]

Gowon's action indicated a shift away from the major ethnic communities, especially the Hausa-Fulanis and Ibos, to the minorities in the Middle Belt, Mid-West, and non-Ibo areas of the East. The decree culminated an eight-month deadlock among the three major ethnic groups, who tended to favor a confederation of the existing regions, and the smaller communities, especially in the Middle Belt, who supported more states in a strong federation. The six new states in the old Northern Region formalized the decline of the traditional aristocracy in the far North, whose previous hegemony was based on political control of the whole region, comprising a majority of the population in the federation. The new structure cut off two minority states from the previous ruling community in the East, the Ibos. It also severed a major industrial center, Port Harcourt, and a large part of the oil-producing areas from the Ibo majority in the landlocked East-Central state (later Anambra and Imo states).[40] This arrangement was considered by the East to violate the agreement at Aburi for greater regional autonomy. The Eastern leaders, with little support from local non-Ibos, moved 30 May 1967 to protect their regional hegemony by declaring the East the independent Republic of Biafra.

Secession threatened the new ruling elite in Nigeria, the high-ranking military leaders and government servants, and the minority communities, whose interests coincided with a strong central government. The Western Region, contrary to indications early in May by its consultative assembly and its leading spokesman, Chief Awolowo (freed from prison in 1966), remained in the federation, where the region's economic interests lay. Although Ibos held fewer posts in the federal civil service than Yorubas, the Ibos provided strong competition for certain positions, and here was a chance for Westerners to make gains at the center by supporting the federation against Eastern secession. Also enough federal troops (primarily Northerners) were present in the West to enforce the federal will against opposition.[41]

Finally, the appointment of Awolowo to be top civilian in the government, deputy chairman of the newly-created Federal Executive Council, and finance commissioner, and the Biafran attack on a Western city, were also important factors in the West's decision to opt for the federation.[42]

In 1966, in the revulsion against civilian rule, the military overlooked functions that politicans had performed, like representing and aggregating divergent interests and providing a sense of participation by newly mobilized groups. Until it faced the prospect of immediate disintegration of the federation after the July 1966 coup, the military did not realize the necessity of fulfilling a political function even though there were no longer any formal parliamentary institutions.[43] Despite the persistent deep mistrust of politicians by many of the regional military governors, Gowon eventually provided for more representation and articulation of the views of major political interest groups than Ironsi had.

CONCLUSION

British colonial rule helped create or exacerbate regional differences and identities that contributed to political instability. The higher literacy, greater parliamentary experience, and more developed capitalist institutions in southern Nigeria than in the North are legacies, in part, of British colonial policy.

Two major factors contributing to disintegration from World War II through the 1960s were the struggles between majority and minority groups within each region, and the contentions among elites of the Eastern, Western, and Northern Regions. One regional elite could attain political and economic security only at the expense of another. The Northern rulers and administrators, through the sanction of religion, coercion, and the control of major economic benefits, prevented opposition elements in the Middle Belt and Kano province from making inroads into their parliamentary representation. Control of the giant Northern Region was sufficient for federal dominance. But it threatened the security of government officials and new elites in the south, who faced a dilemma between aligning with the conservative North or joining radical socialist groups in the south and the opposition parties in the North in a "progressive" coalition.

Membership in a ruling federal coalition aligned to the North was a powerful attraction for the major southern parties. A federal opposition party even risked losing a position of control in the regional assembly, because a ruling federal coalition had substantial patronage and sanctions available to undermine rivals in the regions.

A coalition aligned to the North was inclined toward conservatism, opposing trade union programs, leftist intellectuals, and radical civil servants. Nevertheless, during 1960-62, Chief Awolowo, the leader of the opposition party in the federal parliament who had long been personally inclined towards socialism, reacted to his somewhat vulnerable position by trying to become the spokesman against imperialism and for the dispossessed and underprivileged. Subsequent attempts by the conservative federal coalition to crush the A.G. during 1962-63, and the A.G.-N.C.N.C. alliance during 1964-65, set the stage for army intervention into politics, and the civil war.

NOTES

1. I.F. Nicolson, *The Administration of Nigeria, 1900-1960: Men, Methods, and Myths* (Oxford: Clarendon Press, 1969), pp. 216, 246, 304-305.

2. J.D. Fage, *A History of West Africa: An Introductory Survey* (4th ed., Cambridge: Cambridge University Press, 1969), pp. 69-70, 78-79.

3. Ibid., p. 80, James S. Coleman, *Nigeria: Background to Nationalism* (Berkeley and Los Angeles: University of California Press, 1958), p. 36, and Michael Crowder, *The Story of Nigeria* (London: Faber and Faber, 1962), pp. 110-4.

4. Nicolson, *Administration of Nigeria*, p. 11, Crowder, *The Story of Nigeria*, pp. 135, 151-2, and Coleman, *Nigeria*, p. 36.

African states and political entities in pre-colonial Nigeria were not united in opposing British conquest. Obaro Ikime indicates how inter-African politics explain patterns of collaboration with and resistance to the British in the nineteenth century. "Colonial Conquest and Resistance in Southern Nigeria," *Journal of the Historical Society of Nigeria*, VI, No. 3 (December 1972), 251-70.

5. Coleman, *Nigeria*, p. 42.

6. Strictly speaking, Nigeria was a protectorate, except for the Lagos crown colony.

7. Coleman, *Nigeria*, pp. 42-65.

8. Crowder, *The Story of Nigeria*, pp. 165-9, 178; C.S. Whitaker, Jr., *The Politics of Tradition: Continuity and Change in Northern Nigeria, 1946-1966* (Princeton, N.J.: Princeton University Press, 1970), pp. 259-63, and Coleman, *Nigeria*, pp. 45-53.

9. Coleman, *Nigeria*, p. 153.

10. Ibid., pp. 54, 162-3, and F.D. Lugard, *The Dual Mandate in British Tropical Africa* (4th ed.: London: William Blackwood, 1929), p. 86.

11. Coleman, *Nigeria*, pp. 162-3.

12. James O'Connell, "Political Integration: The Nigerian Case," in *African Integration and Disintegration: Case Studies in Economic and Political Integration*, Arthur Hazlewood, ed. (London: Oxford University Press, 1967), p. 156; and John P. Mackintosh, *Nigerian Government and Politics* (Evanston, Ill.: Northwestern University Press, 1966), p. 163.

13. J.W. Burton, *Systems, States, Diplomacy and Rules* (Cambridge: Cambridge University Press, 1966), p. 124; and Frantz Fanon, *The Wretched of the Earth* (New York: Grove Press, 1963).

14. Coleman, *Nigeria*, pp. 50-2, 192-210.

15. A.G. Hopkins, *An Economic History of West Africa* (London: Longman, 1973), pp. 180-5.

16. Coleman, *Nigeria*, pp. 252-9; Wogu Ananaba, *The Trade Union Movement in Nigeria* (New York: Africana Publishing Corporation, 1969), pp. 26-65; and P.C. Lloyd, *Power and Independence: Urban Africans' Perception of Social Inequality* (London: Routledge & Kegan Paul, 1974), pp. 67-8.

17. Paul Beckett and James O'Connell, *Education and Power in Nigeria* (New York: Africana Publishing Co., 1978), p. 64.

18. For a superb political biography of Adegoke Adelabu, a man

caught between loyalties to the Ibo-led nationalist movement and Yoruba nationalism, see Kenneth W.J. Post and George D. Jenkins, *The Price of Liberty: Personality and Politics in Colonial Nigeria* (Cambridge: Cambridge University Press, 1973).

19. Although not a region after 1939, the "south" included what became the Western, Mid-West, and Eastern Regions, and Lagos, the federal territory, in 1963-67 (see figure 1.1).

20. The far North consisted of what was later Borno (predominantly Kanuri rather than Hausa-Fulani), Bauchi (partly Hausa-Fulani), Kano, Kaduna, and Sokoto states (predominantly Hausa-Fulani), while the Northern Middle Belt included Kwara, Niger, Plateau, and Gongola states (see figure 1.3).

21. Richard L. Sklar, *Nigerian Political Parties: Power in an Emergent African Nation* (Princeton, N.J.: Princeton University Press, 1963); B.I.C. Ijomah, "The Social Characteristics of Nigeria's Political Leaders Before Independence," *The Conch*, V, Nos. 1 & 2 (1973), 105-28; and Whitaker, *The Politics of Tradition*, pp. 299-374.

22. In discussing abuses by Nigerian elites, the concept "corruption" is about as useful as that of "sin." Ronald Wraith and Edgar Simpkins, *Corruption in Developing Countries* (London: George Allen & Unwin, 1963), pp. 12-13, contend that "there was never a time in the history of corruption in the public life of Britain when there were not powerful forces fighting against it. In the end these won. . . . In Africa corruption flourishes as luxuriantly as the bush and the weeds which it so much resembles, taking the goodness from the soil and suffocating the growth of plants which have been carefully, and expensively, bred and tended." B.J. Dudley, *Instability and Political Order: Politics and Crisis in Nigeria* (Ibadan: Ibadan University Press, 1973), p. 46, even represents the relationship between violence and corruption graphically. Neither these sources nor Samuel P. Huntington, *Political Order in Changing Societies* (New Haven, Conn.: Yale University Press, 1968), pp. 59-71, however, has a clear standard for defining corrupt behaviour. For a lucid discussion of corruption, see James C. Scott, *Comparative Political Corruption* (Englewood Cliffs, N.J.: Prentice-Hall, 1972).

23. Dudley, *Instability and Political Order*, p. 75 (italics in the original).

24. Whitaker, *Politics of Tradition*, pp. 373-4.

25. Stanley Diamond, *Nigeria: Model of a Colonial Failure* (New York: American Committee on Africa, 1966), p. 34; and Margery Perham, *Native Administration in Nigeria* (London: Oxford University Press, 1962), p. 234.

26. Robert Melson, "Marxists in the Nigerian Labor Movement" (Ph.D. dissertation, Massachusetts Institute of Technology, 1967), pp. 35-84.

27. K.W. Post, *The Nigerian Federal Election of 1959--Politics and Administration in a Developing Political System* (London: Oxford University Press, 1963), p. 395; and James O'Connell, "Political Integration," in *African Integration and Disintegration*, Hazlewood, ed., pp. 155-6.

28. For more on the political struggle in the West, see Richard L. Sklar, "Nigerian Politics: The Ordeal of Chief Awolowo,

1960-65," in *Politics in Africa: Seven Cases*, Gwendolen M. Carter, ed. (New York: Harcourt, Brace & World, Inc., 1966), pp. 119-65.

29. O'Connell, "Political Integration," in *African Integration*, Hazlewood, ed., p. 170; Mackintosh, *Nigerian Government*, pp. 586-7; and Robin Luckham, *The Nigerian Military--A Sociological Analysis of Authority and Revolt, 1960-67* (Cambridge: Cambridge University Press, 1971), pp. 237-8.

30. Kenneth Post and Michael Vickers, *Structure and Conflict in Nigeria, 1960-1966* (Madison, Wis.: University of Wisconsin Press, 1973), pp. 220-33.

31. Dudley, *Instability and Political Order*, p. 100.

32. For example, among the twelve officers promoted to lieutenant colonel in May 1966 to fill the gaps from the January coup, eight were Ibo. Nevertheless, none of the Ibos were advanced above non-Ibo officers of equivalent or greater seniority. Thus, Luckham, *The Nigerian Military*, p. 57, argues, "If one's starting point is the normal working of the promotional system according to the principles of seniority and merit, then there is little or no evidence of systematic discrimination in favour of the Ibos as a group."

33. Ibid., pp. 264-6; and A.H.M. Kirk-Greene, *Crisis and Conflict in Nigeria: A Documentary Sourcebook, 1966-1969*, I (London: Oxford University Press, 1971), 42-3, 48-9.

34. Dudley, *Instability and Political Order*, pp. 132-3; and Luckham, *Nigerian Military*, pp. 272-3.

J.H. Smith, "The Impact of the Creation of States upon the Public Service of Northern Nigeria," unpublished manuscript, (Rhodes House, Oxford, England, ca. 1969), maintains that the Northern bureaucracy, which reacted strongly against Decrees 33 and 34, favored Northern secession after the July 1966 coup. These views were strengthened by army troops in Lagos consisting primarily of Northerners.

35. Dudley, *Instability and Political Order*, pp. 129-32.

36. John de St. Jorre, *The Nigerian Civil War* (London: Hodder and Stoughton, 1972), p. 80.

37. John J. Stremlau, *The International Politics of the Nigerian Civil War, 1967-1970* (Princeton, N.J.: Princeton University Press, 1977), p. 46.

38. S.K. Panter-Brick, ed., *Nigerian Politics and Military Rule: Prelude to the Civil War* (London: The Athlone Press, 1970), pp. 48-9.

39. In his address to heads of diplomatic missions in Lagos 24 April 1967, Gowon had warned Ojukwu, "I want to make it abundantly clear that in the event of Lt.-Col. Ojukwu carrying out his threat to secede, this will be a clear signal in the first place to create a COR-State [Calabar-Ogoja-Rivers State, the creation of which was a constant objective of minority groups in Eastern Nigeria during the 1950s] for the protection of the minorities in Eastern Nigeria whom we know do not want to part from the rest of the country. This action of creating the COR-State will be backed by the use of force if need be." See Document 103 in A.H.M. Kirk-Greene, *Crisis and Conflict*, I, 414.

40. See Howard Wolpe, *Urban Politics in Nigeria: A Study of Port Harcourt* (Berkeley and Los Angeles: University of California

Press, 1974), pp. 213-28.

41. As indicated in chapter 4, the leaders of the Western Region had asked in early 1967 that Northern troops be removed from the region.

42. See B. J. Dudley, "Western Nigeria and the Nigerian Crisis," in *Nigerian Politics and Military Rule: Prelude to the Civil War*, S.K. Panter-Brick, ed. (London: The Athlone Press, 1970), pp. 106-9, for a discussion of divisions between (and among) federalists and confederalists in the West, and reasons why the West did not secede and become "neutral" in the war between the East and the North, a position consistent with the view of Chief Awolowo and the confederalists in early 1967.

43. M.J. Dent, "The Military and Politicians," ibid., pp. 78-80.

2 Transnational Linkages after Independence

In Nigeria, 1960 to 1966 was a period of a decline in the colonial nexus and a "diversification of the pattern of economic relations inherited at independence,"[1] even though the country still depended highly on Britain for foreign trade, aid and investment, political support, and military assistance. Callaway argues that Nigeria is a neo-colonial state because political independence did not significantly affect her economic dependency before the oil boom, after 1970.

For Callaway, neo-colonialism is the process by which colonial patterns of dependency are sustained after formal political independence is granted. Neo-colonialism's primary objective is to maintain the former colony as a controlled source of raw materials and a market for investment and sale of manufactured goods.[2]

Under Callaway's definition Nigeria was not a "neo-colonial state." But it was if we use a commoner concept that focuses on continued dependence on developed capitalist countries, not just the colonial power.

Some of Nigeria's economic and political dependence on the former colonial power, Britain, was replaced by dependence on other industrialized, capitalist countries, such as the United States and the original six members of the European Economic Community. Even though Nigeria's overall dependence on foreign countries gradually declined in 1960-66, her economic dependence on capitalist countries in the 1960s was still substantial enough to severely limit the ability of her political system to cope with domestic political crises.

INTERNATIONAL TRADE

Nigeria's role in the international division of labor between primary and secondary commodities continued in the post-independence era. As late as 1965, despite a substantial growth in the relative importance of secondary exports, 7.8 percent of exports and 80.9 percent of imports were secondary products (chemicals, machinery, transport equipment, and manufactured goods), while 91.8 percent of exports and 17.8 percent of imports were primary products (food, raw materials, minerals, and organic oils and fats).

Despite the rapid increase in trade with the U.S. and

continental Western Europe, and the relative decline in the importance of commerce with Britain in the previous decade, 38.5 percent of exports and 30.9 percent of imports were with that nation in 1965 (table 2.1). Almost all Nigeria's trade was with the developed capitalist economies, with only a trace (less than 5 percent) with the socialist and less developed countries.[3] That pattern, a legacy from the colonial period, remained fairly strong, even after independence. Policies of the Nigerian government attached little importance to indigenous industrial ventures, maintained economic dependency, and integrated its economy into the world capitalist system.

FOREIGN INVESTMENT

In November 1960, just after independence, Chief Festus Okotie-Eboh, minister of finance and leader of the House of Representatives, made Nigeria's favorable position toward foreign capital clear in a speech to the House.

> A new nation like Nigeria cannot be built on the basis of nationalization. I need, perhaps, only refer to the examples of America and Canada to illustrate how rapid and orderly development has been achieved by private enterprise efforts; including a large measure of foreign capital, but without the over-hanging threat of nationalization. . . . Nationalization, based on quasi-Communist ideas, is alien to our philosophy.[4]

Although Nigeria lacks a consistent source of information on foreign investment over time, the data available suggest that direct private foreign investment as a percentage of gross fixed investment probably increased between the 1950s and 1960s,[5] and that Britain's share of the percentage of estimated investment in fixed assets by foreign companies between 1953-59 and 1962-66 stayed at about 60-70 percent.[6]

In 1962, most foreign private capital was in three sectors: £N85.8 million, trading and services; £N80.6 million, mining and quarrying (including petroleum); and £N36.8 million, manufacturing and processing [7] (table 2.2). From 1961 through 1966, the share of foreign private investment in mining and quarrying expanded but the share in trading and business services fluctuated around a declining trend line (table 2.3).

Nigerian businessmen encroached more on foreign dominance in trade in the 1950s and early 1960s than in manufacturing and mining. From the 1920s through the 1940s, the Nigerian market, especially for import trade, was dominated by a relatively few large, highly integrated European merchant firms, like the United Africa Company (a Unilever affiliate), *Compagnie Francaise de l'Afrique Occidentale* (CFAO), *Societé Commerciale de L'Ouest Africain* (SCOA), John Holt, Paterson Zochonis, and the Swiss Union Trading Company (UTC).

As import demand grew and capital requirements for entry into trade fell during the two decades after World War II, Nigerian traders' share of import trade increased from 5 percent in 1949 to

TABLE 2.1
Nigerian Exports and Imports, 1955-66

Year	Total Exports[a] (£N 000s) (1)	Total Imports (£N 000s) (2)	Exports to U.K./ Col. 1	Imports from U.K./ Col. 2	Exports of S.I.T.C.,0, 1[b]/Col. 1	Exports of S.I.T.C.,2[b] /Col. 1	Exports of S.I.T.C.,3, 4[b]/Col. 1	Exports of S.I.T.C.,5, 6,7,8[b]/ Col. 1	Imports of S.I.T.C.,0, 1[b]/Col. 2	Imports of S.I.T.C.,2, 3,4,[b]/ Col. 2	Imports of S.I.T.C.,5, 6,7,8[b]/ Col. 2
1955	129,816	136,117	.699	.467	.235	.617	.127	.018	.132	.060	.786
1956	132,261	152,713	.645	.448	.214	.620	.145	.019	.139	.060	.779
1957	124,177	152,468	.631	.434	.250	.577	.152	.019	.156	.066	.755
1958	135,550	166,274	.554	.437	.243	.601	.134	.018	.142	.066	.774
1959	163,497	178,405	.505	.454	.274	.574	.133	.017	.149	.070	.765
1960	165,619	215,891	.481	.423	.259	.569	.144	.026	.139	.062	.774
1961	170,067	222,519	.448	.382	.217	.580	.176	.024	.129	.071	.781
1962	164,013	230,217	.429	.320	.228	.501	.196	.073	.139	.081	.762
1963	184,865	207,477	.399	.341	.200	.523	.197	.078	.119	.090	.771
1964	210,462	253,880	.383	.309	.224	.442	.245	.086	.092	.091	.802
1965	263,246	275,148	.385	.309	.188	.380	.350	.078	.091	.087	.809
1966	278,697	286,372	.377	.297	.135	.360	.422	.082	.109	.043	.835

[a]Includes only domestic exports, not re-exports.

[b]The number for S.I.T.C. sections refer to:

0,1	Food, beverages, and tobacco
2	Crude materials (inedible) except fuels
3,4	Mineral fuels, lubricants, related materials, animal and vegetable oils, and fats
5,6,7,8	Chemicals, machinery, transport equipment, and manufactured goods.

Note: Other exports were never more than 0.4 percent of total exports, while other imports never exceeded 2.5 percent of the total.

Sources: Nigeria, Office of Statistics, *Annual Abstract of Statistics: Nigeria, 1963* (Lagos, 1963), pp. 62, 85-91; and *Annual Abstract, 1967* (Lagos, 1968), pp. 87-90.

TABLE 2.2
Foreign Private Capital[a] in Nigeria, 1962 (by type of activity)

	(£N millions)
Mining and quarrying	80.6
Manufacturing and processing	36.8
Agriculture, forestry and fishing	4.3
Transport and communication	2.4
Building and construction	7.6
Trading and services	85.8
Miscellaneous activity	0.9
Total	218.4

[a]Net worth of foreign private enterprises.

Source: Ranald S. May, "Direct Overseas Investment in Nigeria, 1953-63: Some Aspects of its Constitution and Contribution to Nigeria's Economic Development," *Scottish Journal of Political Economy*, XII (November 1965), 246.

about 20 percent in 1963. And Indian, Lebanese, Greek, and Syrian merchants, and European manufacturers began to compete with the established European merchant firms.[8] Before independence, Nigerians were more highly represented in domestic trade than in industry and international trade,[9] and their share of the internal market increased in the early 1960s.

Although Nigeria's output in 1965-66 was only about one-sixth of that in 1973-74 (see table 6.1), it was the world's thirteenth ranking oil producer, with recognized potential for rapid expansion. Foreign private annual investment and cumulative capital in mining and quarrying (largely petroleum) in 1966 exceeded these figures in any other sector of the economy (tables 2.2 and 2.3). At that time, the seven major international oil companies (with headquarters in the United States, the United Kingdom, and the Netherlands) dominated the world's crude petroleum market. A buyer's market meant that the head office of the oil company would periodically reassess its world marketing position, and then reallocate output to various producing areas by choosing the most promising investment alternatives, based partly on the policies of the producing countries, and other relationships with the international majors.

Nigeria had little voice in matters of pricing, royalties, calculating profits, or distribution of earnings among the oil-producing countries and the importing countries. Still the Lagos government had little alternative but to ask large foreign oil corporations to search for and produce oil in the country. Producing petroleum required complex technology and large capital investment. Nigeria had only limited expertise in oil, and the market for crude petroleum for nonintegrated oil companies was

TABLE 2.3
Analysis of Foreign Private Investment, 1961-66 (£N millions)

	1961	1962	1963	1964	1965	1966	Cumulative 1961-66
Type of activity							
Mining & quarrying	5.8	4.5	12.5	35.5	35.7	47.8	141.8
Manufacturing & processing	5.0	12.0	11.0	9.3	10.9	5.0	53.2
Agriculture, forestry & fishing	- 0.9	- 0.1	0.6	0.5	0.2	- 0.8	- 0.5
Transport & communication	0.3	0.1	0.2	0.9	2.3	0.7	4.5
Building & construction	0.5	2.8	2.4	1.4	7.8	-10.6	4.3
Trading & business services	12.3	- 9.1	11.5	4.8	- 8.4	13.0	24.1
Miscellaneous activity	--	0.2	- 0.3	10.6	6.7	- 5.7	11.5
Total	23.0	10.4	37.9	63.0	55.2	49.4	238.9
Source of funds							
Unremitted profits	2.7	7.9	13.4	17.8	37.8	59.5	139.1
Changes in foreign share & loan capital (net)	8.7	4.9	10.5	20.8	2.4	1.4	48.7
Trade & suppliers' credit (net)	2.3	2.3	1.8	4.6	4.8	1.4	17.2
Other foreign liabilities (net)	3.4	1.7	1.4	1.3	0.6	3.6	12.0
Liabilities to head offices	10.2	0.9	10.8	18.5	9.6	-16.5	33.5
Total	27.3	17.7	37.9	63.0	55.2	49.4	250.5

Note: Totals by *type of activity* differ from the totals by *source of funds* in 1961 and 1962 because source of funds was revised.

Source: World Bank, *Nigeria: Options for Long-term Development* (Baltimore: The Johns Hopkins University Press, 1974), p. 220.

TABLE 2.4
The Relative Size of Foreign Ownership and of Employment in Nigerian Manufacturing Industries, 1965

ISIC No.[a]	Ind.[a]	Cap.[c] (£N'000)	For. Pri./ Pri. Own.[d]	Ng. Pub./ Ng. Own.[e]	Ng. Pri./ Tot. Own.[f]	For. Pri./ Tot. Own[g]	Tot. Emp.[h]	For. Emp./ Tot. Emp.[i]	For. W&S/ Tot. W&S[j]
201	Meat	393	0.569	0.508	0.298	0.394	1,056	0.020	0.275
202	Dairy	153	0.940	0.833	0.046	0.725	256	0.030	0.352
203	Fruit	--	--	--	--	--	524	0.004	0.130
205	Grain	1,104	0.935	0.833	0.022	0.869	584	0.059	0.470
206	Bak'y	572	0.537	0.144	0.404	0.468	2,559	0.007	0.120
208	Sugar	490	0.639	0.000	0.361	0.640	950	0.027	0.232
207,211	Disti	1,887	0.899	0.952	0.018	0.161	2,857	0.012	0.241
209,220	Food	6,354	0.903	0.128	0.095	0.890	2,563	0.018	0.189
213	Beer	5,228	0.803	0.306	0.134	0.545	2,984	0.030	0.278
214	Drink	797	0.970	0.969	0.015	0.503	868	0.029	0.311
231,232	Txtls	5,962	0.952	0.894	0.033	0.662	11,554	0.027	0.293
241	Ftwr	732	0.696	0.485	0.234	0.535	1,761	0.029	0.292
243	Wear	110	0.600	0.000	0.400	0.600	652	0.013	0.136
244	TxGd	476	0.589	0.562	0.269	0.386	1,379	0.024	0.348
251	SwMl	2,910	0.557	0.244	0.387	0.487	8,176	0.009	0.194
259	Wood	5	0.000	0.000	1.000	0.000	104	0.000	0.000
260	Frntr	801	0.688	0.200	0.289	0.639	4,251	0.019	0.176
272	Paper	970	0.669	0.000	0.330	0.669	686	0.035	0.384
280	Print	2,824	0.646	0.858	0.095	0.193	5,708	0.035	0.086
291,293	TnTr	336	0.892	0.359	0.080	0.666	726	0.023	0.218
300	Rub'r	6,218	0.842	0.589	0.120	0.643	6,843	0.017	0.268
311	Chem	300	0.912	0.816	0.063	0.660	295	0.057	0.428
312	VgOM	3,612	0.908	0.616	0.065	0.650	7,057	0.007	0.163
313	Paint	816	0.934	0.600	0.025	0.938	407	0.078	0.488
331	BrTl	245	0.910	0.000	0.090	0.910	352	0.034	0.338
332,333	Potry	380	0.871	0.935	0.021	0.144	882	0.011	0.172
334	Cemnt	5,261	0.335	0.312	0.253	0.127	2,393	0.022	0.201
339	Cncrt	2,792	0.959	0.857	0.038	0.737	1,480	0.025	0.387
341,342	BsMt	1,250	0.971	0.826	0.025	0.857	694	0.057	0.455
350	MtPd	4,006	0.954	0.589	0.043	0.896	6,620	0.045	0.351
370	Elctl	369	0.902	0.330	0.092	0.853	759	0.023	0.253
381	Boat	60	0.000	1.000	0.000	0.000	352	0.011	0.125
383,385	Vhcl	1,105	1.000	0.000	0.000	1.000	1,880	0.024	0.263
	Other[b]	9,037	0.950	0.853	0.046	0.726	15,530	0.213	0.278
	Total	67,467	0.848	0.676	0.111	0.619	97,051	0.024	0.247

Source: Nigeria, Office of Statistics, *Industrial Survey of Nigeria, 1964 and 1965* (Lagos, 1968), pp. 32, 34, 37.

TABLE 2.4 (continued)

[a]The following industries correspond to the International Standard Industrial Classification (ISIC) code in the table.

ISIC No.	Industries	ISIC No.	Industries
201	Meat products	272	Paper products
202	Dairy products	280	Printing
203	Fruit canning	291,293	Tanning and travel goods
205	Grain mill products	300	Rubber products
206	Bakery products	311	Basic industrial chemicals
208	Sugar confectionary	312	Vegetable oil milling
207,211	Sugar and spirit distillery	313	Paints
209,220	Miscellaneous food products	331	Bricks and tiles
213	Beer brewing	332,333	Pottery and glass products
214	Soft drinks	334	Cement
231,232	Manufacture of textiles	339	Concrete products
241	Footwear	341,342	Basic metals
243	Wearing apparel	350	Metal products
244	Made-up textile goods (excluding wearing apparel)	370	Electrical equipment
251	Saw milling	381	Boat building and repairs
259	Other wood products	383,385	Motor vehicle and bicycle assembly
260	Furniture and fixtures		

[b]ISIC numbers for other industries are 319, 321, 329, 360, 384, 391, 394, and 399.

[c]Paid up capital.

[d]Foreign private ownership/total private ownership.

[e]Nigerian public ownership/total Nigerian ownership.

[f]Nigerian private ownership/total ownership.

[g]Foreign private ownership/total ownership.

[h]Total employed, refering to the total number of workers engaged, i.e. working proprietors, paid employees, unpaid apprentices, and unpaid family workers.

[i]Number of non-Nigerians employed/total employed.

[j]Wages and salaries of non-Nigerians/total wages and salaries.

restricted because the oil-exporting countries had not yet attained bargaining strength. Three producing companies, Shell-British Petroleum (British-Dutch), Gulf (American), and Safrap (French), and six others with concessions in 1966 each held 100 percent ownership in exploring and producing companies in Nigeria.[10]

Hakam's estimates indicated that in 1964 nearly 75 percent of the book value of industrial assets of firms in Nigeria with a value of £N25,000 (about $70,000) or more was foreign; the British accounted for slightly more than 50 percent of the total.[11] The 1965 *Industrial Survey* of manufacturing establishments with ten or more employed,[12] showed that foreign private ownership comprised 62 percent of total ownership and 85 percent of total private ownership in the manufacturing sector in Nigeria (with ownership shares measured by paid-up capital) (table 2.4). Foreign interests continued to dominate new registrations of manufacturing companies on the eve of the 1966 army mutiny; 78 percent of the thirty-three largest manufacturing companies registered during 1964-65 represented some foreign ownership or management. Lewis estimated that Nigerian income comprised less than 30 percent of the 1963 value-added in foreign, large-scale manufacturing firms.[13]

That foreigners in Nigerian manufacturing in 1965 accounted for as much as 24.7 percent of the total wages and salaries but only 2.4 percent of the total employment (table 2.4) shows that they were highly represented among high-level personnel in the industrial sector. According to estimates from table 2.5, 55.3 percent of the 2,355 professional and managerial personnel in manufacturing firms in Nigeria in 1965 with 100 or more employed were foreign.

Foreign firms frequently obtained access to markets, labor, inputs, and government officials through local intermediaries. These middlemen, usually Nigerian businessmen, acted as "importers, exporters, representatives for foreign salesmen and marketing firms, representatives for foreign firms seeking a particular contract, job-finders, advisers, facilitators, intermediaries, brokers, agents, contact men, and assistants of all varieties." For this service, the middleman received a fee or kickback.

Some such income may have been paid to state officials who made the transaction possible. Thus, there were usually indigenous intermediaries and government officials who also benefited from the establishment of foreign enterprises in Nigeria.[14]

INTERNATIONAL AID AND FINANCE

Nearly all of Nigeria's foreign exchange assets before the 1970s were sterling. Under the post-World War II modified gold-exchange standard of the International Monetary Fund, British sterling was a key currency in international trade. In essence, a country that accumulates sterling, as Nigeria did in the 20 years before 1955, extends credit to Britain, facilitating her long-term investments in underdeveloped economies.

During the period of restrictions on converting sterling from World War II to 1958, Nigeria contributed more dollar earnings to the common sterling pool than she withdrew, and she restricted non-sterling imports in a way to increase the importance of imports

TABLE 2.5
Estimates of Professional and Managerial Employees in Nigerian Manufacturing Firms with 10 or More Employed, 1965[a]

Size of firm (by employment)	Number of indigenous firms	Number of foreign firms	Total number of firms	Number of indigenous professional and managerial personnel in indigenous firms	Number of indigenous professional and managerial personnel in foreign firms	Number of foreign professional and managerial personnel in all manufacturing firms	Number of professional and managerial personnel in all manufacturing firms
10-24	1,888	42	1,930	3,766	82	174	4,022
25-49	318	94	412	957	216	286	1,459
50-99	112	75	187	468	227	511	1,206
100-199	52	47	99	223	155	362	740
200-499	27	38	65	170	190	423	783
500-999	8	16	24	71	106	252	429
1000-1999	3	4	7	36	41	141	218
2000 & over	2	3	5	27	34	124	185
Total	2,410	319	2,729	5,718	1,051	2,273	9,042

Source: E. Wayne Nafziger, *African Capitalism: A Case Study in Nigerian Entrepreneurship* (Stanford, Calif.: Hoover Institution Press, 1977), pp. 84-5.

from the United Kingdom.[15] That strengthened both the balance-of-payments position of the sterling area and the international financial position of the U.K.

The Central Bank, created in 1958, issued a new Nigerian currency on par with the pound sterling, and was required to maintain 80 percent sterling assets and balances in Britain to support local issues of the currency. In 1961, the 80 percent requirement was lowered to 40 percent, and as much as 20 percent of foreign exchange holdings could be held in gold or U.S. dollars.[16]

Between 1946 and 1958, Britain's grant of £27 million through the Colonial Development and Welfare Act was virtually the sole source of Nigeria's external economic assistance. After independence, however, partly as a result of Nigeria's policy of diversification, the sources expanded to a consortium representing the World Bank group and the rich capitalist countries, i.e., the United States, Canada, the present European Economic Community countries, Japan, and Sweden.[17]

For the First National Development Plan, 1962-68, foreign aid comprised one-half of planned public sector investment.[18] Firm offers of foreign aid for this plan, during 1962-64, from the aid consortium were £156.72 million (or 91.6 percent of the total, £N171.72 million). But only £N25.19 million (or 14.7 percent of the offers) was from the British government, which because of a weakened international balance-of-payments position, could not maintain her previous rate of expanding economic aid after 1962.

Apart from scholarships, the only direct assistance from the Soviet bloc before 1966 was, an unspecified amount of credit in March 1962, a £N15 million loan granted by Poland in June 1962, and a £N5 million loan by Czechoslovakia in September 1965. In late 1960, the newly independent government rejected an offer by the Soviet Union for an interest-free loan of £N30 million.[19]

Debt servicing became a major problem just before the Nigerian civil war, as the net international outflow of private direct income exceeded the net inflow of private direct investment by £N73.4 million to £N55.0 million in 1966, a reversal from 1965 when it was less than the net inflow by £N61.4 million to £N53.4 million, and 1960-64 when its annual average was less than the net inflow by £N33.0 million to £N12.3 million.[20]

Largest shares of the $441.047 million of external public debt outstanding 31 December 1965, repayable in foreign currency to nonprivate sources, were held by the following: 41.1 percent by the International Bank for Reconstruction and Development (or 49.1 percent by the World Bank group), 21.6 percent by the United Kingdom, and 13.9 percent by the United States. The aid consortium held 98.9 percent of the total.[21] Nigeria temporarily suspended certain foreign exchange payments during the war, which hampered her ability to obtain credit and crucial imports.

FOREIGN DOMINANCE, INDUSTRIAL CONCENTRATION, AND TECHNOLOGICAL TRANSFER

Another colonial legacy partially responsible for the primacy of the foreign industrial sector was the dominance of overseas banks. The principals of these banks, especially the Bank of West

Africa (largely owned by Lloyds Bank, the Westminster Bank, the National Bank, and the Standard Bank) and Barclays Bank D.C.O., were dubious concerning the viability of indigenous firms. As late as 1965, 90 percent of total demand deposits were held in banks where foreign capital was at least a majority.

The Nigerian government favored the foreign sector through its industrial policies. The government granted "pioneer" status, which included income-tax holidays of 2-5 years, to new enterprises of high priority, mostly large-scale and relatively heavy industry, which was primarily foreign. Of the 145 companies designated "pioneer" between 1952 and 1966, only six were exclusively Nigerian. Foreign firms benefited disproportionately from many other governmental concessions, such as accelerated depreciation allowances, import duty relief, equity and loan finance, and land acquisition provisions, as well as improved public services.[22]

Unlike most developed countries in early stages of industrialization, in Nigeria foreign merchants and manufacturers, rather than domestic entrepreneurs, took the lead in developing import-substitution industries. A prime motive for establishing foreign enterprise, according to empirical studies, was to change a highly competitive market in international trade to one with competition virtually eliminated. Ironically, the greatest pressure for increased protection for manufacturing was not from the government, or even from domestic producers, but from foreign capitalists and their local collaborators.[23]

Foreign dominance of the manufacturing sector was accompanied by high rates of industrial concentration. Table 2.6 indicates that the total value-added of the largest four establishments in 31 manufacturing industries as a percentage of the total value-added in the 31 industries was 69.0 percent in Nigeria in 1965 compared with 3.7 percent in the same 31 industries in the U.S. in 1947. In addition, total employment by the largest four firms in these industries was 72.2 percent of total employment in Nigeria compared with 3.3 percent in the U.S. (The appendix to this chapter indicates that Nigerian and U.S. data are highly comparable. Also see the appendix for the basis for selecting industries, and the method of computing concentration rates.)

The overwhelming majority of the foreign firms have been multinational corporations, companies with headquarters outside Nigeria. Although foreign subsidiary firms dominated production in Nigeria's nascent industrial sector, output of the subsidiary enterprises usually was only a fraction of the output of the parent companies.

Control of technology in Nigeria has been concentrated in the advanced economies of North America, Western Europe, and Japan. Müller's data on patents granted by a group of mixed and capitalist less developed countries indicate that more than 90 percent were granted to foreigners. If the number of patents is weighed by their economic or technological worth (i.e., volume of sales or value-added), the patents granted to foreigners by these less developed countries exceeded 99 percent.[24]

A major argument by Nigerian elites for overseas investment was the necessity to transfer techniques of modern production to Nigeria. But the advantages to Nigeria from the foreign firms'

TABLE 2.6
Concentration Rates[a] of Value-added and Employment Compared in Selected Manufacturing Industries in Nigeria, 1965, and the U.S., 1947

ISIC No.[b]	Ind.[b]	No. Es-tab Ng.[c]	No. Es-tab. U.S.[d]	Tot. Emp. Ng.[e]	Tot. Emp. U.S.[f]	Emp. Conc Rate[g] Ng.	Emp. Conc Rate[g] U.S.	Value added CR[h] Ng.	Value added CR[h] U.S.
201	Meat	10	3,974	1,056	275,441	0.747	0.097	0.869	0.055
202	Dairy	4	7,816	256	207,669	1.000	0.018	1.000	0.021
205	Grain	6	4,206	584	113,217	0.963	0.066	0.999	0.069
206	Bak'y	70	7,123	2,559	297,368	0.297	0.028	0.408	0.044
208	Sugar	6	1,754	250	91,710	0.908	0.085	0.782	0.113
207,211	Disti	3	825	2,857	73,542	1.000	0.090	1.000	0.124
209,220	Food	9	6,691	2,563	150,794	0.884	0.049	1.000	0.072
213	Beer	6	493	2,984	85,058	0.767	0.138	0.590	0.164
214	Drink	13	5,618	868	79,397	0.647	0.031	0.788	0.036
231,232	Txtls	34	3,715	11,554	864,309	0.553	0.025	0.715	0.024
241	Ftwr	21	1,314	1,761	257,428	0.566	0.084	0.587	0.102
243	Wear	15	24,706	652	940,939	0.440	0.011	0.357	0.010
244	TxGd	6	6,254	1,379	127,631	0.950	0.077	0.894	0.055
251	SwMl	46	19,039	8,176	380,456	0.729	0.203	0.750	0.290
259	Wood	4	2,349	104	65,514	1.000	0.059	1.000	0.037
260	Frntr	55	7,687	4,251	322,384	0.312	0.031	0.582	0.037
272	Paper	8	8,315	686	701,296	0.855	0.015	0.864	0.010
280	Print	77	28,986	5,708	715,450	0.374	0.025	0.452	0.047
300	Rub'r	35	849	6,843	230,967	0.441	0.116	0.255	0.094
311	Chem	6	975	295	271,624	0.902	0.085	0.941	0.079
312	Vg OM	62	1,194	7,057	43,431	0.481	0.066	0.490	0.077
313	Paint	8	1,456	407	67,807	0.730	0.096	0.840	0.089
331	BrTl	7	711	352	36,945	0.871	0.084	0.791	0.088
332,333	Potry	7	1,792	882	148,633	0.939	0.085	0.979	0.096
334	Cemnt	5	155	2,073	35,662	0.969	0.083	0.959	0.084
339	Cncrt	12	6,158	1,480	46,821	0.680	0.027	0.371	0.031
341,342	BsMt	3	4,552	694	1,030,042	1.000	0.026	1.000	0.019
350	MtPd	40	17,545	6,620	1,020,490	0.360	0.020	0.340	0.015
370	Elctl	10	3,973	759	801,359	0.674	0.044	0.853	0.037
381	Boat	3	809	352	19,455	1.000	0.232	1.000	0.211
383,385	Vhcl	11	1,980	1,880	716,736	0.854	0.197	0.932	0.032
	Total	613	183,014	80,221	10,118,075	0.722	0.033	0.690	0.037

Source: Nigeria, *Industrial Survey, 1964 and 1965*, pp. 40-1; and U.S., Department of Commerce, Bureau of the Census, *Census of Manufacturers: 1947*, Vol. II, *Statistics by Industry* (Washington, D.C.: U.S. Government Printing Office, 1949).

TABLE 2.6 (continued)

[a]Concentration rate refers to the size of the four largest establishments in the industry/the size of the total industry.

[b]For the industries that correspond to the ISIC code in the table, see note a, table 2.4.

[c]Total number of establishments, Nigeria.

[d]Total number of establishments, U.S.

[e]Total employment, Nigeria (see footnote h, table 2.4).

[f]Total employment, U.S.

[g]Total number employed by the largest four establishments in each industry in terms of employment size/total number employed in the industry.

[h]Total value-added of the largest four establishments in each industry in terms of employment size/total value-added in the industry.

contributions to national output should be weighed against some possible disadvantages. To retain control of operations and markets within the company, large foreign firms discouraged transmission of knowledge or skills to high-level domestic personnel.

Moreover, the pecuniary interests of many indigenous capitalists and middlemen became linked with those of their foreign partners or benefactors. And in the manufacturing sector, small-scale indigenous enterprises, which were weak and vulnerable in industries with high concentration rates and high foreign ownership percentages, rarely expanded enough to reach the threshold of a large industrial unit (i.e., £N25,000 assets or more).[25]

Manufacturing concerns controlled by Lebanese, Greeks, Syrians, Cypriots, and Palestinians (referred to here as "Levantines") need to be distinguished from western and Japanese industrial enterprises. Although most Levantine business families came to Nigeria between 1900 and 1940, they were considered foreign by the Nigerian government, despite their quasi-permanent residence in Nigeria. They proceeded from small beginnings in transport and small-scale trade to develop several important industrial units. Their operations were smaller than those of westerners,[26] and few had headquarters outside Nigeria.[27] The Lebanese were especially resented by their Nigerian competitors, even though the 1964 book value of their industrial assets, from firms in Nigeria with a value of £N25,000 or more, was only 8 percent of assets held by Europeans or North Americans.[28] Levantine firms in the footwear industry resisted the Nigerianization of management and capital as much as did European footwear firms.[29]

ECONOMIC INTERESTS AND FOREIGN POLICIES

The political elite profited from foreign investment during the civilian regime, 1960-66. In some cases, external interests formed partnerships with members of the governing elite or their business constituents, or with the quasi-government corporations, which widened the elite's patronage and income base. Frequently, leading politicians benefited from foreign firms through "rake-offs" on their contracts, intermediary roles in land deals, sales in inputs and services, positions on the boards of directors, jobs for clients, and political financing.

One example, the "turnkey" project, in which the seller of machinery arranges to have the plant built and management provided "so that the factory is ready to come into operation on the turn of a key," has been fairly widespread in the public sector in Nigeria. Kilby suggests a political explanation for this: "Prestigious capital-intensive projects can be achieved quickly, they provide well paid directorship for politicians as well as jobs for the unemployed, they are an important source of party finance via the 'kick-back,' and they do not require any money down--they are financed on the basis of supplier credit." However, he asserts that, as of December 1966, not a single indigenous unit in Nigeria was earning a profit from a "turnkey" project. Furthermore, sizeable deferred foreign exchange costs had a substantial negative impact on the balance of payments. Some reasons for these projects' lack of viability were the extensive corruption of the political leadership, the poor matching of various pieces of machinery and equipment in the production process, excessive charges for capital costs, over-staffing, and poor management and technical personnel.[30]

The headquarters countries of multinational corporations in Nigeria usually extended political, military, and/or economic assistance, partly to help support those who wished to keep the country open to foreign investment and trade. British capital and aid helped reinforce the pro-British sympathy of the Northern-dominated civilian government.

The Northern ruling aristocracy, highly sympathetic to British economic and military interests in Nigeria, and opposed to the influence of communist countries, could reasonably expect the British to resist any threat to Northern hegemony and regional security, including threats from radical socialists or from potential southern-dominated ruling coalitions. By attracting British capital and assistance, the North minimized the threat of a high concentration of southern entrepreneurship, technical expertise, and labor in its economy; the British were more sensitive to regional employment preferences in the North, and they respected the old authoritarian social system.

The analysis in this chapter, together with the discussion in chapter 4 on interregional and international trade flows, suggests that Nigeria is highly integrated into the international capitalist economy. The North was at least as dependent on the capitalist world for trade and investment as the other regions. According to Hakam, employment and output in foreign firms were greater in Northern Nigeria than any other region. And before the expansion of petroleum production in the Eastern Region in the 1960s, Northern Nigeria received as much export revenue from primary products, mainly groundnuts and seed cotton, as any other region.[31]

Nigeria's military forces during the civilian era were

especially dependent on foreign personnel, equipment, and assistance. Although the Nigeria regiment traced its origin to local forces raised to carry out the British conquest in the second half of the nineteenth century, there were few efforts to commission Nigerians as officers before 1948-49. The War Office in London, the ultimate authority in the army, before April 1958, was effectively insulated from pressures for Nigerianization. At independence, only 22 percent of the army officers was Nigerian (61 of 283); the rest were British. A Nigerian first became a battalion commander in January 1961, a brigade commander in January 1963, and a general officer commanding the Nigerian Army in March 1965.

Until the end of 1966, all Nigerian officers had received at least part of their training in foreign military academies (Britain, Australia, Canada, Ethiopia, India, Pakistan, and the U.S.). And almost everything used in the Nigerian armed forces (except items such as khaki and leather goods) was manufactured in foreign countries. Even as late as 1966-67, the first new ordnance factory, built on a turnkey basis by a West German firm after Nigerian independence, did no primary manufacturing, only maintenance and repairs. Depending on outside powers for equipment, weaponry, and military expertise limited the sovereignty of Nigeria over its internal affairs, as indicated below.[32]

Britain did not need military force or aggressive diplomacy to protect her interests during the Nigerian crisis of 1966-67 because Nigeria depended on Britain (and its western allies) for trade, aid, capital flows, and military supplies. British foreign policy, however, consistently supported an economically integrated Nigerian federation open to international trade and investment. The mutineers of 15 January 1966, whose objective seems to have been to establish a radical socialist regime, surrendered a few days later to General Ironsi, who announced that policies favorable to foreign capital would be continued. How much Sir Francis Cumming-Bruce, the British high commissioner, influenced the meeting of the Nigerian federal cabinet the day after the coup is not certain. In early 1966, slowly but quietly, the ousted Northern politicians, with the aid of Britons still employed in the administrative, professional, and high technical classes of the regional civil service, capitalized on the growing fears of Ibo domination that the Ironsi regime posed, especially after the 24 May 1966 decree which imposed a unitary government and civil service.[33]

After the 28-29 July 1966 coup, Sir Cumming-Bruce, and the American ambassador, Elbert Mathews, visited Lieutenant Colonel Yakubu Gowon at the Ikeja barracks and pleaded with him to keep the country together. "They told me," Gowon later recalled in an interview with Stremlau, "that not another dime in foreign assistance would come to Nigeria" if the regions separated.[34] Pressure by Cumming-Bruce and Mathews may have helped avert an announcement by Gowon of Northern secession and the break-up of the federation in his broadcast to the country 1 August 1966.[35] Opposition by British diplomats helped dissuade Nigerian civilian leaders at the September 1966 constitutional conference, and military leaders at the January 1967 conference in Aburi, Ghana, from agreeing on confederation. British mediation supported

General J.A. Ankrah, head of Ghana's military government, in his efforts to bring together the Supreme Military Council (the Eastern military governor, Colonel Ojukwu, the three other military governors, and Gowon) for the Aburi meeting. However, federation was clearly unacceptable to the East, which had been close to de facto secession by October 1966. Insistence upon a strong federation helped foreclose a possible compromise based on a looser confederation between the East and the rest of Nigeria.

In the second quarter of 1967, the British and American governments assured Lagos they favored Nigerian unity and would not support Eastern secession. But the two governments declined to take sides in what they regarded an internal dispute.[36] Although Britain, for example, did not encourage Biafran secession, she discouraged the Nigerian declaration of war to put the secession down. In the months before the federal military government initiated its "police action" against Biafra 6 June 1967, British officials advised the Nigerian government that a war against the East probably would not be winable, and might result in total national disintegration.[37] These views, undoubtably known to Eastern leaders, may have contributed to their confidence in Biafra's viability.

When secession occurred, British oil interest faced a dilemma of whether to pay revenue to Nigeria or Biafra. On 21 June, Ojukwu ordered that all oil revenues in Biafra be paid into the Bank of Biafra. To underline his order, he had Stanley Gray, managing director of Shell-British Petroleum, the major firm producing oil in the East, incarcerated--in the plush Presidential Hotel in Enugu. Later Gray, pleading *force majeure* under international law, offered a token payment of £250,000 under protest, on the £7 million oil royalties demanded by Biafra.[38] In early July, Nigeria, in response to this offer and no royalty from Shell-B.P., mounted a boycott and newspaper attack against the firm, extended its blockade on Biafran ports to oil tankers, and announced a "police action" to crush the secession.

In July, a federal naval amphibious force captured the ocean oil terminal intact at Bonny, in the Rivers area. The Bonny victory convinced the British government and Shell-B.P. that their interests lay with the federal government.[39] Soon after, the offer by Shell-B.P. was countermanded by the British government, a majority holder in the company. The Bank of England, presumably instructed by the British treasury, refused exchange control permission for the payment.

In the wake of disruption of oil supplied from West Asia, Britain doubtless did not want to risk severing her increasing share of oil originating outside Biafra, in the Mid-West and offshore oil wells. Nor did she want to lose her substantial influence in Nigeria to other powers.

In August 1967, Nigeria, in response to British and U.S. governments' refusal to provide aircraft and arms, purchased arms from the Soviet Union. By the end of 1967, in response to Nigeria's capture of Biafra's oil terminal, Soviet arms sales to the federal government, and Biafra's indirect purchases of two B-26 bombers from a French arms dealer, Britain became the dominant supplier of arms to the federal government. The United Kingdom's military sales and diplomatic support of the federation, in addition to maps, navigational charts, weather information, and some transportation for invading troops provided by British subsidiary firms, were factors contributing to the eventual Nigerian victory.[40]

CONCLUSION

In the early 1960s, Nigeria's political elite was highly dependent on western countries for trade, capital, technical transfers, economic and military assistance, and military equipment. The economic and political interests of the Nigerian elite were much influenced by the rewards and sanctions available to such foreign powers as Britain and the United States. Nigeria's depending on foreign decisions and actions helped create domestic political enmities, and prevented the Lagos government from coping with them. In particular, consistent British (and American) insistence on a federated Nigeria hampered an agreement for a confederation. And Nigeria's depending on British military and economic assistance prevented a substantial military effort by the Lagos government to quell the Biafran secession within a month or two. But by the end of 1967, Britain's support was a major factor strengthening Nigeria's military position in what became a long war of attrition.[41]

APPENDIX: THE MEASUREMENTS OF CONCENTRATION IN NIGERIAN AND U.S. MANUFACTURING

This appendix explains how the intra-industry concentration rates in manufacturing in Nigeria in 1965, and in the U.S. in 1947 were derived. They are based on data obtained by making assumptions essential to find a correspondence between individual firms, and on quantitative data on value-added and employment in the *Industrial Survey of Nigeria, 1964 and 1965*, the last survey before the civil war, and the U.S. Department of Commerce, Bureau of the Census, *Census of Manufacturers: 1947*.

The Nigerian data were taken from the Industrial Survey of 1965. Several types of information collected in 1964, particularly on paid-up capital, were not valid because of ambiguities in the questionnaire, which were clarified in 1965.[42] The U.S. 1947 *Census of Manufacturers* was chosen, as I was unaware of any other census volume that had data by industry comparable to Nigeria's industry classification in 1965.

Of the 33 Nigerian industries of 1965 (table 2.4), each producing goods that are more or less satisfactory substitutes for each other, 31 U.S. industries (table 2.6) could be delineated in a similar fashion. Because establishments with fewer than 10 employed are not included for Nigerian industry, establishments with 1-9 employed were deleted from computations of concentration in the U.S. Otherwise the categories of average employment size are fairly comparable. In Nigeria the categories are 10-19, 20-49, 50-99, 100-299, 300-499, 500-999, and 1,000 and more. The only variations in the U.S. categories are a division between 249 and 250 (rather than between 299 and 300), and an extra category of

2,500 employees and more. The addition has little impact on relative concentration rates, as only 10 of 613 establishments in Nigeria in table 2.6 employed 1,000 or more.[43] Finally, the definition of employment in Nigeria and the U.S. is the same.

To measure the degree of industrial concentration in Nigerian and U.S. manufacturing, the concept of a concentration rate was used because it indicates the proportion of value-added and employment contributed by the largest four establishments of an industry. The delineation of an industry in the Nigerian *Industrial Survey* conforms to one or two three-digit numbers, classified according to the International Standard Industrial Classification (ISIC) code.

Packard's study of concentration in manufacturing in 1963 and 1965 indicated that it is not possible to identify intra-industry concentration in Nigeria.[44] However, the key to the data in the Nigerian *Industrial Survey* and the U.S. *Census of Manufacturers* for measuring intra-industry concentration in value-added (i.e., total value-added of the largest four establishments in each industry in terms of employment size as a percentage of the total value-added) is to make the following two simplifying assumptions: (1) All establishments in a given employment size (i.e., 10-19, 20-49, 50-99, 100-299, 300-499, 500-999, 1,000 and more) have the same value-added--namely the total value-added for that employment size category divided by the number of establishments. (Although that assumption tends to understate slightly the concentration in value-added, because value-added varies somewhat among establishments in the same employment size category, there is no reason to believe that the understatement introduced any systematic bias into the comparative figures for the U.S. or Nigeria.) (2) Each establishment in a higher employment size category also has a greater value-added than any of the establishments in a lower employment size category.

For 1965, the *Industrial Survey* indicates the distribution of establishments within each industry group by employment size, and the distribution of value-added within each industry by the employment size of establishments. In computing total value-added of the largest four firms in the vegetable-oil milling industry (ISIC No. 312) in 1965, e.g., assumption (1) allows the addition of £N1.296 million (for the one establishment that employed more than 1,000) to £N0.737 million (the aggregate for the two establishments employing 500-999) to £N03.72 million (for one of the four establishments tied for fourth place employing 300-499, whose value-added is calculated by dividing the aggregate value-added for the four establishments, £N1.487 million by 4) to get value-added equal to £N2.405 million, which is 49.0 percent (the concentration rate) of total value-added in the industry, £N4.912 million.[45]

Assumption (2) lets a person eliminate from consideration the 55 firms with fewer than 300 employed when computing the value-added of the largest four establishments.

The way to measure intra-industry concentration in employment (i.e., total number employed from the largest four firms in each industry in terms of employment size as a percentage of the total number employed) is to use Bain's technique[46] for averaging the statistically possible maximum and statistically possible minimum values for employment. For example, in the vegetable-oil milling industry, I added 1,889 (the employment for one establishment employing more than 1,000) to 1,059 (the aggregate employment for the two establishments employing 500-999) to 499 (the statistical maximum for the largest establishments, in terms of employment, of the four establishments in the employment size category of 300-499 whose total employment is 1,556) to obtain 3,447, the statistical maximum. The statistical minimum for the fourth largest establishment in employment, 389 (calculated by assuming that all four establishments in the employment size category, 300-499, have the same number of employees), is added to 1,889 plus 1,059 to obtain 3,337, the statistical minimum for the aggregate employment of the four largest establishments.

The average of the statistically possible minimum and statistically possible maximum for the aggregate employment of the four largest establishments is 3,392, which divided by 7,057 (the total employment in the industry), gives a concentration rate of 48.1 percent (table 2.6).[47]

NOTES

1. Olasupo Ojedokun, "The Changing Pattern of Nigeria's International Economic Relations: The Decline of the Colonial Nexus, 1960-1966," *The Journal of Developing Areas*, VI (July 1972), 535-54.

2. Barbara Callaway, "The Political Economy of Nigeria," in *The Political Economy of Africa*, Richard Harris, ed. (Cambridge, Mass.: Schenkman Publishing Co., 1975), p. 103.

3. Nigeria's pattern of international trade with Britain was close to that of its trade with the world as a whole in 1965, with secondary products accounting for 14.1 percent of exports and 91.8 percent of imports, and primary products making up 85.9 percent of exports and 8.2 percent of imports. Nigeria, Office of Statistics, *Annual Abstract of Statistics: Nigeria, 1967* (Lagos, 1968), pp. 87-90.

In 1963-65, the Soviet bloc accounted for 2.3 percent of the imports, and less than 1 percent of the exports of Nigeria. Olatunde J.B. Ojo, "Nigerian-Soviet Relations: Retrospect and Prospect," *African Studies Review*, XIX, No. 3 (December 1976), 49.

4. Gordon J. Idang, *Nigeria: Internal Politics and Foreign Policy, 1960-1966* (Ibadan: Ibadan University Press, 1973), p. 143.

5. This percentage decreased from 0.25 in 1952-54 and 0.27 in 1955-57 to 0.18 in 1958/59-1960/61, after which it increased to 0.33 in 1961/62-1963/64 and 0.40 in 1964/65-1966/67. World Bank, *Nigeria: Options for Long-term Development* (Baltimore: The Johns Hopkins University Press, 1974), p. 15.

6. Nigeria, Office of Statistics, *Annual Abstract of Statistics: Nigeria, 1964* (Lagos, 1964), p. 105, and Central Bank of Nigeria, *Economic and Financial Review*, VI, No. 2 (December 1968), 24.

7. The Nigerian pound, which was on par with sterling before its devaluation in November 1967, exchanged for $2.80. Since 1 January 1973, two old Nigerian pounds (£N) have been equal to one naira (₦1).

8. Peter Kilby, *Industrialization in an Open Economy: Nigeria, 1945-1966* (Cambridge: Cambridge University Press, 1969), pp. 59-62.

9. Peter T. Bauer, *West African Trade: A Study of Competition, Oligopoly and Monopoly in a Changing Economy* (Cambridge: Cambridge University Press, 1954), pp. 22-67.

10. Scott R. Pearson, *Petroleum and the Nigerian Economy* (Stanford, Calif.: Stanford University Press, 1970), pp. 12-30; and Eno J. Usoro, "Foreign Oil Companies and Recent Nigerian Petroleum Oil Policies," *Nigerian Journal of Economic and Social Studies*, XIV, No. 3 (November 1972), 301-14.

11. "Industrial" refers to manufacturing, assembling, and processing. A.N. Hakam, "The Motivation to Invest and the Locational Pattern of Foreign Private Industrial Investments in Nigeria," *Nigerian Journal of Economic and Social Studies*, VIII, No. 7 (March 1966), 49-65. See Central Bank of Nigeria, "Foreign Private Investment in 1969 and 1970," *Economic and Financial Review*, XI, No. 1 (June 1973), 19, on total foreign private investment by country of origin, 1965-70.

12. See footnote h, table 2.4, for the definition of employment.

13. "Foreign large-scale manufacturing" refers to firms with ten or more persons employed where all paid-up capital has been supplied by non-Nigerians. Permanent and quasi-permanent residents of non-African origin are considered foreign. Samuel A. Aluko, *Fiscal Incentives for Industrial Development in Nigeria* (New York: United Nations Department of Economic and Social Affairs, 1967), p. 14; W. Arthur Lewis, *Reflections on Nigeria's Economic Growth* (Paris: Organisation for Economic Cooperation and Development, 1967), p. 26; and Nigeria, *Annual Abstract, 1967*, p. 4.

14. Terisa Turner, "Commercial Capitalism and the 1975 Coup," in *Soldiers and Oil: The Political Transformation of Nigeria*, Keith Panter-Brick, ed. (London: Frank Cass, 1978), pp. 168-9.

Steven Hymer, "The Efficiency (Contradictions) of Multinational Corporations," *American Economic Review*, LX, No. 2 (May 1970), 447, contends that the richest one-third of the population in less developed economies gains from multinational corporations at the expense of the remaining two-thirds of the population.

15. H.M.A. Onitiri, "Nigeria's International Economic Relations: A Survey," *Nigerian Journal of Economic and Social Sciences*, III, No. 3 (November 1961), 15-18.

16. Ojedokun, *Journal of Developing Areas*, VI, 539, 542.

17. Major private foundations and commercial firms in the west spent substantial money on market and feasibility studies. Between 1954 and the late 1960s the Ford Foundation gave more than $20 million to various projects, including support for the key (foreign) personnel in the Economic Planning Unit of the Federal Ministry of Economic Development responsible for developing the First National Development Plan, 1962-68. The Carnegie Foundation gave $700,000 to the Ashby Commission, which studied the Nigerian educational system. The Rockefeller Brothers Fund, which established a Lagos office in 1956, and Arthur D. Little, Inc., which advised the Nigerian government on investment policy

beginning in 1962, helped prepare feasibility studies for U.S. investors. Africa Research Group, "The Other Side of Nigeria's Civil War: A Class Based Probe into the War's Origins and Implication," Cambridge, Mass., April 1970, pp. 6-9; and Callaway, "The Political Economy of Nigeria," in *The Political Economy of Africa*, Harris, ed., p. 103.

18. Nigeria, Ministry of Economic Development, *National Development Plan, 1962-68* (Lagos, n.d.), p. 33.

19. Ibid., pp. 537-8, 543-4; Nigeria, Ministry of Economic Development, *National Development Plan: Progress Report, 1964* (Lagos, 1965), p. 31; and Gordon J. Idang, *Nigeria: Internal Politics and Foreign Policy (1960-1966)* (Ibadan: Ibadan University Press, 1973), p. 139.

According to Ojo, the Soviet Union's offer of aid to Nigeria took the form of credits granted only after the specifics of the "intended agricultural processing plants and training centers" had been worked out. The kind of details wanted--"elaborate documentation on project analysis, completion of site surveys, materials required, cost estimates and engineering and architectural designs"--was bound to overtax the executive capacity of Nigeria's administrative service. Since there was no guarantee that once satisfied, the Soviet Union would give the full upper limit of £N60 million in credits, it just did not seem worth the trouble for Nigeria to undertake the negotiations. *African Studies Review*, XIX, No. 3, 50.

Although the Soviet embassy opened in Lagos in March 1961, Nigeria did not open an embassy in Moscow until 1963.

20. Nigeria, *Annual Abstract, 1967*, p. 94.

21. Nigeria, Office of Statistics.

22. Ola Oni, "Development and Features of the Nigerian Financial System--A Marxist Approach," *Nigerian Journal of Economic and Social Studies* VIII, No. 3 (November 1966), 386-91; Aluko, *Fiscal Incentives*, pp. 58-146; and Okwudiba Nnoli, "The Nigeria-Biafra Conflict--A Political Analysis," in *Nigeria: Dilemma of Nationhood--An African Analysis of the Biafran Conflict*, Joseph Okpubu, ed. (Westport, Conn.: Greenwood Publishing Co., 1972), pp. 133, 137.

23. Kilby, *Industrialization*, pp. 48-59; and Hakam, *Nigerian Journal*, VIII, No. 1, 49-65.

24. Ronald Müller, "The Multinational Corporation and the Underdevelopment of the Third World," in *The Political Economy of Development and Underdevelopment*, Charles K. Wilber, ed. (New York: Random House, 1973), pp. 126-7.

25. Turner, "Commercial Capitalism and the 1975 Coup," in *Soldiers and Oil*, Panter-Brick, ed., pp. 166-79; and Nafziger, *African Capitalism*.

26. Kilby, *Industrialization*, p. 61.

27. For the origin of the Lebanese businessmen in West Africa, see Michael Crowder, *West Africa under Colonial Rule* (London: Hutchinson, 1968), pp. 293-8.

28. Greeks, Syrians, Cypriots, and Palestinians are not mentioned in the statistics, although some may be included in the category, "other," whose holdings of industrial assets are 11 percent of citizens from Europe or the United States. Hakam,

Nigerian Journal, VIII, No. 1, 65.

29. Nafziger, *African Capitalism*, p. 63.

30. Kilby, *Industrialization*, pp. 78-9.

31. Abebayo Adedeji, *Nigerian Federal Finance: Its Development, Problems, and Prospects* (London: Hutchinson, 1969), pp. 122-4; P.N.C. Okigbo, *Nigerian National Accounts, 1950-57* (Enugu: Federal Ministry of Economic Development, 1961), pp. 52-9; and Hakam, *Nigerian Journal*, VIII, No. 1, 59-60.

32. Boniface I. Obichere, "Military Dependence in Historical Perspective: The Case of Nigeria," *The Conch*, V, Nos. 1 & 2 (1973), 82-104; N.J. Miners, *The Nigerian Army, 1956-1966* (London: Methuen & Co. Ltd., 1971), pp. 12-58, 108; and Robin Luckham, *The Nigerian Military: A Sociological Analysis of Authority and Revolt, 1960-67* (Cambridge: Cambridge University Press, 1971), pp. 163, 232-9.

33. Callaway, "The Political Economy of Nigeria," in *The Political Economy of Africa*, Harris, ed., p. 118.

34. John J. Stremlau, *The International Politics of the Nigerian Civil War, 1967-1970* (Princeton, N.J.: Princeton University Press, 1977), p. 35.

35. The decision to take out references to the break-up occurred at the last minute after Gowon had achieved wide support. John de St. Jorre, *The Nigerian Civil War* (London: Hodder and Stoughton, 1972), p. 75. Some have argued that a phrase in the broadcast, "the basis of unity is not there," indicates that Gowon's original intention was Northern secession, while others maintain that it merely indicates a plan to revoke Decrees 33 and 34 of 24 May 1966, which imposed a unitary central government and unified civil service.

36. Stremlau, *International Politics*, pp. 62-3.

37. The source for these two sentences is Olajide Aluko, "The Civil War and Nigerian Foreign Policy," *Political Quarterly*, XLII, No. 2 (April-June 1970), 178.

By and large, after the Biafran secession, the United States supported Britain's efforts in the Nigerian conflict. A crude indication of this was Dean Rusk's blunder in early June 1967 that angered Nigerians. Rusk, U.S. secretary of state, remarked that "We regard Nigeria as part of Britain's sphere of influence."

38. de St. Jorre, *The Nigerian Civil War*, p. 141.

39. Stremlau, *International Politics*, pp. xv, 76.

40. Roy Lewis, "Britain and Biafra: Commonwealth Civil War," *Round Table: The Commonwealth Quarterly* (July 1970), p. 242; Ojo, *African Studies Review*, XIX, No. 3, 54-6; Walter Schwarz, "Foreign Powers and the Nigerian War," *African Report* XV, No. 2, (February 1970), 12-13; *Petroleum Press Service*, July 1975, p. 265, and August 1967, p. 306; B.J. Dudley, *Instability and Political Order: Politics and Crisis in Nigeria* (Ibadan: Ibadan University Press, 1973), p. 106; A.H.M. Kirk-Greene, *Crisis and Conflict in Nigeria: A Documentary Sourcebook, 1966-1970*, vol. I, *January 1966-July 1967* (London: Oxford University Press, 1971), pp. 104-5; and Nnoli, "The Nigeria-Biafra Conflict," in *Nigeria: Dilemma*, Okpabu, ed., pp. 141-2.

No other country had the stake in Nigeria's petroleum that Britain did.

This study focuses on the economic factors affecting political violence, and the economic impact of political violence. Thus, the scope of the study precludes a detailed consideration of factors contributing to successful secessions, such as Texas, Panama, and Bangladesh, and failures, such as Biafra. One obvious similarity in the successes was the support of a powerful neighboring country, the United States for Texas in the 1830s and Panama at the turn of the twentieth century, and India for Bangladesh in 1971. In addition to Indian troops for Bangladesh in December 1971, Pakistan faced insurmountable logistical problems transporting supplies a thousand miles across hostile Indian territory, or almost three thousand miles by ship around India. Biafra, on the other hand, received little military or diplomatic assistance from abroad before September 1968 (see chapter 7), and lacked the international support to insure its continued production of oil. The major powers observed the blockade of Biafran ports by Nigeria's small navy.

41. Douglas G. Anglin contends that the economic alignment of Nigeria with the west in the early 1960s did not prevent its political nonalignment. For him, the "personal and political conviction [of the Nigerian foreign policy elite] may be a better clue to an understanding of Nigerian foreign policy than crude economic determinism." In several instances cited by Anglin where strong national interests and sentiments dictated--the abrogation of the Anglo-Nigerian Defence Pact in January 1962, the rejection of associate status in the European Economic Community in 1962, and the 1961 breaking of diplomatic relations with France after her third atomic explosion in the Sahara--Nigeria asserted its independence from ties with the west. ["Nigeria: Political Non-alignment and Economic Alignment," *The Journal of Modern African Studies*, II, No. 2 (1964), 247-63.] However, the renunciation of the pact did not affect military relations between Britain and Nigeria, as most of the arrangements covered by the pact were to continue under informal arrangements for Commonwealth consultation and cooperation. In addition, posting Dr. Pius C.N. Okigbo as Nigeria's ambassador to the European Community in 1963 was an attempt to seek other trading arrangments with the EEC. Furthermore, the refusal to recognize East Germany for fear of losing substantial West German aid, the concentration of the first diplomatic posts outside Africa in the west, the limited number of overseas missions in communist countries, and the decision to remain within the Commonwealth indicated a concern for external economic ties with the west. Finally, the foregoing discussion in this chapter suggests how Nigeria's foreign (and internal) policies were constrained by the nexus of economic dependence on the west.

For Sir Abubakar Tafawa Balewa, the prime minister from 1957 to 1966, the western powers, especially Britain and the United States, were Nigeria's best friends. In his independence broadcast Sir Abubakar told the nation, "We are grateful to the British whom we have known first as masters, then as leaders, and finally as partners, but always as friends." Six days later he warned the General Assembly that Nigeria "shall not forget" her old western friends under his leadership. Idang, *Nigeria: Internal Politics and Foreign Policy*, pp. 49, 137, 144.

Lloyd A Free, *The Attitudes, Hopes and Fears of Nigerians* (Princeton, N.J.: Princeton University Institute for International Social Research, 1964), pp. 5-18, indicates that the pro-western views of Balewa were similar to Nigerian members of the federal House of Representatives in 1962-63. Forty-one percent of his random sample of these representatives sided with the United States and Britain in the cold war, 2 percent with the Soviet Union, 50 percent with neither, and 7 percent gave qualified answers.

42. *Industrial Survey of Nigeria, 1964 and 1965*, p. 21.

43. Ibid., p. 38.

44. Philip C. Packard, "A Note on Concentration and Profit Rates within the Manufacturing Sector, 1963 and 1965," *Nigerian Journal of Economic and Social Studies*, XI, No. 3 (November 1969), 386.

45. *Industrial Survey*, pp. 38, 41.

46. Joe S. Bain, *International Differences in Industrial Structure: Eight Nations in the 1950's* (New Haven, Conn.: Yale University Press, 1966), pp. 27-28.

47. The figures for the calculation are in *Industrial Survey, 1964 and 1965*, pp. 38, 41.

3
Class Conflict and Economic Discontent

Those who lead the country into the abyss
Call ruling too difficult
For the ordinary.
Those who take the meat from the table
Teach contentment.
Those for whom the contribution is destined
Demand sacrifice.
Those who eat their fill speak to the hungry
Of wonderful times to come.
Bertolt Brecht, *From a German Primer*, 1937.

The rarity of slave rebellions and of uprisings among the disinherited and dowtrodden is notorious; on the few occasions when they occurred it was precisely "mad fury" that turned dreams into nightmares for everybody.
Hannah Arendt, *On Violence*, 1969

Broadly speaking, there are three classes of people in Nigeria. First, the educated classes consisting of the professional men and women, teachers, and clerks; second, the "enlightened" classes consisting mainly of traders and artisans; and third, the ignorant masses.

The number of educated persons is put at 2½ percent. This figure is probably incorrect; it is not unlikely that there are as many as 5 percent. Of this number only a very small percentage are politically conscious. The rest, together with the enlightened class, are indifferent.

As for the remaining masses, they are ignorant and will not be bothered by politics. Their sole preoccupation is to search for food, clothing, and shelter of a wretched type. To them, it does not seem to matter who rules the country, so long as in the process they are allowed to live their lives in peace and crude comfort.
Obafemi Awolowo, *Path to Nigerian Freedom*, 1947.

None of these conflicts (in Nigeria in the 1960s) was of poor with rich, workers with capitalists, or Nigerians

> with foreigners . . . Nigerian society, like most societies contained in national boundaries, is fissured ethnically and in other ways; if we do not observe great social classes in dramatic conflict, one reason is that the society is too heterogeneous to allow their formation.
>
> Douglas Rimmer, "Elements of the Political Economy," in *Soldiers and Oil*, Keith Panter-Brick, ed., 1978.

The position, interaction, and conflict of classes and occupational and economic groups while decolonizing and modernizing are important as background factors explaining internal war.[1] The relative position and regional distribution of economic groups and their representation in the Nigerian power elite affected regional identities and competition, and the potential for civil war.

The Nigerian political conflict of the 1960s did not follow Marx's scenerio of a united working class overthrowing a capitalist state. Even the Nigerianists at the Soviet Academy of Sciences admitted when I was in Moscow in May 1978, that Nigeria's industrial proletariat was too weak for such a revolutionary role.[2] But the conflict involved more than ethnic and regional strife.

THE SCOPE OF THE CHAPTER

This chapter is divided into two sections. The first examines discontent by relatively deprived classes and economic groups that contributed to increased political conflict in Nigeria in the early and middle 1960s. Included are: (1) discontent among younger graduates concerning the decline in vacancies in government, the military, business, and the universities; (2) the low morale of junior army officers resulting from a drop in openings and promotions; (3) labor discontent from the wide gap between wages of white-collar and blue-collar workers; and (4) grievances by cocoa cultivators regarding their contributions to marketing board surpluses. The second section analyzes elite interests in development planning and economic policy which affected political dissatisfaction by nonelites.

CLASS CONFLICT

Discontent among Younger Graduates

A major restive element in Nigeria has been the relatively deprived and politically discontented members of the educated classes.[3] During the decolonization process (1950s and 60s) many elite positions in the civil service, armed forces, police, government corporations, private business, and universities were opened in a short period of time as a result of rapid indigenization. For example, in the 1950s, the first Nigerian permanent secretaries in the Western Region had an average of ten years' service. During the same period, the first Nigerian professors and heads of departments at the University of Ibadan gained their chairs on the average seven years after beginning as assistant lecturer with a newly won Ph.D.

By the mid 1960s, however, vacancies were scarce because many foreigners had given way to Nigerians, and because those recently recruited were relatively young. New university graduates, with high aspirations for good positions and rapid promotion, based on observing careers of slightly older men, became frustrated with the abrupt decline in openings, especially at the top levels of the hierarchy, where salaries were disproportionately high.

Nigerians in the more than 4,000 senior posts in the federal public service increased from 19.3 percent in 1953 to 74.9 percent in 1961 to virtually 100 percent in 1965. In addition, Nigerians filled the majority of new positions created after the regional public services commenced in 1954. Returning university graduates from the Western Region in the mid 1950s were welcomed into a government position with its privileges and perquisites; in the mid 1960s this region inaugurated civil service examinations and was no longer bound to find jobs for those whose training it had financed.[4] Aspirants for government and university posts in 1965, for instance, may have been only slightly junior to those holding positions, and more qualified by education and training.

The frustration of educated southerners was exacerbated when less qualified Northerners were advanced over them to give regional balance to the federal civil service. Northerners also had access to more jobs in the Northern public service where fewer foreigners had retired during 1955-64. The southern governing elites expanded the number of senior posts and intensified policies of regional discrimination in employment in reaction to the decline in openings at the higher levels and the increase in unemployment rates for those with primary and secondary school certificates. But there was a limit to the growth of white-collar jobs that the political class could provide to placate disgruntled graduates.

Economic regionalization, though it exacerbated the geographical segmentation of the labor market, could not increase overall employment opportunities, but only contributed to greater regional conflict. By the mid 1960s the scramble for the few remaining posts was intense, and a perception of ethnic competition for them contributed to the enmity and bitterness, which set the spark for the crises of 1966 and 1967 (see chapter 4).

University graduates with good honors degrees, however, still received senior positions in the civil service. Although other graduates were not guaranteed the positions, they experienced virtually no unemployment because university graduates represented a mere 0.4 percent of the total labor force in Nigeria in 1965 (and even much less in Northern Nigeria). In the 1960s, Nigerian university students, who were expected soon to join the elite, consistently supported the dominant political and administrative elites in the region. During the general strike of June 1964, students, who organized essential campus services to prevent disruptions during final examinations, and workers at the University of Ibadan engaged in confrontation, which might have degenerated into bloody conflict, had the acting vice-chancellor not intervened. Student protests at Ahmadu Bello University in Zaria, Northern Nigeria, against the decree that replaced the regional federation with a unitary administration, and the repudiation of regional preference in employment very likely provided the spark for the riots of 29-30 May 1966 in which Ibos were killed and their property destroyed (chapter 1). A major center of support for Eastern secession was the University of Nigeria, Nsukka, where student enrollment increased from 2,500 to about 4,000 with the exodus from other regions after the July 1966 coup. In contrast, Pakistani university students, who faced high rates of unemployment upon graduation, were the most politically mobilized segment of the population in the late 1950s and early 1960s, and formed the vanguard of the revolts against the rule of General Ayub Khan in the 1960s.[5]

Low Morale among Junior Army Officers

A drop in the rate of openings and promotions was important in explaining the alienation and low morale in the army before the revolt by the majors in January 1966. The Nigerian army's distorted age structure and promotional pattern were determined by the rapid indigenization of the officer corps from 1 January 1960, when only 18 percent of the 278 officers were Nigerian, to 1 January 1964, when 89 percent of 419 were Nigerian, and 1 January 1966 when all 511 were Nigerian.

Rates of promotion for the small groups of officers commissioned before 1960 were especially high, particularly for a country not at war. (The Nigerian army did, however, assist in a series of "peacekeeping" operations in Cameroun, 1959-60, Zaïre, 1960-64, and Tanzania, 1964.[6]) An officer recruited at the age of nineteen or twenty in 1952-54 could expect to receive his commission after army training at the Royal Military Academy, Sandhurst, England, in 1954-56, and attain the rank of lieutenant colonel in 1963-55 when only thirty-one or thirty-two years old.

Promotions to the rank of major were even faster for the officers commissioned in the late 1950s, including the majors who initiated the January coup. By the end of 1965, officers in the middle ranks, majors and captains, faced distinctly longer waits for promotion than their predecessors.[7]

The waiting contributed to a feeling of deprivation among middle-rank officers, and a weakening of established patterns of discipline because sharp gradations in formal status and prestige existed alongside small gaps in age and experience between officers in command and those in subordinate positions. In addition, the top command (colonel and above) had been recruited from the ranks with no more than primary school, while subordinates generally had secondary education, and a direct commission after training at an army academy.[8]

Labor Unrest

The most visible aspect of class conflict was that between workers and the government in its dual role of ruler and major employer. From 1-12 June 1964, about 800,000 Nigerian workers, predominantly from the south, went on strike, defied the call of the prime minister to return to work, almost induced the collapse of his government, and won a large portion of their demands.

What was the basis for labor discontent that culminated in the

1964 general strike, state of emergency, and threat to the authority of the civilian government? Huntington argues that "the industrial worker in most modernizing countries is almost a member of the elite; he is economically far better off than the rural population, and he is usually in a favored position from governmental policy."[9] Several observers of labor problems in Nigeria, drawing upon Engels's concept of an "aristocracy among the working class" in late nineteenth century Britain, have emphasized the privileges of the regularly employed.[10] For Kilby

> Rather than being an exploited group, organized labour is already a highly privileged minority. Whether initiated by modernizing nationalists or the departing colonial benefactor, the full range of welfare measures contained in the ILO conventions (e.g., minimum factory conditions, workmen's compensation, a limited working week, paid holidays, old age and medical insurance, etc.) have now been implemented in the unionized sectors of nearly all the countries of Latin America, Africa, Asia, and the Middle East. . . . Likewise on the wages side, the labourer's earnings considerably exceed his opportunity income outside the organized employment market--in short, he is enjoying a higher standard of living than he has ever before known.
>
> The problems and tensions arising out of the adaptation to the industrial way of life in the less developed areas have proved to be far less significant than nineteenth-century history or twentieth-century sociological theorizing would indicate. Indeed it is difficult to find instances of *industrial* unrest in backward economies. There is much *labour* unrest but it has little to do with the absolute wage or conditions of work; rather it is, as in Nigeria, an expression of relative deprivation by the "haves" *vis-à-vis* the even smaller minority of the "have-mores." [Italics in the original.][11]

Dudley's policy prescription for 1970, when real[12] and relative remuneration of workers was no higher than in the prewar period, is like that of many scholars who oppose making concessions to the "privileged" urban workers. "Logically--and ideally--one would have expected that there was in fact only one option open to the [Adebo Wages and Salaries] Commission: to rule against any increases in wages and salaries." One reason for opposition to these increases is that, "Even at the lower [end of the range for minimum pay], the urban worker is already earning almost three times the average per capita income."[13]

Per capita income, however, is not comparable with average wages of workers. While per capita income figures are derived by dividing gross income (or product) by both the working and nonworking population, average wages are computed by dividing wages *only* by the working population.

To be sure, the ratio of the average annual wages of

daily-paid and semi-skilled workers in the public services to the gross domestic product (GDP) per capita in Nigeria even in 1963-64 was 3.7:1 (in contrast to rough estimates for comparable ratios of 2:1 in the U.S. and 1.5:1 in Western Europe).[14] However, the ratio of the total number in the labor force to the total population in Nigeria was 1:3. Thus, the 1963-64 GDP per capita of members of the households of daily-paid and semi-skilled Nigerian workers was only slightly above that of the total labor force[15] which consisted of 56 percent in the low-income agricultural sector.[16]

Moreover, the limited evidence available on West African laborers suggests that the average number of dependents supported by wage-earners exceeded considerably the ratio of the labor force to population. For example, Pfefferman's survey of wage-earners in Senegal, biased somewhat in the direction of better-off employees, found that the average worker supported 9.6 persons.[17] Furthermore, the wages of workers in the government service were likely to be higher than those in the private sector, so the per capita income of members of the households of workers may be lower than that of the total labor force. There may have been "labor aristocrats" around, but they did not comprise the bulk of wage-earners, who were unskilled or semi-skilled workers with low wages.[18]

Labor discontent resulted from a growing sense of injustice at the wide gap between the wages of white-collar and blue-collar workers. In the fiscal year 1963/64 (beginning 1 April), supervisors were paid 33 times as much as daily-paid and semi-skilled workers in the Nigerian public service, compared with a multiple of 5 to 10 in the United States and about 5 in the U.S.S.R.[19] According to Teriba and Philips, the personal income distribution in Western Nigeria in 1966/67 was more unequal than that in the United States, the United Kingdom, and the "average" less developed country.[20] Furthermore, personal income tax rates were low (i.e., a 3.2-6.0 percent average rate for single persons in the top-income class, the 99th percentile--an annual income of £N700), and regressive (or, at best, approximately proportional) in all regions except the East.[21] To exacerbate the frustration, the government had not increased wages since 1959-60, despite annual increases in overall prices of 3.1 percent, and an estimated annual real growth in GDP per capita of about 2 percent from the fiscal year 1960/61 to 1963/64.[22]

After independence, with the British no longer the whipping-boy, many workers began to feel that the political elite was making no effort to erase the inequities of the structure of colonial wages and benefits.[23] Conspicuous consumption among several politicians included living in large houses, formerly occupied by the British colonial secretaries, and possessing a fleet of cars, including a costly Rolls Royce (more than £N30,000), Mercedes-Benz (at least £N15,000), or an American automobile.

Since the annual salary of a federal minister was £N2,250-2,700 in 1965, workers assumed that public funds were diverted to provide such high level expenditures. Public indignation against the privileges of those in power grew especially after the unsuccessful austerity campaign of 1961 to reduce salaries and allowances of senior civil servants, members of parliament, and ministers, and the pay raise 1 April 1963 of 10 percent for the last two groups, while workers received no pay increment.[24]

The resentment, together with frequent exposés of corruption among African leaders, eroded the sense of legitimacy attached to the wide income gap, especially among the younger and more articulate urban workers. The high rate of unemployment and the communal competition for jobs, discussed in chapter 4, also contributed to the unrest.

Yet between 1945 and 1963, central trade union organizations were too weak and disorganized to undertake successful industrial action on workers' grievances at the national level. In 1962, wage-paid employment comprised only about 5 percent (compared with 20 percent in Kenya and Ghana, and 67 percent in the Republic of South Africa), and trade union members were only 2 percent (300,000) of the economically active population of 17.6 million, most of whom were "self-employed" in agriculture, petty trade, or crafts. In addition, the reluctance of the British Colonial Office to strengthen trade union rights, dependence on foreign financial support, and thwarting labor political organizations by nationalist leaders, hampered the development of a strong united movement. After the general strike of 1945, the trade unions were divided between the "moderates," supported by western confederations and oriented towards immediate goals of higher wages and better working conditions under the existing capitalist system, and the "leftists," devoted to the creation of a socialist economy and a more centralized government, and affiliated with communist and/or revolutionary pan-African confederations. After independence the "moderates" and Marxists also were each split into factions by leadership struggles, personal feuds, and ideological differences.

Nevertheless, the five superordinate central labor organizations joined during 1963-64 to form the Joint Action Committee (J.A.C.) to pressure the government to raise wages and salaries. As early as 1961, when the federal government failed to consider separate demands for wage increases by rival trade union federations, it had become clear that general pay raises would have to wait for labor unity. The J.A.C. decided at its inaugural meeting 12 September 1963 to call a general strike for 27 September 1963 if the government did not revise wages upward. The workers, some of whom feared greater government repression after Nigeria became a republic 1 October 1963, carried out the threat to strike. The government, afraid that the workers might mar Nigeria's image during the Republic Day celebrations, tried to placate the workers by appointing the Morgan Commission to review the structure of wages and salaries in both public and private sectors.

After a delay in publishing the report of the Commission, and after a wage offer by the government below the Commission's recommended level, the J.A.C. mobilized 800,000 supporters, many of them not unionists, to stop work 1 June 1964. Even though peak participation during the twelve-day general strike represented less than 5 percent of the economically active population, it disrupted the vital economic and administrative services in southern Nigeria, and especially affected the upper-income classes. For included among the strikers were an estimated 100,000 dockers and merchant navymen, 97,000 teachers, 70,000 government officials, 35,000 agricultural workers, 32,000 railway workers, 30,000 trade employees, 15,000 professional workers, 12,000 public workers, 10,000 electricians, 5,000 printing workers, 2,000 hotel workers, and 1,000 bus workers.[25]

After 1950, trade union officers were never prominent among leaders of the major political parties. But the workers got an improvement on the government's original offer, no dismissals during the strike and payment of wages, plus a consideration of the Morgan Commission's recommendations on industrial relations and the machinery for a continuing wage review--partly because the two major southern parties in the federal parliament, the N.C.N.C., a government coalition member, and the A.G., supported their demands.

Although the strike demonstrated the government's fragility, the J.A.C. could not translate this victory into further political strength, because labor unity disintegrated. As the pressure of the federal elections of December 1964 neared, the contending political parties and regional governments improved their offers to segments of organized labor, thereby increasing its fragmentation. The federal government gave preferential treatment to the moderate United Labour Congress. When the U.L.C. surmised it could not hold its position against the "leftists," it lost interest in the J.A.C. Furthermore, the election alignment between radical labor leaders and the A.G.-N.C.N.C. coalition, U.P.G.A., miscarried after the latter refused to endorse the candidates of the labor parties. Finally, the political strike, called by the still-surviving J.A.C. to support U.P.G.A.'s election boycott, largely failed--strengthening the hands of the "moderates."[26]

Labor disaffection, which culminated in the 1964 general strike, was not a direct cause of the January 1966 mutiny, but contributed to the political unrest and violence, which precipitated it. Even though discontented trade unionists and leftist members of the U.P.G.A. had nothing to do with planning or executing the coup by the young majors, all three groups shared major elements of a vision of a reformed Nigeria and continuing opposition to the intrigues and abuses of the government in power.

After the strikers defied a ban on public meetings, illegally marched toward Government House in Lagos, rejected Prime Minister Balewa's call to return to work, clashed with police, pressed for the resignation of the Balewa government, talked openly of seizing political control, and won many of their major demands, many members of the "progressive" alliance perceived the real possibility of gaining control of the government, by political violence, if not by parliamentary means. Also after June 1964, support of the army and police for the government was in question. Strikers at times were openly abetted by the police, whose grievances and wage concerns were included in trade unionists' demands. In addition, the army troops who were ordered to suppress marches and demonstrations of the workers were not entirely unsympathetic to the workers' demands.

Often the weakness of a government only becomes manifest in direct confrontation. The 1964 general strike posed a challenge to the legitimacy of the civilian government, demonstrated its ineptness and powerlessness, raised questions about the future use of the army and police to repress popular demands, and increased the likelihood of further attempts by dissident forces to use political violence to effect political change.[27] Since trade union strength lay primarily in the south, and the federal coalition was dominated by Northerners, the confrontation reinforced regional antagonism (see chapter 4). Also much of organized labor supported the progressive opposition to the ruling coalition in the 1964-65 election boycott and constitutional crisis, and at the end of 1965 workers helped to foment the mass violence directed against a Northern-supported, Western regional government with little popular support. The near-anarchy in the West, together with the rumored punitive response by the Nigerian National Alliance (see chapter 1), precipitated the military mutiny of January 1966, which set the stage for the countercoup and civil war.[28]

Unrest among Farmers

The distribution of farm holdings by size (in hectares) is more nearly equal in Nigeria than in most less developed countries. But, contrary to the myth, there was substantial inequality in wealth and income among those engaged in agriculture. The 1963 average income of the first decile (bottom tenth) of the economically active population in rural areas was £N14.45 compared with £N64.75 for the tenth decile (top tenth), while average incomes were £N23.29 for the first decile and £N309.23 for the tenth decile in urban areas. The average income per economically active person in the rural areas was less than half that in urban areas.

Despite adjustments for the lower purchasing power in the cities, average real incomes in the rural areas were still substantially lower than those in urban areas. The Gini coefficient, which measures income concentration, was the same for urban and rural incomes in 1963. Because of low educational levels and problems of political mobilization and communication among scattered populations, farmers were generally less restive about inequality and relative deprivation than were urban workers.[29] Exceptions were farmers in Ibadan and Ife-Ilesha divisions of Oyo Province and in parts of Ondo, Abeokuta, and Ijebu provinces, the cocoa belt, the most urbanized area of its size in Nigeria with double the national average in per capita income.

Most cocoa cultivators lived in large towns. Thirty-five percent of Ibadan's 1963 population of 627,380 the highest in sub-Saharan black Africa, was engaged in agriculture. More than one-third of the Western Region's 1963 population of 10.3 million depended directly on cocoa cultivating, marketing, and transporting,[30] and many others depended on spending by those in the cocoa sector.

By the last half of 1965, the approaching Western regional parliamentary elections became the new political battleground between the Northern-dominated N.N.A. (the coalition between the Northern Peoples' Congress and the N.N.D.P.) and the progressive southern elements (the U.P.G.A.). The N.N.D.P., the ruling party in the West, made lavish promises of new development schemes, including a £N10-million iron and steel firm for Ondo division "very soon."

But it was cocoa, Nigeria's major agricultural export through 1965 and the primary source of economic prosperity in the West, that received the most attention. Between June and August, farmers in Ekiti division had received loans totaling £N13,400. At the end of August, it was announced that the Agricultural Credit Corporation was to loan £N50,000 to Western farmers. Early in September the Western government indicated that a delegation including farmers would tour other cocoa-exporting countries to try to secure more control by producers over world market prices.[31]

Cocoa cultivators had a long-standing grievance against government resulting from their contributions to marketing-board surpluses, which were used for investment in infra-structure, industry, and other projects of little benefit to the small farmer. At the beginning of September 1965, however, the Western Regional Marketing Board was paying farmers £N120 per ton of cocoa, but receiving, after marketing and distribution costs were subtracted, only £N90 on the world market. Despite the precipitant decline in world cocoa prices in the middle of 1965, the 1964-65 buying price, which subsidized the farmer, was continued beyond the new season, September through mid October 1965, ostensibly to give time to clear away the old crop and to disinfect storage facilities.

The real reason became apparent shortly after polling day, 11 October 1965, when the re-elected N.N.D.P. government lowered the price from £N120 to £N65 a ton. That evidence of the political manipulation of the spread between world and producer prices, together with the blatant rigging of nominations and balloting in the Western elections by an Electoral Commission responsible to the regional government and bureaucracy, was a fillip to revolt. Violence among cocoa farmers gradually spread to the unemployed and other discontented elements of the towns. By December 1965, it was risky to travel by automobile from Ibadan, the Western capital, to Lagos, the federal capital.[32] As indicated in chapter 1, the military intervention in politics in January 1966 was partly in response to anarchy in the West.

ELITE INTERESTS IN DEVELOPMENT PLANNING AND ECONOMIC POLICY

In Nigeria, the federal government pursued projects and policies primarily oriented toward benefits for "modernizing" elites--the politico-bureaucratic elites and their business constituents--and their allies among the traditional rulers and landed aristocracy. Planning and implementing were hamstrung by the desire of the ruling elites to keep control of all bounties that the government distributed.

The earliest national plans, during 1946-55 and 1955-60 (later extended to 1962), were framed by colonial administrators. Even the First National Development Plan, 1962-68, after independence, made available to the United States Agency for International Development and the International Bank for Reconstruction and Development before the Nigerian public saw it, was drawn up primarily by foreign economists (e.g., the two top men in the Economic Planning Unit of the Federal Ministry of Economic Development were U.S. economists). They favored "automatic" decision-making by private units, dismissal of major discrepancies between financial and social profitability, stressing marginal adjustment rather than fundamental structural change, accenting high economic pay-offs from directly productive investments (as opposed to an indirect return from social overheads), eschewal of increased tax rates at high-income levels (for fear of dampening private incentive), a conservative monetary and fiscal policy emphasizing a relatively small plan, an economy open to foreign trade and investment, and substantial reliance on overseas assistance. Foreign aid was set at one-half of public sector investment.[33]

Although political leaders and, to a lesser extent, government officials were involved in selecting certain projects, they provided little overall direction or specification of goals.[34] Despite their lack of involvement in formulating the plan, however, Nigerians were charged with its administration.

Lewis, a Nobel laureate in economics, suggests that the main weaknesses of the 1962-68 plan were incomplete feasibility studies and inadequate evaluation of projects, meager public participation followed by excessive political intervention in making economic decisions, insufficient attention to the small indigenous sector, and unsatisfactory machinery for implementing developments in the public sector.[35] A strong central program designed to redistribute income to and increase participation of the underprivileged classes would have threatened the power and privileges of the ruling elite. Dispersing economic power to the multiplicity of petty traders, craftsmen, and small industrialists, without a quid pro quo, would have threatened the economic interests of the political leaders--the viability and monopoly return of the public corporations that serve as a basis for patronage, and the large private business interests. Only 81.3 percent of the £N676.8 million capital expenditure planned for the public sector was spent.[36] One reason for the shortfall was that the planners did not clearly identify feasible industrial projects, nor give details of supporting government policies. The lack of preparatory work by professional accountants, economists, engineers, managers, and planners resulted from ineffective coordination, shortages of high-level manpower, and the introduction of political criteria for determining projects.

The elite, virtually devoid of goals and priorities that could be articulated to the masses, and preoccupied with preserving their system of patronage, encouraged neither decision making by local authorities nor consultation with the public. Members of parliament energetically pushed projects that would enhance their income, perquisites, and clientage base, regardless of the projects' relationship to the plan's objectives. According to Dudley, a leading Nigerian political scientist in the 1960s and 1970s,

> few, if any, government contracts or loans were given out by the political class unless they were offered ten percent of the value of the contract or loan in return, a return which then went, in part, to the resources needed for side-payments. In this way, the "ten percent" cut

became the criterion for assessing the feasibilty and economic viability of most public projects.

Decisions on expenditures involving millions of pounds were made on the basis of conversations between politicians without documents or expert advice, and with little knowledge of easily ascertainable facts. Parliament was not equipped, nor did it have the will, to make important decisions concerning the plan because its members were preoccupied with distributing the bounty to the faithful.[37]

It is not surprising that the elite had no desire to establish adequate machinery to implement and independently evaluate the plan.[38] If such an apparatus had been controlled by professionals or civil servants not oriented toward the interests of political leaders, it would have undermined a system that they themselves stood to profit by. The lack of departmental annual reports, the secrecy of official information, and the paucity of program evaluation allowed the political elite to keep enhancement of their individual positions paramount. Political intervention was essential to enable them to keep control of the instruments vital for maintaining their influence. An emphasis on socioeconomic development for the low-income classes had no priority with a ruling regime preoccupied with the struggle to retain power and to maintain patron-client relationships.

During civilian rule, high tariffs on inputs used to produce domestic commodities, together with tariff rebates and tax incentives for pioneering companies and other favored applicants benefited selected manufacturing enterprises. Import taxes on a number of industrial materials were so high that many unsuccessful applicants for tariff relief on vital inputs could not afford to stay in business, while favored enterprises, then with little competition, made sizeable gains. Quasi-government corporations dominated by leading politicians, or foreign or indigenous producers allied with them, were more likely to receive tariff rebates.

One widely held prescription for increasing the rate of economic development and modernization, but at the same time enhancing the profits or patronage of the political leaders of the country, has been transferring resources from the agricultural to the industrial sector. Despite the rapid growth in petroleum output, agriculture still accounted for more than 50 percent of the value of Nigeria's exports just before the civil war. But her foreign exchange earnings were used primarily to import industrial capital and consumer goods. The overvaluation of the Nigerian pound in international exchange increased the amount of the transfer. Furthermore, evidence from Helleiner indicates that a sizeable amount of private savings in agriculture was employed in other sectors of the economy. Finally, farmers have borne the bulk of the tax burden during this century, contributing to marketing board surpluses and being assessed export duties, in addition to paying the taxes and import duties also collected from urban groups.[39]

Despite 56.4 percent of GDP in 1965-66 originating in the agricultural sector, only 5.0 percent of the current expenditures and 11.8 percent of the capital expenditures of the federal government in 1965 were for agriculture, and only 13.6 percent of expenditures in the first development plan was for primary production.[40]

Those controlling federal economic policy profited by transferring resources from agriculture to industry, by involving government industrial firms, collaborating with foreign enterprise, "rake-offs" on the contracts of foreigners, intermediary roles in land deals, selling inputs and services, and from positions on the boards of directors, in addition to private industrial enterpreneurial activity. Altogether the transfer of resources from agriculture hampered the economic development of that sector.

Discontent with civilian politicians grew as farmers and workers became increasingly conscious of the way economic policy was being used on behalf of the indigenous governing elite in the independence era.

SUMMARY

By 1964-66, unrest among a number of major classes in Nigeria helped to fuel political discontent. Recent university graduates, especially from southern Nigeria, who encountered a drop in the number of openings in the public service, perceived the scramble for the remaining posts in ethnic terms, and pressured politicians to increase the number of positions. Officers from the middle ranks, particularly from the south, who faced a longer wait for promotion than their predecessors, experienced alienation and low moral before the January 1966 revolt. Discontent among less skilled workers increased as real wages declined between 1959 and 1964, and the gap between white-collar and blue-collar wages widened. Western cocoa farmers revolted in the last part of 1965 as a result of the political manipulation of producer prices.

The interaction of class antagonisms, communal economic enmities, and foreign dependency enhanced the potential for internal war.

In Nigeria, the federal government pursued policies primarily oriented toward benefiting political and bureaucratic leaders, the business elite, the landed aristocracy, and the traditional rulers. As the masses became increasingly aware of the way development planning and economic policies were used on behalf of a small power elite, discontent with the civilian government grew.

NOTES

1. See Barrington Moore, *Social Origins of Dictatorship and Democracy* (Boston: Beacon Press, 1966); and Charles Tilly, *From Mobilization to Revolution* (Reading, Mass.: Addison-Wesley, 1978).

2. This was after a lecture I gave on "The Problem of Nigerian Economic Development and National Integration," to the African Institute of the Soviet Academy of Sciences, 24 May 1978. Soviet Nigerianists had a Marxian explanation for Nigerian political instability. I do not understand their views clearly enough to summarize them. But they do not believe that Nigerian political conflict is simply one between workers and capitalists.

3. Perceptions of the educated elite varied by time and

region in Nigeria. From the 1920s through 1940s, those with a primary school-leaving certificate comprised this elite. By the 1960s, members of the educated elite had at least a primary school certificate in the North, and at least a secondary certificate in the south. The overwhelming majority of the elite was employed in the government bureaucracy. P.C. Lloyd, *Africa in Social Change* (Harmondsworth, Eng.: Penguin, 1967), pp. 125-53, and P.C. Lloyd, *The New Elites of Tropical Africa* (Oxford: Oxford University Press, 1966), p. 7. See chapter 4 below for differences in school enrollment rates between North and south.

4. John P. Mackintosh, *Nigerian Government and Politics: Prelude to the Revolution* (Evanston, Ill.: Northwestern University Press, 1966), pp. 188-9; K.W.J. Post, *The Nigerian Federal Election of 1959: Politics and Administration in a Developing Political System* (London: Oxford University Press, 1963), p. 23; P.C. Lloyd, "The Ethnic Background to the Nigerian Crisis," in *Nigerian Politics and Military Rule: Prelude to the Civil War*, S.K. Panter-Brick, ed. (London: The Athlone Press, 1970), pp. 6-7; and Lloyd, *Africa in Social Change*, p. 149.

5. Wale Oyemakinde, "The Nigerian General Strike of 1964," *Genève-Afrique*, XIII (1974), 67; Pauline H. Baker, "Seeds of Radicalism among an Aspirant Elite," in *Social Change and Economic Development in Nigeria*, Ukandi G. Damachi and Hans Dieter Seibel, eds. (New York: Praeger, 1973), p. 205; John de St. Jorre, *The Nigerian Civil War* (London: Hodder and Stoughton, 1972), p. 112; and Tariq Ali, *Pakistan: Military Rule or People's Power* (New York: William Morrow and Co., 1970).

6. N.J. Miners, *The Nigerian Army, 1956-1966* (London: Methuen, 1971), pp. 71-90.

7. Note the parallels with other armies, such as Pakistan's in 1951 (see chapter 9), which have just been transferred to indigenous control.

8. Robin Luckham, "The Nigerian Military: Disintegration or Integration?" in *Nigerian Politics and Military Rule*, S.K. Panter-Brick, ed., pp. 63-6; and B.J. Dudley, *Instability and Political Order: Politics and Crisis in Nigeria* (Ibadan: Ibadan University Press, 1973), p. 94.

In the 1960s, the United States Air Force faced a similar problem. Top officers commissioned during World War II generally had less education than their immediate subordinates commissioned in the 1950s. This information is based on communication with military historian Robin Higham.

9. Samuel P. Huntington, *Political Order in Changing Societies* (New Haven, Conn.: Yale University Press, 1968), p. 287.

10. In 1859, Engels referred to the British proletariat as "becoming more and more bourgeois." Karl Marx and Friedrich Engels, *On Britain* (Moscow: Foreign Languages House, 1953), pp. 28, 30-1, 491-2. Lenin used the idea of a "labor aristocracy" to explain the development of nationalism at the expense of international worker solidarity. Peter Waterman, "The 'Labour Artistocracy' in Africa: Introduction to a Debate," *Development and Change*, VI, No. 3 (July 1975), 57-9.

One source of confusion is Marx's initial misconception concerning the proletariat. See A.J.P. Taylor's "Introduction" to

Karl Marx and Friedrich Engels, *The Communist Manifesto* (Harmondsworth, Eng.: Penguin, 1972), pp. 18-20.

11. Peter Kilby, *Industrialization in an Open Economy: Nigeria, 1945-1966* (Cambridge: Cambridge University Press, 1969), pp. 301-2.

12. John F. Weeks, "The Impact of Economic Conditions and Institutional Forces on Urban Wages in Nigeria," *Nigerian Journal of Economic and Social Studies*, XIII, No. 1 (November 1971), 331.

13. B.J. Dudley, "The Politics of Adebo," *Quarterly Journal of Administration*, VI, No. 3 (January 1972), 133.

Adrian J. Peace, *Choice, Class, and Conflict: A Study of Southern Nigerian Factory Workers* (Atlantic Highlands, N.J.: Humanities Press, 1979), pp. 11-12, makes a similar error, although he is more skeptical than Dudley about the validity of his findings.

14. S.A. Aluko, "Prices, Wages and Costs," in *Reconstruction and Development in Nigeria--Proceedings of a National Conference*, A.A. Ayida and H.M.A. Onitiri, eds. (Ibadan: Oxford University Press, 1971), pp. 424, 439.

15. If one assumes the figures in this paragraph are accurate, the GDP per capita of workers' households is only 23 percent higher than the average GDP per capita (i.e., 3.7/3 = 1.23).

16. Nigeria, Office of Statistics, *Population Census of Nigeria, 1963*, III (Lagos, 1968), 2, 39-40. Agricultural workers include "farmers, fishermen, hunters, loggers, and related workers." Ibid, p. 39.

17. Douglas Rimmer, "Wage Politics," Faculty of Commerce and Social Science, University of Birmingham, Occational Paper No. 12, February 1970, pp. 56-7; and Guy Pfefferman, *Industrial Labour in Senegal* (New York: Praeger, 1968), pp. 160-70.

18. However, it is not true that 69 percent of the total labor force in 1962 was "'general' (unskilled) labour," as Robin Cohen, *Labour and Politics in Nigeria* (New York: Africana Publishing Co., 1974), pp. 54, 188, indicates on the basis of data from Nigeria, Office of Statistics, *Annual Abstract of Statistics, 1964* (Lagos, 1964), p. 26, which analyzes wage employment, not the total labor force (a concept that includes the "self-employed"). See *Population Census, 1963*, III, 39-40 for information on the total labor force. Furthermore, the number of general unskilled laborers (150,149 of 518,805 employed) was 29 percent, not 69 percent. Cohen's error results from his also including as unskilled, in addition to the "general unskilled labour," the occupational groups: farmers, fishermen, loggers, miners, quarrymen, transport and communication workers, craftsmen, trade apprentices, artisans and production process workers, and service, sports, and recreation workers, only some of whom are unskilled.

19. Aluko, "Wages, Costs and Prices," Conference on National Reconstruction and Development in Nigeria, University of Ibadan, 24-29 March 1969, p. 16.

The wages of blue-collar workers were not only low in a relative sense but in an absolute sense. Rimmer, "Wage Politics," p. 35, on the basis of a report of the International Labour Office points out that "the distribution of African wage-earners by rates of pay [are extremely skewed in West Africa], with around 50 percent of total employees at or close to minimum rates." In 1964, the Morgan Commission, reviewing wages and salaries, concluded that in Lagos a "living wage," providing an "effective minimum level" for a young unskilled worker with a wife and child would be £N16.16. Actual minimum rates then were less than half that amount, and even the minimum wage after the 1964 general strike was only £N10 a month. Ibid., 36; and Nigeria, Ministry of Information, *Report of the Commission on the Review of Wages, Salary and Conditions of Service of the Junior Employees of the Federation and in Private Establishments, 1963-64* (Lagos, 1964), pp. 11-21.

20. O. Teriba and O.A. Phillips, "Income Distribution and National Integration," *Nigerian Journal of Economic and Social Studies*, XIII, No. 1 (March 1971), 91-4. Data primarily from the late 1950s and early 1960s in Irma Adelman and Cynthia Taft Morris, *Economic Growth and Social Equity in Developing Countries* (Stanford, Calif.: Stanford University Press, 1973), p. 152, indicate that distribution of income is more unequal in Nigeria than a sample of forty-three less developed countries from Africa, Asia, and Latin America. According to this source, Nigeria ranks in the middle (a two-way tie for twenty-first place) in the percentage share of income by the poorest 40 percent of the population, and in the 63rd percentile (the sixteenth highest in concentration) in the share of income of the richest 20 percent of the population. However, the distribution of income among the economically active population in Nigeria in 1963 was less unequal than in Latin American countries, which have been characterized by high inequality. Egon Vielrose, "Distribution of Income in Nigeria," Nigerian Institute for Social and Economic Research, University of Ibadan, Ibadan, 1975, pp. 56, 59-60; United Nations, Economic Commission for Latin America, *Income Distribution in Latin America* (New York: United Nations, 1971), pp. 7, 11, 12; Shail Jain, *Size Distribution of Income: A Compilation of Data* (Washington: The World Bank, 1975), pp. 13-15, 24, 34, 36, 87, 89, 118; and Hollis Chenery, Montek S. Ahluwalia, C.L.G. Bell, John H. Duloy, and Richard Jolly, *Redistribution with Growth* (Oxford: Oxford University Press, 1974), pp. 8-9.

21. Adebayo Adedeji, *Nigerian Federal Finance--Its Development, Problems and Prospects* (New York: Africana Publishing Corporation, 1969), pp. 188-9.

Additionally personal income tax evasion was widespread in Nigeria, especially by wealthy self-employed individuals. P. Ada Omorogiuwa, "Personal Income Taxation and Income Distribution in Nigeria" (Paper presented to a Conference on Income Distribution in Nigeria, University of Lagos, Department of Economics, January-February 1979).

22. The real growth rate in GDP was 4.5 percent per annum, while an educated guess for population growth was 2.5 percent per year. Nigeria, Office of Statistics, *Gross Domestic Product of Nigeria, 1958/59-1966/67* (Lagos, 1968), pp. 25. 30; Nigeria, Ministry of Information, *Second National Development Plan, 1970-74* (Lagos, 1971), P. 77; and Ifagun I.U. Eke, "Population of Nigeria, 1952-65," *Nigerian Journal of Economics and Social Studies*, VIII, No. 3 (November 1968), 308-9.

23. Kwame Nkrumah, *Class Struggle in Africa* (New York: International Publishers, 1970), pp. 15, 32, writes: "In [the] colonialist situation, African workers regarded the colonialists, foreign firms and foreign planters, as the exploiters. Thus their class struggle became in the first instance anti-imperialist, and not directed against the indigenous bourgeoisie. It is this which has been responsible in some degree for the relatively slow awakening of the African worker and peasant to the existence of their true class enemy--the indigenous bourgeoisie. . . . In the post-independence period . . . there emerged what may be termed the 'party *nouveaux riches*,' an elite which developed from among the ranks of the Party which successfully won political freedom from the colonial power."

24. Kilby, *Industrialization*, p. 287; and Oyemakinde, *Geneve-Afrique*, XIII (1974), 54.

25. Kilby, *Industrialization*, pp. 202, 267; Wogu Ananaba, *The Trade Union Movement in Nigeria* (New York: Africana Publishing Corporation, 1970), pp. 213-52; Oyemakinde, *Geneve-Afrique*, XIII, 55-9; A.K. Essack, "Nigeria at the Crossroads," *Economic and Political Weekly*, VI, No. 11 (13 March 1971), 613; and Richard Sandbrook and Robin Cohen, eds., *The Development of an African Working Class: Studies in Class Formation and Action* (London: Longman, 1975), p. 130.

26. William F. Friedland, "Paradoxes of African Trade Unionism: Organizational Chaos and Political Potential," *Africa Report*, X, No. 6 (June 1965), 6-10; Robert Melson, "Marxists in the Nigerian Labor Movement" (Ph.D. dissertation, Massachusetts Institute of Technology, 1967), pp. 30-87; Kilby, *Industrialization*, p. 288; and Cohen, *Labour and Politics*, p. 172.

27. Hannah Arendt, *On Violence* (New York: Harcourt, Brace & World, 1969), p. 49, and Cohen, *Labour and Politics*, pp. 166-8, 217.

28. For analysis of the descent into chaos in Western Nigeria, see below, and K.W.J. Post and Michael Vickers, *Structure and Conflict in Nigeria, 1960-65* (Madison, Wis.: University of Wisconsin Press, 1973), pp. 219-38.

29. Vielrose, "Distribution of Income in Nigeria," pp. 15, 56, 62; Charles Lewis Taylor and Michael C. Hudson, *World Handbook of Political and Social Indicators* (New Haven, Conn.: Yale University Press, 1972), pp. 267-9; Rural Economy Research Unit, "Farm Income Levels in the Northern States of Nigeria," Samaru Miscellaneous Paper, Institute for Agricultural Research, Ahmadu Bello University, Zaria, 1972; and David W. Norman, David H. Pryor, and Christopher J.N. Gibbs, "Technical Change and the Small Farmer in Hausaland, Northern Nigeria," African Rural Employment Paper No. 19, Michigan State University, East Lansing, Mich. 1979, pp. 72-3, 127. Polly Hill *Rural Hausa: A Village and a Setting* (Cambridge: Cambridge University Press, 1972); Polly Hill, *Population, Prosperity and Poverty: Rural Kano, 1900 and 1970* (Cambridge: Cambridge University Press, 1977); Polly Hill, "The Myth of the Amorphous Peasantry: A Northern Nigerian Case Study," *Nigerian Journal of Economic and Social Studies*, XIII, No. 1 (March 1971), 239-60; and E. Wayne Nafziger, "A Critique of Development Economics in the U.S.," *The Journal of Development Studies*, XIII, No. 1

(October 1976), 20, criticize the widespread assumption in the economics literature that peasant societies are characterized by populations with roughly uniform poverty.

30. Reuben K. Udo, *Geographical Regions of Nigeria* (Berkeley and Los Angeles: University of California Press, 1970), pp. 26-35.

31. Post and Vickers, *Structure and Conflict*, p. 221.

32. Ibid., p. 221-3; B.J. Dudley, "Western Nigeria and the Nigerian Crisis," in *Nigerian Politics and Military Rule*; S.K. Panter-Brick, ed. (London: The Athlone Press, 1970), p. 98; and Central Bank of Nigeria, *Annual Report and Statement of Accounts for the Year Ended 31st December, 1966* (Lagos, 1967), p. 23.

The steady drop in the world price of cocoa in 1965 made the political problems of Ghana's President Kwame Nkrumah more difficult. Henry L. Bretton, *The Rise and Fall of Kwame Nkrumah: A Study of Personal Rule in Africa* (New York: Praeger, 1966), p. 155.

33. Nigeria, Ministry of Economic Development, *National Development Plan, 1962-68* (Lagos, n.d.), p. 33.

34. Wolfgang F. Stolper, Head of the Economic Planning Unit at that time, discusses "The Main Features of the 1962-68 National Plan," *Nigerian Journal of Economic and Social Studies*, IV, No 2, (July 1962), 85-91. Sayre P. Schatz, "Nigeria's First National Development Plan (1962-68): An Appraisal," ibid., V, No. 2, (July 1963), 221-35, and Reginald H. Green, "Four African Development Plans: Ghana, Kenya, Nigeria, and Tanzania," *The Journal of Modern African Studies*, III, No. 2 (1965), 253-74, provide cogent criticisms of the plan.

35. W. Arthur Lewis, *Reflections on Nigeria's Economic Growth* (Paris: Organisation for Economic Cooperation and Development, 1967), pp. 37-9.

36. Nigeria, Ministry of Information, *Second National Development Plan, 1970-74* (Lagos, n.d.), pp. 11-14.

37. Dudley, *Instability and Political Order*, p. 50; and A. Akene Ayida, "Development Objectives," Conference on National Reconstruction and Development in Nigeria, University of Ibadan, 24-29 March 1969, p. 10, modified slightly in *Reconstruction and Development in Nigeria*, Ayida and Onitiri, eds., p. 6. For detailed evidence on kickbacks to the political elite, see Nigeria, *Report of the Coker Commission of Inquiry into the Affairs of Certain Statutory Corporations in Western Nigeria, 1962*, 4 vols. (Lagos, 1962).

38. O. Aboyade has stated that "the [first] plan's control mechanism is more an elegant paper work than an effective guideline for policy makers." "Problems in Plan Révision," *Nigerian Journal of Economic and Social Studies*, VII, No. 2 (July 1965), 129.

39. Gerald K. Helleiner, *Peasant Agriculture, Government, and Economic Growth in Nigeria* (Homewood, Ill.: Richard D. Irwin, 1966), pp. 140-1.

40. Central Bank of Nigeria, *Annual Report and Statement of Accounts for the Year Ended 31st December, 1966* (Lagos, 1967), pp. 70-1; and S.A. Aluko, "Resource Allocation and Overall Strategy," *Quarterly Journal of Administration*, V, No. 3 (April 1971), 276.

4
Regional and Communal Competition, Conflict, and Disintegration

The most salient characteristic of political life in Africa is that it constitutes an almost institutionless arena with conflict and disorder as its most prominent features.

Aristide R. Zolberg, "The Structure of Political Conflict in the New States of Topical Africa," *American Political Science Review*, 1968.

When each [community] has its own opinions, beliefs, laws, and customs, it looks on itself as comprising the whole of humanity and feels touched only by its own sorrows. If war breaks out between peoples of this disposition it is sure to be conducted with barbarity.

Alexis de Tocqueville, *Democracy in America*, Vol. II, 1835.

Cultural pluralism had nothing whatsoever to do with the general causes of insurrection; however, once insurrection occurred, ethnicity did enter the picture as one prism through which individuals and groups sought to understand the social composition of the insurgents and the balance of threat and advantage which the movements offered.

Crawford Young, *The Politics of Cultural Pluralism*, 1976.

The [Nigerian-Biafran] conflict is sometimes said to be a tribal dispute between the Ibos and the Hausa, with the Yoruba having reluctantly to take sides with one or the other. It is also sometimes asserted to be a religious war, a preponderance of Ibos being Christians and preponderance of Hausa being Moslems. Both explanations are gross and misleading simplifications. . . . Obviously tribal animosities and religious differences may become sharpened by, and in turn sharpen, the conflict. They are not, however, major factors in bringing about the . . . conflict.

S.K. Panter-Brick, "The Right to Self-Determination: Its Application to Nigeria," *International Affairs*,

1968.

> Many Christian missionary organizations moved to the support of Biafra, almost seeming to regard the Nigerian Civil War as a re-enactment of the crusades--a religious war rather than a ethnic confrontation. In reality the religious factor in the Nigerian Civil War was at most subsidiary, and certainly not fundamental.
>
> Ali A. Mazrui, "Black Africa and the Arabs," *Foreign Affairs*, 1975.

The low degree of economic integration between regions and ethnic group areas, exacerbated by further economic disintegration in 1966-67, contributed to the civil war by making the cost of secession and benefit of unity low. And communal (regional, ethnic, linguistic religious, etc.) economic conflict and competition, which cut across conflicts between classes and occupational groups, increased the tendency toward political disintegration in Nigeria. The elites accentuated the pre-colonial and colonial identification with traditional political and cultural entities, and--in furtherance of their own special interest--used these sentiments to transfer potential hostility from economic and class differences (within their own communities) to the elites and masses of others.[1]

This chapter focuses on several regional and communal economic factors that contributed to Nigerian political disintegration: (1) the low degree of regional economic integration; (2) rivalry between ethnic and regional communities for employment; (3) the effect of expanding petroleum production in the Eastern Region on its potential domestic and international economic and political position; (4) the interregional conflict over a formula for allocating revenue; and (5) the vulnerable economic position of Northern Nigeria.

LACK OF REGIONAL ECONOMIC INTEGRATION

Political cohesion is partly a function of the extent of interregional trade flows.[2] But it is difficult to ascertain whether the quantitative density of these flows evinces a high degree of salience. Smith suggests that the implication of the volume of interregional trade for national integration can be assessed by dividing this figure by the volume of international trade, or by comparing the salience scores for trade between regions with some norm.[3]

He computes a salience matrix showing the level of relative acceptance for the twelve cells, which indicates the potential connections of each of the four regions--the West (including Lagos, the federal territory), Mid-West, North, and East--with every other region in 1964. He found that although nine of the twelve cells contained positive values for interregional migration, only six of the twelve were positive for interregional trade.[4]

According to Smith, "The regions are much more strongly connected by salience indices for strangers [migrants] than by comparable indices for interregional trade." Of the six possible interregional trade connections, the North-West, Midwest-West, and North-East links are two-way positive connections, and the East-West (two noncontiguous regions), East-Midwest, and Midwest-North connections are two-way negative ones. The relatively low connectivity index seems to suggest low integration.[5] Toscano has suggested that positive salience may be equated with integration, with "the higher the negative salience, the higher the probability for disintegration and conflict."[6]

Smith gives a figure for interregional trade as a percentage of the volume of foreign trade in 1964. However, both Smith and Mobogunje point out that little about Nigerian national integration can be deduced from this single percentage. In the first place, the value of interregional trade can be increased or decreased by varying the number of regions. Secondly, such a percentage has little meaning except when compared with other countries, or with other times in Nigeria. Mabogunje further laments the lack of even simple statistics or indices to indicate the extent of regional economic integration or disintegration in Nigeria.[7]

Although the figures are crude, data on West and East Africa economies roughly comparable to Nigerian figures seem to indicate that the extent of interregional trade in Nigeria was relatively low for a national unit before 1966. From a study by Foltz, one can obtain information on a contiguous free trade area to be called FWA, which consists of five "regions," Senegal, Mali (formerly French Soudan), Guinea, Ivory Coast, and Upper Volta.

As shown in table 4.1, the value of interregional trade as a percentage of gross domestic product (a proxy for the size of the economy) was a fraction of a percentage point higher in FWA in 1956 than in Nigeria in 1964. The value of interregional trade as a percentage of merchandise imports, 60.7 percent in FWA, a unit which Foltz considers highly dependent on external trade, was substantially higher than the 25.8 percent for Nigeria.[8] Thus the relative size of interregional trade was lower in Nigeria than in FWA. This was true, despite that, a priori, one would expect interregional trade to be relatively lower in FWA, as it consisted of more than one nation-state, its figures were earlier in time, its population was lower, it had closer ties to a colonial power, and its trade with three members of the free-trade area, Mauritania, Dahomey, and Niger, was included as noninterterritorial, international trade.

Additionally, in the East African Customs Union, consisting of three contiguous "regions," Kenya, Uganda, and Tanganyika, interregional trade was 4 percent of gross domestic product in 1959[9]--a figure not much less than that for Nigeria in 1964 (see table 4.1). If the Kenya-Uganda-Tanganyika unit had been divided into five units as in the Nigerian case, the percentage for the East African unit would have exceeded that for Nigeria.

Finally, comparing sources of data in FWA, East Africa, and Nigeria indicates that the relative size of interregional trade was likely to be understated. There is no evidence, however, that Nigeria's figures were understated any more than those of the other units.

In light of these comparisons, it is reasonable to believe that the extent of interregional trade in Nigeria before 1966 was

TABLE 4.1
Comparative Data on FWA and Nigeria

	FWA (Senegal, Mali Guinea, Ivory Coast, and Upper Volta)	Nigeria
(1) Year	1956	1964
(2) Number of regions	5	5
(3) Total population	14,189,000	55,670,000
(4) Population of coastal region	7,220,000	25,861,000
(5) (4)/(3)	.509	.463
(6) Value of interregional trade (in wholesale prices)	39,345,000,000 CFA francs	£N65,411,000
(7) Merchandise imports (from other units, c.i.f.)	64,861,000,000 CFA francs	£N253,880,000
(8) (6)/(7)	.607	.258
(9) Gross domestic product	767,000,000,000 CFA francs	£N1,403,000,000
(10) (6)/(9)	.051	.047

Sources: Alan M. Hay and Robert H.T. Smith, *Interregional Trade and Money Flows in Nigeria, 1964* (Ibadan: Oxford University Press, 1970), p. 148; William J. Foltz, *From French West Africa to the Mali Federation* (New Haven, Conn.: Yale University Press, 1965), pp. 33, 36, 40; United Nations, Statistical Office, Department of Economic and Social Affairs, *Statistical Yearbook, 1966* (New York, 1967).

relatively low, even when compared with that of other African countries.

Furthermore, indigenous economic interests were especially unlikely to be involved in producing for interregional trade and thus, benefited less economically from national integration. In 1965 in manufacturing, the major benefits from economic integration accrued to foreign firms, which accounted for 61.9 percent of total paid-up capital, and 84.8 percent of total private paid-up capital in firms with ten or more employed, and a higher percentage in the larger firms (table 2.4). According to Asiodu, permanent secretary in the Federal Ministry of Industries during the civil war, public firms, whose paid-up capital comprised 25.8 percent of the total in manufacturing in 1965 (table 2.4),[10] were oriented primarily to regional markets because of political factors, which led to a lack of regional coordination in determining industrial sites.[11]

Indigenous private industrial firms, which accounted for 11.1 percent of 1965 paid-up capital in firms with ten or more employees (table 2.4), and a lower percentage of larger firms, sold primarily to local markets.[12] There was little interregional trade of agricultural commodities or raw materials, most of which entered international trade or were consumed locally. Thus, in general, indigenous groups were not likely to have a strong vested economic interest in national integration.

Most interregional trade of goods made or grown by indigenous producers was confined to that among members of the same ethnic community. Since most Nigerian businessmen had no access to commercial banking facilities, it usually was necessary sooner or later to advance goods on credit or make cash loans. Although credit was crucial to a large proportion of the transactions between Nigerians in business, there was a dearth of credit facilities among persons from different ethnic groups, for lack of a common language, customary law and cultural traits, and a lack of access to kinship arrangements for checking credit worthiness and guaranteeing against default.[13]

Another factor associated with political integration is interregional migration. Table 4.2 indicates that, if a migrant is defined as a person living in a region other than the home region of his ethnic community (region of origin), 2.5 percent of the population of Nigeria in 1952 was migrants. A study by the Nigerian Institute of Social and Economic Research, which uses the same definition for a migrant, points out that in 1963, 7 percent of the population was migrants.[14] These figures on migration between regions cannot be compared with figures from other countries with different numbers of regions and dissimilar concepts of region of origin. Still, the percentages for Nigeria do not seem peculiarly low for a less developed country.

TABLE 4.2
Internal Migrants in Nigeria, 1952

Ethnic Community	Region of destination					Total Migrants
	Lagos	West	North	East	Mid-West	
Yoruba	-	-	54,364	11,377	16,010	81,751
Hausa	3,847	38,151	-	10,288	3,219	55,505
Ibo	31,887	52,858	166,910	-	57,857	309,512
Edo	5,708	18,979	11,938	4,027	-	40,652
Others	21,168	161,579	85,129	10,840	3,810	282,626
Total	62,610	271,567	318,341	36,532	80,996	770,046
Total population	267,407	4,593,650	16,840,479	7,215,249	1,491,415	30,409,200
Migrants/total population	.234	.059	.019	.005	.054	.025

Source: A.L. Mabogunje, "Inter-regional Trade and National Integration in Nigeria," *Journal of Business and Social Studies*, III, No. 1 (December 1970), 99, based on Nigeria, Office of Statistics, *Population Census of Nigeria, 1952-53* (Lagos, 1956).

Because of economic restriction, however, cultural and language hindrances, or the potential direct physical threat from inter-ethnic conflict or political crisis, very little capital or entrepreneurship moved between regions and ethnic communities to establish firms with large fixed capital (more than £N2000 net worth). In 1965, studies by both Harris and me found less than 5 percent of manufacturing entrepreneurs operated businesses in regions outside their birth. (Lagos is included with the Western Region.)[15] The events of 1966-67, with the forced return of many Nigerians to their region of origin, only reinforced the attitudes that the most prudent course for businessmen with substantial capital was to remain in their region, and that the risk of default was smaller when credit was granted within ethnic groups.[16]

COMMUNAL COMPETITION FOR EMPLOYMENT

As alluded to above, communal identity received its staying power because it was the major framework within which the political elite distributed jobs to clients. The Ibos (later dominant in secessionist Biafra) were at the center of the communal competition for employment and business activity--if we leave aside the clash between the dominant and minority ethnic groups in the regions. Ibos, other southerners (especially Yorubas), and Northerners competed for positions in trade, transportation, civil service, public corporations, and foreign firms in the North. Less than 10 percent of the posts in the federal civil service in the early 1960s was held by Northerners, and these primarily from the Middle Belt.[17] Ibos and Yorubas were the major contenders for key positions in the federal civil service and for other jobs in the modern sectors of the West and Lagos (Yoruba areas).

In 1963 the East's population density was 420 persons per square mile compared with 156 in Nigeria as a whole. Seventy percent of the East's labor force was engaged in agriculture during 1963-64, even though there was little farm land in the region. The Ibo-speaking area, long a food-deficit area, was especially hindered by high density (712 persons per square mile in the Onitsha-Owerri Provinces), and poor agricultural land. The North, in contrast, the most sparsely populated region, had only 106 persons per square mile.[18]

The socio-cultural differences between the Ibo and the Hausa go far back in history and are highly pronounced. Several social scientists, who have attempted to analyze them, describe the Ibo as individualistic, competitive, energetic, opportunistic, and receptive to change, and the Hausa as authoritarian, traditional, and loyal and obedient to superiors. Social scientists also contend that the Ibo social structure is more fluid than the Hausa.[19] In short, overpopulation, together with various socio-historical factors that tended to make them enterprising and aggressive, induced more interregional emigration by Ibos than by any other ethnic group.[20]

Official recognition of indigenous forms of land tenure during British colonialism inhibited the movement of some Nigerians, especially southerners who wanted to acquire land in the North. Although southerners resented the policy most Northerners supported it.

The colonial government pursued distinct policies regarding land ownership between the North and the south. The Northern administration prohibited anyone from acquiring freehold title, whereas in the south individual tenure was the rule in urban and periurban areas. The North's policy created grievances among many southerners with economic interests and aspirations in the North.

Despite the property restrictions, in 1952-53, Ibos constituted more than one-third of the nonindigenous population of the urban centers in the North, and were represented in Lagos and parts of the West.[21] Yet so far as the North was concerned, immigration was possible only because of the protection of the colonial regime.

The growth in the number of southerners in the North paralleled that in the Kano *Sabon Gari* (non-Northern residential ghetto), which changed from about 2,000 in 1921 (mostly Yorubas) to 21,000 in 1954 and 40,000 in 1964 (mostly Ibos). Southerners were dominant in much of the trade and transport, and in employment in the public corporations (e.g., postal services and railways) and foreign firms.

The Kano riots in May 1953, in which 36 died, were directed against southerners, partly because so many local Northerners worried about prospects for employment and business in their own region, with an independent government under the control of non-Northerners. Indeed, even by 1955, there was scarcely a single Northerner in the administrative class of the Northern civil service.[22]

The large numbers of southerners in the Northern economy resulted primarily from their higher formal education. The colonial government's need for an educated class of civil servants and clerks in the North was obviated by "indirect" rule through indigenous chiefs and administrators. In addition, the British cooperated with local rulers in the far North to discourage Christian missions, and their primary and secondary schools, because they threatened the political oligarchy as well as the Islamic faith.[23]

Even during the 1950s, education and modernization in the North were less important to the traditional aristocracy than maintaining its political hegemony. Thus, as late as 1960, the male primary enrollment rate (i.e., males enrolled in primary school as a percentage of males aged 6-14), and the corresponding secondary rate (males aged 13-18 as the denominator) were 11 and 1 percent, respectively, in the North, compared with 81 and 11 percent in the south. Only 84 of the graduates from Nigerian universities in 1966 were from the North, compared with 1,249 from the south.[24]

The policy of Northernization initiated in late 1955, which gave priority in many positions to the local ethnic communities, was a reaction to the uneven economic and educational development in the regions. As a result of this policy, Northerners in the superscale, administrative, professional, executive, and higher technical classes of the Northern civil service increased from virtually none in 1955 to 14 percent in 1958, surpassing 50 percent of mid 1961.

Regionalization was directed more toward southerners than foreigners because southerners represented a potential long run rival to Northern political power in the country. From June 1958 to October 1959, southerners in the Northern public sector declined from 294 to 1.[25]

Regional employment preference helped solidify the bureaucracy as the instrument of the traditional aristocracy and administration, to whom civil servants owed their positions. Northernization, by expanding the employment of educated Northerners, especially benefited the more advanced Middle Belt (especially present-day Kwara, Benue, and Plateau states), and expedited an alliance of convenience (at times shaky) between the upper Northern rulers and the educated classes of the Middle Belt.

In early 1966, however, the modern sector of the Northern private economy was still dominated by southerners, Levantines, and Europeans, who were, in general, sending their earnings out of the North. The alien values, especially of southern Nigerians, threatened the Northern Islamic way of life and social structure. Yet the growing enmity in the urban areas was less a conflict of values than competition for the benefits of modernization, which both groups prized highly, but in which the majority of Northerners were at a disadvantage as a result of arriving late on the scene with less education. In the major Northern centers, there were already the beginnings of a restive group of unemployed (from which political thugs were recruited, as discussed below).

The resentment against southern migrants peaked after 24 May 1966, when General Ironsi (an Ibo) announced the abolition of regions and the establishment of a unitary administration. The uneasiness concerning the impact of this on economic opportunities for Northerners in their own region was one factor that helped ignite the disorders in May and July. Later, at the September ad hoc constitutional discussions, those supporting the Northern traditional rulers were jolted by the North's *volte face* (influenced by younger bureaucrats, academics, and army officers in the Middle Belt) from a position favoring retention of the regions in a confederation to one backing the creation of new states, which, in an environment of distrust and animosity, provided one of the immediate sparks for several days of popular violence and disorders directed against Ibos and other Easterners in the North beginning on "Black Thursday," 29 September 1966[26] and climaxing 1 October when army troups stationed in Kano mutinied against officers restricting them from killing Easterners.[27]

The disorders appeared too far-reaching and well ordered to have been entirely spontaneous, and can be interpreted as a desperate last-ditch strike by the insecure far Northern elite at the most vulnerable group available. An integrated federation with more states threatened the political hegemony of the Northern Region. In all, several thousand Easterners were killed in the North during 1966 (and some Northerners were killed in the East, also). The indiscriminate nature of the massacres of Easterners temporarily unified Ibos and minorities whose interests on regional autonomy were otherwise at variance.

Interregional migration in Nigeria was estimated at about 1.7 million the year ending 1 April 1967. Most were persons returning to the regions of origin and could be classified, according to Aluko, as refugees because they moved from fear or by force or edict. In April 1967, 3 percent of the Nigerian population was characterized as refugees, i.e., persons who had fled from one region to another the previous year.

Aluko's figures indicated that about 96 percent of the

migrants were Ibos and others returning to their ethnic homelands in the East[28] (table 4.3). This region, already overcrowded with about 12 million inhabitants, now was burdened with an increase in population by 15 to 20 percent between January 1966 and the beginning of the civil war, and by the loss of transfer income from other regions. Aluko estimated that only 60,000 Easterners remained in the North by April 1967, compared with more than 1.5 million who left the previous year. Of approximately 9 million Ibos, only a half million, many of whom were Mid-West Ibos, still remained in the federation when Biafra seceded.

TABLE 4.3
Interregional Migration, 1 April 1966 - 31 March 1967
(in thousands of persons)

Region	Exits	Entries	Net population movement
East	20	1,600	+1,580
West	40	10	- 30
Mid-West	13	45	+ 32
North	1,580	6	-1,574
Lagos	10	2	- 8
Total	1,663	1,663	-

Source: Aluko, *West Africa* (15 April 1967), p. 495.

The migration of labor from the overpopulated East had been a powerful factor drawing that region to the federation. In fact, before 1966 the Ibos were perhaps the foremost advocates of Nigerian nationalism and a strong central government.[29] But the exodus of large numbers of Easterners from other parts of Nigeria, and the closing of employment and investment opportunities outside the East, substantially decreased their cost of secession. Some were afraid that the North, which used its political power to realign economic power through Northernization, would do the same in the federation as a whole.[30] Many were concerned that regional quotas (e.g., 50 percent North) for newly commissioned military officers, and lower entry qualifications to accommodate Northerners, in 1961-62, might be broadened to apply to representation and promotion of higher-ranking military officers, as well as civilian federal civil servants.

The major competitors for high-level positions within the federation were Yorubas and Ibos, the two ethnic groups most advanced in education. After World War II the Yorubas, who had previously held almost exclusive control of indigenous jobs in the federal service, were challenged substantially by the Ibos in the rapid opening of positions at the center to Nigerians after 1948. Competitive modernization, channeled into political rivalry between the two communities, culminated in the formation of the Action

Group in 1951 as an alternative to the N.C.N.C. Later in 1964, when it became apparent that vacancies in the government bureaucracy were dwindling sharply, contests for the remaining top posts intensified, and unsuccessful applications and slow promotions tended to be explained in communal terms.

Realignment in the Western Region resulted in the formation of a new party, the Nigerian National Democratic Party (N.N.D.P.), which became the ruling party of the region in March 1964. Communal economic contention was reinforced by political rivalry between the N.N.D.P., allied with the Northern Peoples' Congress in the Nigerian National Alliance, and the Action Group, which joined with the Ibo-dominated N.C.N.C. in the United Progressive Grand Alliance, in 1964.

Newspaper articles, pamphlets and an N.N.D.P. white paper written by Yorubas unremittently charged public corporations with maladministration, nepotism and Ibo favoritism--charges that culminated in the dismissal of the Ibo director of the Nigerian Railway Corporation in May 1965. He was considered directly responsible for the fact that 270 of the 431 senior posts in the corporation were held by Ibos. His dismissal, together with a Provisional Council with a Yoruba majority replacing the Ibo vice-chancellor with a Yoruba at the federal University of Lagos in March 1965, exacerbated communal enmity in Lagos and the East.

In the 1960s, the other federal university, the highly reputed University of Ibadan, was brought to the brink of collapse by ethnic conflict over professorial appointments and control of the University Council. The Ibo vice-chancellor, whose contention with the Yoruba registrar lay at the center of the conflict, resigned in December 1966, indicating the "university would be better served . . . by a vice-chancellor who had the fullest support of the people of the region in which it is situated."

In June 1966, some Yoruba members walked out of or failed to attend the meetings of the federal Joint Economic Planning Committee because of alleged favoritism by Dr. Pius Okigbo, the Ibo chief economic advisor to the Ironsi government, toward the demands of the East. Ibo perceptions of discrimination were reinforced when the Ibo high commissioner in London was replaced with a Yoruba in early 1967.[31] (After Eastern de facto secession in late 1966, the federal military government wanted to be certain of loyalty in its most important diplomatic posts.)

The anti-Ibo feeling in the federation during 1966-67 led to an exodus of many of the intelligentsia. University lecturers (especially from the Universities of Ibadan, Lagos, and Ife) and civil servants migrating to the East, who had severed their previous employment ties, became a powerful lobbying group for an independent Biafra, in which they now had a vested economic interest. During the war the Yorubas and members of other communities who remained loyal to the federation moved into some of the positions vacated by Ibos.[32]

The army was one example of the way in which political enmity exacerbated the regional competition for jobs. Communal affiliation in the army became especially crucial after its politicization, which was particularly strong after the last British officer departed in early 1965. Before the first coup, while the majority of the rank-and-file were from the Northern Middle Belt, about half (27) of the 53 officers who held the rank of major or above were Ibos. This resulted from the rapid development of secondary education in the East, limited alternative employment opportunities, high achievement aspirations, the lack of social impediments, and encouragement of leading ethnic politicians.[33]

The numerical importance of Ibos and Easterners in the officer corps introduced an additional factor in Nigerian politics, as illustrated by their role during the 1964-65 election crisis, the January 1966 coup, and the civil war. The potential viability of Biafran secession was enhanced by the fact that in August 1967, 21 of the 30 militarily active officers with a rank of major or above on 1 January 1966 were Eastern or Mid-Western Ibos or non-Ibos Easterners in the Biafran army.[34] Tension among Ibo and Eastern officers was further exacerbated by regional quotas for the recruitment of officers and the rank-and-file, a *perception* of bias toward more rapid promotion of senior Northern officers, and a fear of future discrimination in promotion at all ranks.[35]

Communal competition was intensified by policies instigated in response to the large body of unemployed. Although there are no standard statistics or concepts in this field, Callaway estimates that more than 500,000 of the urban population of 9 million were unemployed in 1963. He defines an unemployed person as a member of the regular labor force, at least 15 years old, who had not earned enough during the previous 12 months to cover personal food costs.

In 1964 Callaway's survey indicated that 28 percent of the total male labor force was unemployed in Ibadan--the largest city (627,379 in 1963) in sub-Saharan black Africa--the overwhelming majority being male youths who were recent primary or secondary school leavers (graduates) or dropouts. During 1966-67, before the civil war, unemployment increased sharply as both business activity and emigration to alien communal-group areas declined.

In an atmosphere of apprehension and suspicion, the response to such problems was intensification of policies of regional discrimination in employment. The geographical segmentation of the labor market then contributed to numerous cases of specific shortages in one region alongside surpluses elsewhere because migration was no longer an equilibrating device. These regional imbalances probably increased the unemployment rate.

Economists in both Nigeria and Biafra stressed that economic regionalization contributed to the disintegration of the federation, and that pressures for additional states, and for secession, were aimed at solving problems of unemployment.[36] For example, Eke, who became commissioner of information for Biafra, wrote in 1967 as an economist at the University of Nigeria: "No socioeconomic problem in present-day Nigeria rivals the problem of finding employment for its mostly idle, teaming population. The political and economic unification of Nigeria has long been significantly hampered by a high rate of unemployment. Competition by the unemployed for employment and, in the understandable absences of public unemployment benefit payments, pressure on responsible citizens to provide a measure of livelihood, even a subsistence level, for people whom they know, have forced otherwise well-meaning citizens to apply ingenuity in substantially expanding the list of criteria for employment in those areas of the economy under their control. This list has inevitably assigned a low priority to competence."

Eke went on to indicate that birth, language group, patron-client relationship, and political affiliation had become some of the major qualifications to fill positions. He concluded that the problems of regionalism, nepotism, and low productivity in the civil service could be traced to socio-political pressures resulting from the dissatisfaction of the large body of unemployed.[37]

Urban people out of work, particularly school leavers and dropouts, proved to be social dynamite in the hands of the upper classes of the regions. Political thugs, including those used by the Northern elite in September-October 1966, were recruited largely from the ranks of the unemployed. In 1967, the Eastern regional military government argued that it had to take complete control of regional resources, since the federal military government abrogated the agreement reached at Aburi to pay fleeing federal employees who had no alternative employment through 31 March 1967. Furthermore, the large number of displaced and destitute persons in the East constituted a combustible and easily manipulated group for the pursuit of military mobilization, secession, and territorial extension.[38]

PETROLEUM PRODUCTION

Before the war, concessions for exploration and production of crude oil were held by foreign petroleum companies, primarily Shell-B.P., Gulf, and Mobil. Expansion of the Eastern crude-oil industry, with its implications for levels of living, foreign exchange position, government finance, and the international political power of an independent region, contributed to the Biafran secession. The benefits of autonomy for the East increased relative to benefits of continued membership in the federation beginning in 1958 with the output of commercial quantities of crude petroleum.

Even as early as the federal election crisis of 1964-65, the credibility of threats of Eastern secession was linked to the considerable potential of petroleum production in the East.[39] After this crisis, journalists, scholars, and officials in Nigeria increasingly believed that the major reason for the potential separation of the Eastern Region was its crude oil production. A leading observer of Nigerian politics, James O'Connell, then professor of political science at the University of Ibadan, wrote before the civil war, "The Ibo bureaucratic and military elites were alienated by the July [1966] coup and a majority of them took a secessionist stand. Initially they hoped to bring the Mid-West with them into secession. They reckoned that the resources in land and oil that the two regions possessed between them would be adequate for whatever economic problems arose." Alhaji Yahaya Gusau, then federal commissioner for economic development, expressed a common view of federal officials 24 March 1969: "The root cause of the present civil war is really an economic one. For example, I am convinced that if there were no petroleum discovered in large quantities in parts of the former Eastern Region, the secessionist leaders would not have tried to break up Nigeria."[40]

The dominant structural change in the Nigerian economy before the civil war was the rapid increase in the share of output of crude oil. The volume of crude petroleum grew from 5,000 barrels a day in 1958 to 415,000 barrels a day in 1966, or 78 percent annually. By then Nigeria, with an annual output of £N100 million, about two-thirds of which was in the East, ranked thirteenth in the world in crude oil production, from that region alone.[41]

The value of crude oil exports increased from a negligible percentage of total export value in 1958 to 10.3 percent in 1962 to 33.1 percent in 1966.[42] In 1966, the oil sector made a net positive contribution of £N43.4 million to the balance on current and capital account, to counter a deficit of £N54.2 million in other sectors. This is significant in an economy where merchandise exports were £N279.0 million the same year (table 5.9).

The oil sector viewed in 1967, promised to be even more important in the future. Despite a large part of the concession territories having not been intensively investigated, it was estimated that known crude-oil reserves already amounted to 800 million tons, compared with production of 20.7 million tons in 1966. Pearson's low projections, predicated on the assumption of an independent Biafra whose output during 1969-73 would not be disrupted by war, or affected by changes in the pattern of concessions and taxation, indicated that Eastern (onshore and offshore) crude petroleum production would more than triple from 1966 to 925,000 barrels a day in 1973. That would compare with 857,000 barrels a day in the rest of the federation in 1973. The positive balance-of-payments impact of the oil sector, according to Pearson, would be £N111 million in Biafra and £N103 million in Nigeria in 1973, each more than double the total for the entire federation in 1966.

No doubt political and military elites in the East and the federation during the early and middle 1960s foresaw the potentially rapid growth in petroleum production. In the East this perception reinforced the case for autonomy. Biafran secession, authorized by the East's Consultative Assembly 26 May, became inevitable with the announcement 27 May 1967 of the establishment of twelve states. This left the ruling Ibos with control only of the East-Central state, a mere 9.7 percent of Eastern Nigeria's oil output of 380,566 barrels per day in April 1967, and without Nigeria's only oil refinery.[43] Although Ibos were only a fraction of the oil-rich Rivers state, a state severed from the East, 45.1 percent of petroleum production in the state in April 1967 was in Ibo-inhabited areas.[44] By and large, Biafra's potential gain constituted a loss for the federation, as was clear in June 1967 when Shell-B.P. offered a token payment of royalties to Biafra.

Not surprisingly, in July 1967, Nigeria took measures to quash the rebels, including a total economic blockade by its navy of Biafran ports (see chapter 2), and a "police action," that captured several towns in northern Biafra. These measures were necessary for Nigeria to maintain support of British oil interests and to avert the threat of loss of oil revenues to Biafra. These measures, and Biafra's invasion of the Mid-West and West in August 1967 made civil war inevitable.

During the second quarter of 1967, western petroleum interests were ambivalent in their positions toward the Eastern Region and the federation. In late 1966, when the federal government raised the question of renegotiating oil concessions to bring the revenue paid per barrel by the foreign companies to the government to the level received by Algeria, some companies may have encouraged the political autonomy of the East, which was willing to return to pre-1966 terms. At the time, federal supporters erroneously suspected that the Eastern government sold petroleum rights to French oil interests for £7 million in November-December 1966.[45]

Britain, which advised Lagos that a war against the Eastern Region probably could not be won, discouraged military action. But in July 1967, the British government, a majority shareholder in Shell-British Petroleum, countermanded its offer of a token payment of £250,000 on the oil royalties demanded by Biafra. With Britain's withdrawal east of Aden, the closing of the Suez Canal in June 1967, and the increasing uncertainty of obtaining oil from West Asia, the United Kingdom doubtless did not wish to risk severing the increasing share of oil in Nigeria originating outside the East.[46] During the course of events, British military and diplomatic assistance to Nigeria helped contribute to its eventual victory. (Chapter 2 elaborates on Britain's role in Nigerian disintegration.)

INTERREGIONAL FINANCIAL ALLOCATION

A major source of interregional contention was determining a formula for allocating oil revenue. Before 1959, all revenues from mineral and agricultural products had been retained by the producing region. But after 1959, only a fraction of the revenue from mineral and mineral oil production was received by the region of production, which was a major source of the East's dissatisfaction. For example, none of the profits tax and only half the rents and royalties from crude petroleum were received by the producing region. In contrast, after 1959 all the revenue from agricultural exports was retained by regional marketing boards. The agricultural exports of the Eastern Region, unlike those in other regions, were relatively small. In 1965/66, the Eastern government received only £N2.90 million from agricultural export duties compared with £N6.07 million received by the North, and £N5.03 million by the West.[47]

In 1967, despite the disruption of war, revenue from onshore and offshore crude oil produced in the East was £N18.1 million. Had all of it been retained by that region, it would have equaled 59 percent of the approved estimates for current revenue, £N30.7 million. According to the formula for allocation, the share of the East in the oil revenue originating in its region was £N9.4 million, or 31 percent of approved current revenue in 1967. With the creation of new states, the Ibo-dominated East-Central state would have received only £N2.6 million, 14 percent of the oil revenue from the old Eastern Region. Finally, with growing oil production, the relative share of the industry's payment to the federal government, which taxed petroleum profits, would have increased, and the proportion to the state of origin, which received one-half of rents and royalties, would have decreased.[48] The potential impact of a viable Biafra on the control of the Ibo military, political, and bureaucratic elite over national revenue was very clear.

Since 1946, when a legislative council was established for the whole country, there have been complaints of discrimination in the distribution of funds and projects. Ironically, the projects with top priority in the 1962-68 educational program, the three national secondary schools to promote political integration, were located in Sokoto, Warri, and Afikpo, home towns of the three ministers who chose the locations. Despite the lack of a detailed feasibility study to support even one steel mill in the country, the National Economic Council agreed in May 1964 to award costly steel plants to both the North and East, the respective regional power bases of the N.P.C. and N.C.N.C., the parties in the ruling federal coalition.

The West and the North alleged that during the 1940s and early 1950s they were contributing more to the central treasury than they were receiving, with the chief beneficiary being the East. In the period 1959-67, the East joined the West in complaining about alleged discrimination favoring the North. Discontent of the East peaked in early 1967 when its Ministry of Information charged that the region had benefited least from the siting of federal investment projects.[49]

REGIONAL ECONOMIC POWER

On the eve of secession, the Economic Planning Commission of the Eastern Region apparently estimated that growth in the region's gross domestic product (GDP) from 1962/63 to 1964/65 (at constant 1962/63 prices) exceeded 8 percent annually and that the region's GDP comprised 33.3 percent of Nigeria's total in 1964/65. However, Ojukwu, whose speeches frequently emphasized the theme of southern unity in late 1966 and early 1967, expected the West and the Mid-West to unite with the East, secede as independent states, or, at least, remain neutral in a conflict between Biafra and the North.[50]

In early 1967, the Yoruba elite had increased demands for removal of the Northern "army of occupation" from the West and creation of an autonomous Oduduwa state. As late as 3 May 1967, a policy resolution by the Western assembly on constitutional proposals reiterated Chief Obafemi Awolowo's position that if the East seceded, the West should also become a sovereign state.[51] In this event, the Mid-West, which had a substantial Ibo minority and was in a weak strategic position between the East and the West probably would have seceded also.

Eastern leaders may have been encouraged to take an independent course, hoping to be in a strong bargaining position because of the potential economic vulnerability of a landlocked North if the southern regions seceded. It is estimated that the North, with 45.5 percent of the GDP of Nigeria compared with 53.5 percent of its population, had the lowest GDP per capita in the federation in 1964/65.[52] But a more important logistic factor was that the North depended on the south for an outlet to the sea and a market for its agricultural products.

When the East severed its ties with the federation 30 May 1967, the West did not follow suit. In fact, Chief Awolowo accepted an offer by General Gowon to be federal commissioner of finance, and deputy chairman of the Federal Executive Council, virtually equivalent to the position of prime minister. Awolowo's support of the federation may have been influenced by several other factors. (1) Ojukwu refused to listen to the peace proposal by the National Reconciliation Committee, which included Awolowo. (2) He may have disagreed with Ojukwu on respective roles in a southern alliance. (3) Gowon solicited advice and support from Awolowo. (4) Awolowo also may have been apprehensive concerning a loss of influence in the federal government to other Yorubas. (5) He may have feared a repeat of 1963 when he was jailed for treason. (6) The creation of twelve states was similar to Awolowo's proposal, first advanced in 1953, which included dividing the North and East into more states.[53]

In addition, Yorubas were drawn to the federation by the declaration of emergency in the federation, the presence of Northern troops in the West, the large stake in federal civil service positions, and the opportunity to make gains in federal positions as Ibos were withdrawn; and Yorubas were repelled from ties to the East by its explusion of all non-Easterners in September 1966.

In August 1967, the Biafran head of state, Lieutenant Colonel Odumegwu Ojukwu, embarked on a strategy of conquest of southern Nigeria. Although Biafran leaders may have expected that the invasion of the Mid-West, a neighboring region where Ibos formed a majority of the officer corps, and the West would encourage secession from the North, it appeared rather to strengthen the resolve to remain with the federation, especially in the West.

Non-Ibos from the Eastern coast were the Trojan horse in Biafran territory that Mid-Western Ibos were in federal Nigeria. Although Eastern minorities, resentful of discrimination by the ruling Ibos in government jobs and favorable toward Gowon's decree on new states, did not rise against Ojukwu, many welcomed the invading federal troops and cooperated with them in April-May 1968.[54] Despite the fact that federal forces, in May 1968, captured the area containing the oil refinery and a large part of prewar oil production in the Eastern Region, output of onshore crude and refined oil in the East was not resumed until after the war (see chapter 6).

CONCLUSION

British colonial policy in Nigeria helped create or exacerbate such regional differences as the more rapid development of southern compared with Northern Nigeria in education, parliamentary experience, and capitalist institutions. Between 1949 and independence in 1960, the British handed over positions, patronage, and economic benefits to a new southern elite, consisting of politicians, bureaucrats, professionals, and businessmen, who together with the Northern traditional aristocracy and its allies, became the indigenous political leaders of the 1950s and early 1960s. Political elites from majority parties in the regional assemblies, who also cooperated with the ruling federal coalition, dispensed a wide range of rewards and sanctions in their regions to retain or enhance their own positions. After independence, however, it became increasingly clear that there were not enough political resources available to reward all the major parties, particularly the Action Group, which tried to acquire a broader constituency, including the dispossessed from all regions. The A.G., which under Chief Obafemi Awolowo, became the first major party to try to mobilize its support on a pan-regional and class basis, was undercut by the ruling, regionally oriented parties. The attempts by the conservative federal coalition to crush the A.G. during 1962-3, and the A.G.-N.C.N.C. alliance during 1964-5, set the stage for army intervention into politics and the civil war.

During the first republic, Nigeria depended heavily on such western capitalist countries as Britain and the United States for trade, aid, investment, technology, political support, and military assistance and equipment. A large portion of the Nigerian political elite and local bourgeoisie relied upon and profited by economic and military assistance and support from rich countries. Indigenous elites served as traders, agents, advisors, representatives, facilitators, intermediaries, and contact men for foreign economic interests, and obtained from them employment and income for clients and supporters. The elite of Nigeria depending on foreign decisions and support prevented Nigeria from competently coping with internal political crises.

Foreign economic, political, and military relations helped shape the formation of regional elites and upper classes, and thus, conflicts between classes and elites. Foreign aid for the First National Plan, 1962-68, helped the federal government pursue projects and policies oriented toward benefits for "modernizing" elites and their political allies. But the alliance lacked enough resources to alleviate the growing frustration of workers, farmers, junior army officers, and the younger educated classes.

Communal conflict and competition cut across class antagonsims. Elites emphasized communal differences partly to distract from class antagonisms, which were more threatening to their positions. Policies of regional economic discrimination, used to increase employment opportunities in the region, had a negative impact on aggregate employment. In late 1966, in a climate of regional economic and political chauvinism, many Easterners were forced to flee from other parts of Nigeria where they had settled. Closing employment and investment opportunities outside the Eastern Region substantially decreased its cost of secession. Animosity also increased between the two major communities, Yorubas and Ibos, competing for high-level employment after prominent Ibos in leading public service positions were dismissed in 1964-66.

Additionally, the disproportional representation of Ibos among army officers and the increased threat to their recruitment and promotion, increased tensions in the army. Moreover, the expansion of the Eastern crude-oil industry, with its implication for economic development, government revenue, and international economic position, contributed to the Biafran secession. The economic vulnerability of the landlocked Northern Region to secession by southern regions was another factor encouraging Lieutenant Colonel Odumegwu Ojukwu to secede. Indigenous businessmen had very little vested interest in Nigeria's interregional economic and political integration. Thus, regional economic competition, which interacted with other economic variables like foreign dependence and class conflict, was a major factor contributing to the Biafran secession and the Nigerian civil war.

NOTES

1. A parallel exists in Lebanon, where the lower classes tended to join religious-confessional parties instead of those that promised to improve their economic condition. Michael W. Suleiman, *Political Parties in Lebanon: The Challenge of a Fragmented Political Culture* (Ithaca, N.Y.: Cornell University Press, 1967) pp. 276-7.

2. Philip E. Jacob and Henry Teune, "The Integrative Process: Guidelines for Analysis of the Bases of Political Community," in *The Integration of Political Communities*, Philip E. Jacob and James V. Toscano, eds. (Philadelphia: J.B. Lippincott Company, 1964), pp. 23-30.

3. Robert H.T. Smith, "Interregional Trade in Nigeria--A Constraint of National Unity?" Proceedings of the Conference on *Problems of Integration and Disintegration in Nigeria*, Northwestern University, Evanston, Ill., 31 March-2 April, 1967, pp. 84, 86; and A.L. Mabogunje, "Inter-regional Trade and National Integration in Nigeria," *Journal of Business and Social Studies*, III, No. 1 (December 1970), 101-2.

4. Relative acceptance from region i to region j (RA), is calculated from the expression

$$RA_{ij} = \frac{A_{ij} - E_{ij}}{E_{ij}}$$

where A_{ij} = actual payments associated with shipments of locally produced final commodities from region i and region j, and E_{ij} = expected payments associated with shipments of locally produced final commodities from region i to region j. The calculation of expected flows is based on an assumption of origin-destination independence, i.e., that flows of payments from region i to region j are distributed only on the basis of the amount of payments received by region j. Thus, as the Mid-West receives 9.6 percent of all payments for traded commodities, then 9.6 percent of the payments from the East to other regions should be received by the Mid-West. Smith, "Interregional Trade," pp. 86, 88, 98-9.

5. If two-way connections between regions (i.e., positive salience for flows in both directions, e.g., from both North to West, and West to North) are given a weight of one, and one-way

links (i.e., positive salience in only one direction, e.g., from North to West, but not West to North) a score of one-half, an index of connectivity would be the sum of these scores divided by the number of possible two-way links. The connectivity index for migration between regions was 0.925, compared with an index of 0.5 for interregional trade. *Ibid.*, pp. 88-91.

6. James V. Toscano, "Transaction Flow Analysis in Metropolitan Areas: Some Preliminary Explorations," in *Integration of Political Communities*, Jacob and Toscano, eds., pp. 98-119.

7. Smith, "Interregional Trade," pp. 84, 86; and Mabogunje, *Journal of Business and Social Studies*, III, No. 1, 101-2.

8. William J. Foltz, *From French West Africa to the Mali Federation* (New Haven, Conn.: Yale University Press, 1965), pp. 31-48.

9. Joseph S. Nye, Jr., *Pan-Africanism and East African Integration* (Cambridge, Mass.: Harvard University Press, 1965), pp. 142-3.

10. Nigerian public ownership/ total ownership = Nigerian public ownership/ total Nigerian ownership X (1 - foreign private ownership/ total ownership). Computed from the information in table 2.4.

11. P.C. Asiodu, "Planning for Further Industrial Development in Nigeria," Conference on National Reconstruction and Development in Nigeria, University of Ibadan, 24-29 March 1969, pp. 7-9, 20.

12. John R. Harris and Mary P. Rowe, "Entrepreneurial Attitudes and National Integration: The Nigerian Case," in *Nigeria: Modernization and the Politics of Communalism*, Robert Melson and Howard Wolpe, eds. (East Lansing, Mich.: Michigan State University Press, 1971), p. 148; and Peter Kilby, *Development of Small Industries in Eastern Nigeria* (Enugu: Eastern Ministry of Information, 1963), pp. 18-20.

13. E. Wayne Nafziger, "Inter-regional Economic Relations in the Nigerian Footwear Industry," *Journal of Modern African Studies*, VI, No. 4 (1968), 535-40; Smith, "Inter-regional Trade," p. 84; and Alan M. Hay and Robert H.T. Smith, *Interregional Trade and Money Flows in Nigeria, 1964* (Ibadan: Oxford University Press, 1970), pp. 17-26.

14. Nigerian Institute of Social and Economic Research, "Nigeria: Population Models for National Regional Planning, 1952-67," Ibadan, March 1969, p. 18.

15. Among 81 manufacturing entrepreneurs I interviewed in the footwear industry, only 3 were operating businesses in a region outside their birth, and only 2 were operating businesses in an area dominated by another ethnic community. The two businessmen operating in another communal group area returned to their "home" areas in 1965-66. *Journal of Modern African Studies*, VI, No 4, 538-9. John R. Harris, in a study of the sawmill, furniture, printing, rubber-processing, and garment-making industries, found only 5 of 101 entrepreneurs operating businesses outside the regions of their birth. "Industrial Entrepreneurship in Nigeria" (Ph.D. dissertation, Northwestern University, 1967), p. 252.

16. Nafziger, *Journal of Modern African Studies*, VI, No. 4, 539; and Smith, "Interregional Trade," p. 84.

17. Paul Beckett and James O'Connell, *Education and Power in*

Nigeria (New York: Africana Publishing Co., 1978), pp. 54, 57.

18. Nigeria, Office of Statistics, *Population Census of Nigeria, 1963*, III (Lagos, July 1968), 54, 57.

19. Robert A. LeVine and others, *Dreams and Deeds: Achievement Motivation in Nigeria* (Chicago: University of Chicago Press, 1966), pp. 25-37, 92-4; James S. Coleman, *Nigeria: Background to Nationalism* (Berkeley and Los Angeles: University of California Press, 1958), pp. 64, 333-6; Simon Ottenberg, "Ibo Receptivity to Change," in *Continuity and Change in African Cultures*, W.R. Bascom and M.J. Herskovits, eds. (Chicago: University of Chicago Press, 1958), pp. 130-43; and Phoebe Ottenberg, "The Afikpo Ibo of Eastern Nigeria," in *Peoples of Africa*, James L. Gibbs, Jr., ed. (New York: Holt, Rinehart and Winston, 1965), pp. 1-39.

20. See table 4.2, and Nigerian Institute of Social and Economic Research, "Nigeria: Population Models," p. 8.

21. Coleman, *Nigeria*, pp. 58-60, 76-7.

22. John N. Paden, "Communal Competition, Conflict and Violence in Kano," in *Nigeria*, Melson and Wolpe, eds., pp. 121-2; and B.J. Dudley, *Parties and Politics in Northern Nigeria* (London: Frank Cass and Company, 1968), p. 219.

23. Some western journalists and scholars perceived the Nigerian civil war as a religious war between the Muslim North and the Christian south. True, according to the 1963 census, more than 77 percent of the Eastern Region was Christian and less than 1 percent Muslim, while only about 10 percent of the Northern Region was Christian and 72 percent Muslim. In addition, religious identity was used to stir up fervor in the war. Muslim Northerners often regarded Ibos as "pagans," with a facade of Christianity, and not "people of the book." On the other hand, even nominal Ibo Christians used Christianity as a part of Ibo nationalism, and during the civil war, a part of Biafran nationalism. Biafran diplomatic officials, supported by some missionaries and church relief personnel, especially stressed Christian identity in their appeals to western Christendom. Moreover, for many Nigerians, Christian-Muslim differences were symbolic of other sources of enmity, as religion was correlated with ethnicity, westernization, modernization, educational attainment, social structure, and colonial experience. Furthermore, as indicated in the text above, colonial rule and administration, and missionary and educational policy in the Northern Islamic emirates were different from the rest of Nigeria, especially from the south.

One point that contradicts the stereotype about the Nigerian-Biafran war as a Muslim-Christian war was the fact that a majority of the federal troops were Christians from the Middle Belt, not Muslims from the far North.

Another point refuting this stereotype was the religious composition of the Western population. The West, according to the 1963 census, was 49 percent Christian and 43 percent Muslim. As Trimingham argues, among Yoruba in Western Nigeria where religion has been secularized, "individual changes of allegiance [between Christianity and Islam] can take place without causing any outcry from the community, for it is not thought to menace family solidarity or undermine the fabric of society. Many Yoruba families have Muslim, Christian, and pagan members and all join happily in each other's religious festivals, for they are merely acts of social custom like the observance of Christmas in the western world. . . . Both Islam and Christianity have gained large numbers of adherents, especially Islam, yet neither of these religions hold together the social edifice, they are simply the religious department of life." Similarly, religion has little political salience. J. Spencer Trimingham, *Islam in West Africa* (Oxford: Oxford University Press, 1959), pp. 221-2. As Ali A. Mazrui indicates, "In reality the religious factor in the Nigerian Civil War was at most subsidiary, and certainly not fundamental." "Black Africa and the Arabs," *Foreign Affairs*, LIII (July 1975), 737.

24. Peter Kilby, "Technical Education in Nigeria," *Bulletin of the Oxford University Institute of Economic and Statistics*, XXVI, No. 2 (May 1964), 183-4; and Nigeria, Office of Statistics, *Annual Abstract of Statistics, 1967* (Lagos, 1968), pp. 154-5.

25. Dudley, *Parties and Politics*, pp. 220-1.

26. Official blame was laid on Radio Cotonou (Dahomey) for broadcasting inflammatory reports of Northerners being killed in the East, which were repeated over Radio Kaduna. Nigeria, Ministry of Information, *Background Notes on the Nigerian Crisis* (Lagos, 1967), p. 5; and A.H.M. Kirk-Greene, *Crisis and Conflict in Nigeria: A Documentary Sourcebook, 1966-1970*, I (London: Oxford University Press, 1971), 63.

27. B.J. Dudley, *Instability and Political Order: Politics and Crisis in Nigeria* (Ibadan: Ibadan University Press, 1973), p. 165.

28. In addition, about 2 percent of the migrants were Mid-Western Ibos returning to their region of origin. Samuel A. Aluko, "Displaced Nigerians," *West Africa* (15 April 1967), pp. 495-8.

29. Coleman, *Nigeria*, pp. 332-43; and Alan Peshkin, "Education and National Integration in Nigeria," *Journal of Modern African Studies*, V, No. 3, (1967) 323-34.

30. John N Paden, "Northern Region: Relations with Southern Nigeria" (Paper presented to a Conference on Problems of Integration and Disintegration in Nigeria, Northwestern University, Evanston, Ill., 31 March - 2 April 1967).

31. Kenneth Post and Michael Vickers, *Structure and Conflict in Nigeria, 1960-1966* (Madison, Wis.: University of Wisconsin Press, 1973), pp. 120-2, 209-11; John P. Mackintosh, *Nigerian Government and Politics: Prelude to the Revolution* (Evanston, Ill.: Northwestern University Press, 1966), p. 559; P.C. Lloyd, "The Ethnic Background to the Nigerian Crisis," in *Nigerian Politics and Military Rule: Prelude to the Civil War*, S.K. Panter-Brick, ed. (London: The Athlone Press, 1970), p. 10; B.J. Dudley, "Western Nigeria and the Nigerian Crisis," ibid., p. 99; K. Whiteman, "Enugu: The Psychology of Secession," ibid., p. 119; and "Professor Dike Quits Ibadan Varsity Post," *West African Pilot* (21 December 1966).

32. The Ibos, partly as a result of their control of the levers of power in the Eastern Region, dominated entrepreneurial activity and jobs in the modern sector in many of the non-Ibo

communities of the East. This was an irritant especially in the Rivers area, where Ibos obtained much of the employment connected with the rapidly expanding oil sector.

33. "Matchet's Diary," *West Africa* (29 January 1966), p. 111; W.F. Gutteridge, *The Military in African Politics* (London: Methuen and Company, 1969), p. 93; and Robin Luckham, *The Nigerian Military: A Sociological Analysis of Authority and Revolt, 1960-67* (Cambridge: Cambridge University Press, 1971), pp. 188-90. Luckham suggests that, since the educated Ibos arrived on the scene later than the Yorubas, the Ibos were driven to seek advancement in occupations like the army where others were not already entrenched.

34. Robin Luckham, "The Nigerian Military: Disintegration or Integration?" in *Nigerian Politics and Military Rule*, Panter-Brick, ed., pp. 60-2.

35. Luckham, *The Nigerian Military*, pp. 192, 230-1, 243-6.

36. I.I.U. Eke, "Unemployment in Nigeria: A Study of the Strategy of Development for Nigeria," Economic Development Institute, University of Nigeria, Enugu, 1967; Archibald Callaway, "Creating Employment for Nigeria's School Leavers," *Quarterly Journal of Administration*, III, No. 1 (October 1969), 1-11, and "Education Expansion and the Rise of Youth Unemployment," in *The City of Ibadan*, P.C. Lloyd, A.L. Mabogunje, and B. Awe, eds. (London: Cambridge University Press, 1967), pp. 198-203; and T.M. Yesufu, "Manpower and Educational Objectives for Nigeria's Reconstruction and Development," Reconstruction and Development Conference, 1969.

37. Eke, "Unemployment in Nigeria," pp. 2-3.

38. Ukpabi Asika, "Rehabilitation and Resettlement," Reconstruction and Development Conference, 1969, p. 11.

39. "Nigeria's Oil Revolution Begins," *West Africa* (27 February 1965), p. 233; and K. Whiteman, "Enugu: The Psychology of Secession, 29 July 1966 to 30 May 1967," in *Nigerian Politics and Military Rule*, Panter-Brick, ed., p. 118.

40. James O'Connell, "Political Integration: The Nigerian Case," in *African Integration and Disintegration: Case Studies in Economic and Political Union*, Arthur Hazlewood, ed. (London: Oxford University Press, 1967), p. 177 and Alhaji Yahaya Gusau, "Opening Addresses," in *Reconstruction and Development in Nigeria--Proceedings of a National Conference*, A.A. Ayida and H.M.A. Onitiri, eds. (Ibadan: Oxford University Press, 1971), p. 747.

41. Scott R. Pearson, *Petroleum and the Nigerian Economy* (Stanford, Calif.: Stanford University Press, 1970). See also chapter 7 below.

42. Nigerian Institute of Social and Economic Research, "Economic and Social Survey, 1958 to 1968," Reconstruction and Development Conference, 1969.

Before the 1970s, when the international oil companies were integrated from prospecting for crude petroleum to marketing petroleum products, and when the full proceeds from the exports of petroleum did not directly accrue to oil exporting countries, the "price" used for the output of petroleum overestimated the percentage of GDP originating in the oil sector, and the value of crude oil output and exports. This "price" was for most companies an intra-firm transfer price, which was important in determining the taxes paid to the exporting country. Despite this, the data on petroleum exports are useful for indicating the change in petroleum's relative importance over time. Kathleen M. Langley, "Financing Development in Nigeria: An Appraisal," in *South of the Sahara: Development in African Economies*, Sayre P. Schatz, ed. (Philadelphia: Temple University Press, 1972), pp. 234, 240.

43. See chapter 1 for more details on the actions and reactions by the East and the federation in early 1967.

44. Ironically only 19.5 pecent of petroleum production in the East-Central state and only 42.6 percent in the Eastern Region were in Ibo ethnic areas. Pearson, *Petroleum and the Nigerian Economy*, pp. 137-52. Different researchers may not agree on the breakdown between Ibo and non-Ibo ethnic areas, since neither the identification of the Ibo nor the size or boundary of the appropriate geographical unit is exact.

45. Dudley, *Instability and Political Order*, p. 197, discusses the encouragement of the East's political ambitions by foreign oil companies and the suspicion concerning French oil interests.

46. The Union blockade in the American civil war proved that Europe could more easily survive without southern cotton than it could get along without northern wheat. American Heritage, *Picture History of the Civil War* (New York: American Heritage, 1960), p. 401. Contrary to the Eastern leaders' calculations, Britain could more readily forego the short run acquisition of the East's oil than to alienate the federation, and lose its increasing share of Nigeria's oil from the Mid-Western and offshore oils.

47. Abedayo Adedeji, *Nigerian Federal Finance: Its Development, Problems and Prospects* (New York: Africana Publishing Corporation, 1969), pp. 151-4, 165-6, 179-85, 253-4.

48. Although the federation and the East must have foreseen the growing importance of petroleum revenues, especially petroleum profits revenue, they may not have envisioned the magnitude of the increase. By 1975, petroleum revenue comprised 78 percent of total revenue collected by the Nigerian federal government, £N2,136 million. Petroleum profits taxes as a percentage of total petroleum revenue increased from 15 percent in 1966/67 to 78 percent in 1971/72. Pearson, *Petroleum and the Nigerian Economy*, pp. 142-5; Nigeria, Office of Statistics, *Digest of Statistics*, XVII, No. 4 (October 1968), 87; Lawrence A. Rupley, "A Survey of the Nigerian Fiscal System," Ahmadu Bello University, Zaria, April 1976, table A-1; and table 8.4 below.

49. Adedeji, *Nigerian Federal Finance*, pp. 55-6, 63, 151, 252-4; James O'Connell, "The Political Class and Economic Growth," *Nigerian Journal of Economic and Social Studies*, VIII, No. 1 (March 1966), 137, and John P. Mackintosh, *Nigerian Government and Politics: Prelude to the Revolution* (Evanston, Ill.: Northwestern University Press, 1966), pp. 560-1.

50. See Ojukwu's speeches, in documents from Kirk-Greene, *Crisis and Conflict*, I, 294-5, 397, 423, 442-3, 451.

51. Chief Awolowo stated in a speech made to Western "leaders of thought" in Ibadan 1 May 1967, "If the Eastern Region is allowed by acts of omission or commission to secede from or opt out of Nigeria, then the Western Region and Lagos must also stay out of

the Federation." *Daily Times*, 2 May 1967, reprinted as document 104 in Kirk-Greene, *Crisis and Conflict*, I, 415.

52. O. Aboyade and A. Ayida, "The War Economy in Perspective," *Nigerian Journal of Economic and Social Studies*, XIII, No. 1 (March 1971), 16-17; Dudley, *Instability and Political Order*, p. 187; Robin Cohen, "'A Greater South': or What Might Have Happened in the Nigerian Civil War," Faculty of Commerce and Social Science, University of Birmingham, Series C, Occasional Paper No. 22, February 1971; Adedeji, *Nigerian Federal Finance*, p. 291; and Nigeria, Office of Statistics, *Annual Abstract of Statistics, 1964* (Lagos, 1964), p 12.

53. Cohen, "'A Greater South,'" pp. 14-15; Dudley, *Instability and Political Order*, pp. 199-200; S.K. Panter-Brick, "From Military Coup to Civil War, January 1966 to May 1967," in *Nigerian Politics and Military Rule*, Panter-Brick, ed., pp. 54-5; and Dudley, "Western Nigeria and the Nigerian Crisis," ibid., p. 109.

54. K. Whiteman, "Enugu: The Psychology of Secession, 29 July 1966 to 30 May 1967," ibid., pp. 114-19.

Part 2

The Economic Impacts of the War

5
Output, Prices, Wages, Employment, and the Balance of Payments

Few events alter the socioeconomic structure of a country as radically as the convulsions and displacements concomitant with war and political upheaval. In Nigeria, the two coups d'état of 1966 and the civil war of 1967-70 profoundly affected economic activity. In contrast to chapters 1-4, where the economic variable tended to be independent and the political factor dependent, chapters 5-7 treat economic activity as dependent on the political variable (disintegration and war).

In this chapter, I examine the movement of the macro-variables during the war--output, prices, wages, employment, and the balance of payments--and their relationship to government policies, especially domestic financial and international trade policies. The last section of the chapter assesses costs and benefits of the war. In chapter 6, the major sectors affected by the war--oil, manufacturing, transportation, domestic trade, and agriculture--are analyzed with primary emphasis on the federal Nigerian economy. In chapter 7, to the extent that evidence is available, a view of the Biafran economy is presented.

DOMESTIC AGGREGATES

The reliability of estimates of Nigerian national-income statistics even in peacetime is limited by meager industry-wide data (especially where commodities are consumed domestically), difficulties in assessing the representation of sample inquiries, and the arbitrariness of quantification based on subjective and qualitative judgements of provincial officers.[1] In addition, there were sources of inaccuracies (above those in "normal" years) in Nigerian national-income accounts during the war, 1967/68 through 1969/70, resulting from the lack of documentation in Biafran territory.[2] Despite the deficiencies in aggregate economic statistics in Nigeria, a few general tendencies concerning output, prices, wages, and the rate of employment are clear.

Official figures indicate that gross domestic product (GDP) at *current* prices in the fiscal year 1966/67 (beginning 1 April) was £N1,605.0 million, or about £N35 (or $98) per capita.[3] Growth in real GDP (at 1962/63 factor cost) went from 6.0 percent per annum from fiscal 1958/59 to 1965/66, to 2.6 percent from 1965/66 to 1966/67, -7.6 percent from 1966/67-1967/68, 0.9 percent from

TABLE 5.1
Estimated All-Nigerian Gross Domestic Product at Constant (1962/63) Factor Cost, 1958/59-72/73 (£N millions)

Sector	1958/59	1959/60	1960/61	1961/62	1962/63	1963/64	1964/65
Agriculture, livestock, forestry & fishing	672.2	704.5	799.9	776.9	804.8	870.8	866.7
Mining	10.2	12.1	15.8	22.3	26.8	31.3	47.5
Manufacturing and crafts	45.3	52.0	57.0	63.8	75.9	76.8	78.8
Electricity and water supply	2.8	3.5	4.2	5.2	6.0	7.3	8.1
Building and construction	35.3	47.0	55.4	57.9	57.5	66.0	65.0
Distribution	127.9	136.1	154.7	155.5	161.1	180.9	194.9
Transport and communication	40.8	44.3	53.4	59.3	60.9	68.1	67.2
General government	39.8	47.8	49.7	49.6	51.3	51.3	52.1
Education	23.8	28.1	29.5	32.2	35.7	37.8	43.0
Health	4.0	4.6	5.3	5.2	7.2	7.5	9.4
Other services	21.8	22.7	25.3	28.1	20.2	27.9	30.7
Total	1023.9	1102.7	1250.2	1256.0	1315.4	1425.7	1463.4

Sources: For 1958/59-1966/67, Nigeria, Office of Statistics, *Gross Domestic Product of Nigeria, 1958/59-1966/67* (Lagos, August 1968), p. 30. For 1966/67-1969/70, O. Aboyade and A. Ayida, "The War Economy in Perspective," *Nigerian Journal of Economic and Social Studies*, XIII, No. 1 (March 1971), p. 29, who use the figures of the Federal Office of Statistics for 1966/67. For the series to the right of the double bar, 1969/70-1972/73, not comparable to the former series, Nigeria, Central Planning Office, Ministry of Economic Development and Reconstruction, *Second National Development Plan, 1970-74: Second Progress Report* (Lagos, 1974), p. 12.

TABLE 5.1 (continued)

1965/66	1966/67	*1967/68*[a]	*1968/69*[a]	*1969/70*[a]	*1969/70*[a]	1970/71	1971/72	1972/73
870.9	869.5	*817.3*	*805.8*	*801.8*	*762.3*	912.1	1068.6	1122.0
82.4	114.4	*51.5*	*55.6*	*68.4*	*129.4*	251.9	339.0	400.8
91.7	93.1	*108.9*	*126.3*	*142.7*	*131.7*	158.8	178.3	205.1
9.2	10.7	*10.0*	*10.5*	*11.2*	*10.4*	12.0	13.4	15.0
80.0	81.3	*72.3*	*73.4*	*76.3*	*75.8*	121.6	188.3	208.5
202.7	200.9	*193.9*	*191.0*	*190.0*	*205.7*	266.6	273.8	300.2
64.8	62.7	*57.9*	*57.6*	*58.5*	*53.7*	69.2	72.5	76.0
51.6	51.6	*48.1*	*49.1*	*52.0*	*104.0*	166.6	177.7	201.6
43.7	48.2	*46.3*	*47.3*	*49.2*	*33.4*	50.9	61.1	67.4
9.8	9.3	*9.0*	*9.1*	*9.7*	*12.3*	21.4	24.6	27.8
36.2	41.4	*47.2*	*50.5*	*54.0*	*44.7*	58.1	66.8	76.8
1543.0	1583.1	*1462.4*	*1475.2*	*1513.8*	*1563.4*	2089.2	2464.1	2701.2

[a]Includes Biafra.

1967/68-1968/69, and 2.6 percent from 1968/69-1969/70. (Biafran territory is included in data for the fiscal years, 1967/68-69/70.)

Estimates of the Central Planning Office based on a series not parallel to the figures for 1958/59-1969/70 indicate a real growth rate of 33.6 percent per annum from 1969/70, the last year of the war, to 1970/71, 17.9 percent in 1970/71-1971/72, and 9.6 percent in 1971/72-1972/73 (table 5.1).[4] Apparently the rate of growth was slow in 1966/67-1968/69 and rapid in 1969/70-72/73, compared with 1958/59-65/66.

Real gross domestic product dropped by 1.5 percent per annum from fiscal years 1966/67 (which ended two months before the Eastern secession) to 1969/70 (which ended three months after the war). Although the data are unreliable, the consensus of economists was that population was growing 2.5-3.0 percent per annum during the middle and last part of the 1960s.[5] Thus, real GDP per capita is likely to have decreased substantially during the war.

Real net domestic product (NDP) per capita probably declined even more precipitiously. It is misleading to stress figures of GDP during the war. Economists widely recognize that net product--where "capital exhaustion" (capital consumption plus capital destruction)[6] is subtracted--is more appropriate as a measure of economic well-being than gross product. Because of difficulties in measuring exhaustion, economists usually settle for figures of gross product, assuming a rough parallel between growths in net and gross products. In "normal" times, this assumption may not seriously distort the picture of growth, but in wartime, impressions of growth are greatly distorted where capital destruction, together with depreciation, is not subtracted from gross product to obtain net product.[7]

Even though there are no precise figures, a conservative estimate for capital destruction/gross domestic product during the war would be 5-10 percent annually.[8] Because of the destruction, GDP figures severely understate the decline in NDP from 1966/67 to 1967/68, the first year of the war, and substantially understate the growth of NDP from 1969/70, the last year of the war, and 1970/71.

The rapid expansion in output of military goods from 1967/68 through 1969/70 was at the expense of both civilian producer and consumer goods, so the percentage decrease in the consumption of civilian goods per capita was even greater than the decline in NDP per capita.

Part of the decline in growth during 1966/67 to 1967/68 can be explained by weakening private investment, especially from overseas,[9] as a result of growing anxieties about the strength of the Nigerian economy following evidences of political instability in 1965-67. Also, the political impotence and government turnover in this period added to administrative difficulties in submitting viable and well-planned projects within the framework of the First National Development Plan (1962-68).

Other factors accounting for the slow growth were the drop in oil and manufacturing output in the secessionist East after the embargo instituted in mid 1967, the disruption in transportation, communication, and internal trade sectors stemming from the forced exodus of skilled personnel to their ethnic homelands in 1966/67, the breakdown of economic relations with the East, and the loss of human lives and damage of capital assets.[10]

The apparent increase in real GDP in 1968/69 and 1969/70 resulted from several factors. In the last quarter of 1968, crude-oil production was resumed in the Rivers area, recaptured by federal forces earlier that year. Manufacturing output expanded during the period as a result of import substitution in response to the tightening of trade restrictions. Other sectors expanded their output as transportation bottlenecks were alleviated and trading networks were altered in response to losses in secessionist areas.

Nigeria avoided much of the severe inflationary pressures usually accompanying wartime. The annual change in the overall price level for 1965/66 through 1969/70 did not exceed 3 percent. The rate of increase from 1965/66 to 1969/70 was 2.0 percent per annum, less than the annual rate of increase in overall prices from 1960/61 to 1965/66, 2.1 percent (table 5.2). Even though the figures on the change in price level, which are based on the GDP price deflator, are subject to some error during the crisis, it is clear that overall prices were stable.

TABLE 5.2
Annual Percentage Change in the Overall Price Level, 1960/61-1969/70

Fiscal year	Change in prices (%)
1960/61-1961/62	+5.2
1961/62-1962/63	+5.8
1962/63-1963/64	-1.6
1963/64-1964/65	+1.2
1964/65-1965/66	+0.3
1965/66-1966/67	+1.6
1966/67-1967/68	*+2.9*
1967/68-1968/69	*+2.0*
1968/69-1969/70	*+1.7*

Sources: Nigeria, Office of Statistics, *Gross Domestic Product of Nigeria, 1958/59-1966/67* (Lagos, August 1968), pp. 25, 30; and Aboyade and Ayida, *Nigerian Journal*, XIII, No. 1, pp. 28-9.

Consumer prices in federal territory were also stable. The stable prices (i.e., single-digit price rises) characteristic of the five years before 1966 continued throughout the crises, except in 1966 and 1969.

In 1966 the average consumer price index for major cities increased 6 percent for middle-income groups and 10 percent for lower-income groups. The 20 percent increase in food prices in 1966 resulted largely from shortages after traders departed from their customary markets during the political disturbances. Substantial increase in prices also can be attributed to uncertainties accompanying political events, which traders and transporters exploited to their advantage, and to increases in customs and excise duties early in the year.[11]

The average consumer price index for lower-income groups decreased in both 1967 and 1968. The comparable index for middle-income groups decreased in 1967, and increased moderately in 1968 (table 5.3). Partly as a result of the mass exodus of Easterners and Mid-Westerners from other regions to their ethnic homelands in 1966-67, consumer prices increased substantially within the East and Mid-West, and decreased elsewhere in 1967. Food prices actually fell in federal Nigeria in the last half of 1967 and in 1968, as many supplies were diverted from the blockaded East, a food-deficit area, to other parts of the country (table 5.3). Restrictive financial policies, which curbed expenditure in the civilian sector, added to the restraint on the general price level in 1967 and 1968. Prices would have remained even more stable except for the major transport crisis in 1967-68, resulting from the severance of the East and the loss of its skilled manpower.[12] Because changes in food prices form a smaller percentage of the living costs of high-income classes, and because of greater import restrictions on luxury items, upper-income groups probably experienced a higher increase in 1967-68 prices than lower-and middle-income groups.

The average consumer price index for lower- and middle-income groups increased 10 and 6 percent, respectively, in 1969, and 14 and 9 percent, respectively, in 1970. Pressure on prices was exerted by rising government spending financed by the commercial banking system, and the demand for food and sustenance and their high distribution costs in war-damaged areas regained from Biafra. Food prices rose by 19 percent in 1969 and 23 percent in 1970,[13] an especially onerous burden for lower- and middle-income classes in the urban areas.

The all-cities consumer price index increased 37 percent, with food prices rising 56 percent (table 5.3), as money wages paid by government remained constant from 1964 to 1970. By 1969, real wage rates for unskilled labor had declined to rates below 1955. Under military rule, trade union leadership was weak, with its influence through party politics destroyed and strikes decreed illegal. Grassroots labor unrest and peasant revolts came in reaction to deterioration of wages, a compulsory savings scheme (which involved a 5 percent deduction from all wages and salaries except for the lowest-paid workers), increased taxes for low- and middle-income earners, a rise in excise and import duties, and the introduction of import restrictions. Labor agitation during early 1968 led to a decree in June 1968 restricting the right to strike.[14] Later, in response to inflation and dissension, the government banned strikes and wage increases for the twelve months after December 1969.

The price control board established in May 1970 to fix prices of twenty-three commodities could not control the major items in the budget of low-income groups. Most food they consumed was produced locally in a competitive market, which is almost impossible to control. Where detailed qualitative standards are not specified, sellers of such highly differentiated products as textiles and clothing can lower the quality of the goods when

TABLE 5.3
Consumer Price Indices, 1960-77

Year	(1) All-cities index for lower-income groups[a]	(2) Percentage change in (1) from previous year	(3) All-cities index for food for lower-income groups[a]	(4) Percentage change in (3) from previous year	(5) Lagos index for middle-income groups	(6) Percentage change in (5) from previous year
1960	100.0	-	100.0	-	100[b]	-
1961	106.4	+ 6.4	109.8	+ 9.8		
1962	112.0	+ 5.2	118.0	+ 7.5	115[b]	n.a.
1963	108.9	- 2.8	106.7	- 9.6		
1964	110.1	+ 1.1	105.7	- 0.9	117.0	n.a.
1965	114.4	+ 3.9	110.5	+ 4.5	121.8	+ 4.1
1966	125.5	+ 9.7	133.1	+20.5	129.6	+ 6.4
1967	120.8	- 3.8	119.3	-10.4	127.2	- 1.9
1968	120.3	- 0.4	112.6	- 5.6	131.3	+ 3.2
1969	132.3	+10.0	133.9	+18.9	139.7	+ 6.4
1970	150.6	+13.8	164.5	+22.9	152.7	+ 9.3
1971	174.7	+16.0	211.4	+28.5	165.4	+ 8.3
1972	179.6	+ 2.8	216.6	+ 2.5	172.5	+ 4.3
1973	189.3	+ 5.4	223.6	+ 3.2	181.5	+ 5.2
1974	213.6	+12.8	261.4	+16.9	211.9	+16.7
1975	285.4	+33.6	367.7	+40.7	274.6	+29.6
1976	348.1	+22.0	464.7	+26.4	320.4	+16.7
1977	423.1	+21.5	592.2	+27.4	387.4	+20.9

[a]Weighted average price indices in Benin, Ibadan, Kaduna, Kano, Lagos, Zaria, Enugu, and Port Harcourt from 1960 through 1969, with Enugu omitted in 1970-75, and Port Harcourt replaced by Sapele, Warri, and Ilorin in 1970-77. Lower-income groups were those earning less than £N400 per annum in 1964-68.

[b]Data not given beyond whole numbers.

[c]Middle-income groups are those earning £N400 or more but less than £N700 per annum, for 1964-68.

Sources: Central Bank of Nigeria, *Annual Reports and Statements of Accounts*, (Lagos).

Note: The composite consumer price index for both rural and urban centers computed by the Federal Office of Statistics replaced the all-cities index for lower-income groups and Lagos index for middle-income groups in 1978. The change in this composite price index was 24.3 percent from 1975 to 1976, 13.8 percent from 1976 to 1977, 24.4 percent from 1977 to 1978, 11.8 percent from 1978 to 1979, and 9.9 percent from 1979 to 1980. The change in the composite price index for food for both rural and urban centers was 28.1 percent from 1975 to 1976, 21.1 percent from 1976 to 1977, 26.5 percent from 1977 to 1978, 8.0 percent from 1978 to 1979, and 7.6 percent from 1979 to 1980. Central Bank of Nigeria, *Annual Report and Statement of Accounts for the Year Ended 31st December, 1978* (Lagos, 1979), p. 29; Central Bank of Nigeria, *Annual Report and Statement of Accounts for the Year Ended 31st December, 1979* (Lagos, 1980), p. 28; Central Bank of Nigeria, *Annual Report and Statement of Accounts for the Year Ended 31st December 1980* (Lagos, 1981), p. 35.

prices are controlled. Finally, producers selling at controlled prices have a limited impact upon prices to the final consumer where there are middlemen in distributive trades.[15]

The pent-up worker dissatisfaction at the end of the civil war, together with government concern about reorientation of the economy toward consumer goods, led to the establishment of the Wages and Salaries Review Commission in July 1970 under the chairmanship of Chief S.O. Adebo. In December 1970, the Commission recommended an interim award backdated to 1 April 1970 to low- and middle-income earners (i.e., those receiving less than £N500 per annum) in the government sector, with the private employers to follow suit.

Despite the annual renewal of the prohibition to strike, the number of strikes in 1971 exceeded that of any year since 1940 except 1964, largely because foreign firms took advantage of the federal government's vacillation to resist the recommendation of an Abedo award to the private sector. Although in August 1971, the Commission's second report recommended a general wage increase, including additional increments for those awarded an interim raise, the increase was lower than the rise in the consumer price index between 1964 and 1971.[16] Furthermore, public service gradings remained unchanged, although percentage increases in wages to low-income workers exceeded those for high-income workers.

The Office of Statistics and the economics ministries in Nigeria have no series on unemployment, perhaps because it was long assumed that unemployment would be reduced by rapid economic growth.[17] The only longitudinal data on unemployment are those of the Central Bank of Nigeria, based on the number of registered unemployed persons at labor exchanges throughout the country. Even though registered unemployment represents a fraction of total unemployment, the two figures likely move in the same direction. Still, confidence in the data as a basis for the following discussion is not high.

The rate of unemployment increased in 1966-67, before the civil war, as business activity and emigration to other regions and other communal group areas were reduced.[18] Although regional discrimination in employment opportunities had been present since the 1950s, emphasis on regionalism increased between 1966 and 1970. The creation of more states, together with their increasing self-sufficiency during the political crises, intensified the geographical segmentation of the labor market--especially in the North, where a single market for public employees gave way to separate markets for each of the six states under the preference by employing agencies for "sons of the state." Only Kwara state was generally able to fill most of the established public service posts at all levels with staff of the right seniority and experience.[19] Numerous shortages of a given type of labor in one state existed alongside surpluses in other states, for lack of labor migration as an equilibrating device. For example Kwara state had a surplus of civil servants and school teachers in 1968-69 when Kano state had shortages.

By 1968, however, additional unemployment resulting from the increased segmentation of the labor market was overwhelmed by mobilization of the armed forces. Expansion of the armed forces from 10,500 in January 1966 to 180,000-200,000 on the two sides in 1969, reduced the unemployment below that of 1966.

Despite maintaining that size army through 1975, unemployment rose steadily from 1970 through 1973, with a disproportionate share in areas surrendered by Biafra. Statistics from the Central Bank on the registered unemployed suggested that the unemployment rate declined modestly in 1974, but reverted to its 1973 rate in 1975, then decreased in both 1976 and 1977. Fresh school-leavers made up about one-third of the registered unemployed throughout the early and middle 1970s.[20]

MONETARY AND FISCAL POLICIES

Financial policy was directed toward raising sufficient funds to finance the war, while preventing rapid inflation and deterioration in the balance of payments. From the beginning of the war, monetary policy was designed to ease government borrowing, while restricting bank credit to the private sector to restrain the growth of internal demand. Fiscal policy, on the other hand, was geared to increasing tax rates and decreasing nondefense expenditure, to dampen the expansionary impact of the budget.

Current federal government spending on general administration, social and community welfare, and economic services was reduced from £N43.7 million in 1966 and £N37.4 million in 1967, and to £N34.5 million in 1968, while capital expenditures were reduced from £N52.0 million in 1966 and £N51.7 million in 1967 to £N34.5 million in 1968. These reductions helped raise expenditure on defense and internal security from £N17.7 million in 1966 to £N32.0 million in 1967 and £N75.0 million in 1968 (tables 5.4 and 5.5) although the figures for the last two years are understated for reasons of national security.[21]

Several measures were used to expand revenue sources including a compulsory savings scheme for wage and salary earners, a surcharge on import duties on a number of consumer goods, a super tax on companies, and increased import and excise duties. Notwithstanding the increase in tax rate, current revenue, which averaged more than £N160 million per annum during 1964-67, dropped to £N142.4 million in 1968 (table 5.6), partly because of dampened demand from restrictive measures on the civilian goods sector, destruction and dislocation of economic activities, and the loss of revenue in the East--especially from the crude-oil industry. Despite the measures undertaken to reduce expenditures and increase receipts, table 5.7 shows a large increase in current expenditures, and a substantial deficit in the 1968 recurrent budget--the first such deficit since independence.

The overall government budget deficit rose from £N48.3 million in 1966 to £N141.7 million in 1968, in spite of attempts by fiscal authorities to curb the stimulating effect of the budget. By the last part of 1969, the demand of the federal government for funds to prosecute the war and provide rehabilitation and relief for wartorn areas convinced the financial authorities that direct wage and price controls were necessary.

The expansionary impact of borrowing by the federal government to finance the deficit was modest--especially before 1969. The

TABLE 5.4
Current Expenditure, 1964-74 (in £N millions and percentages)

Functions	1964		1965		1966		*1967*		*1968*	
	£Nm	%	£Nm	%	£Nm	%	£Nm	%	£Nm	%
Defense & internal security	15.3	10.6	16.5	11.3	17.7	11.8	*32.0*	*20.8*	*75.0*	*35.9*
General administration	33.7	23.6	16.7	11.5	21.7	14.6	*17.5*	*11.3*	*18.1*	*8.7*
Social & community serv.	41.2	28.8	10.1	6.9	9.1	6.1	*10.1*	*6.6*	*6.7*	*3.2*
Economic services	28.8	20.1	16.8	11.6	12.9	8.6	*9.8*	*6.4*	*9.7*	*4.6*
Transfers	24.1	16.9	85.3	58.7	88.1	58.9	*84.4*	*54.9*	*99.4*	*47.6*
Total	143.1	100.0	145.4	100.0	149.5	100.0	*153.8*	*100.0*	*208.9*	*100.0*

Sources: Central Bank of Nigeria, *Annual Report and Statement of Accounts for the Year Ended 31st December, 1966* (Lagos, 1967), p. 70, Central Bank, *Annual Report for the Year Ended 31st December, 1967* (Lagos, 1968), p. 51, Central Bank of Nigeria, *Annual Report for the Year Ended 31st December, 1968* (Lagos, 1969), p. 59; Central Bank, *Annual Report, 1969*, p. 64; Central Bank of Nigeria, *Annual Report for the Year Ended 31st December, 1972* (Lagos, 1973), p. 73; and Central Bank of Nigeria, *Annual Report for the Year Ended 31st December, 1974* (Lagos, 1975), p. 71.

Note: Beginning 1 January 1973, Nigeria introduced a new decimal currency, the naira (₦), equal to two Nigerian pounds (£N). Figures after 31 December 1972 for chapters 5-7 are reported in their equivalence in Nigerian pounds.

TABLE 5.4 (continued)

1969		*1970*[a]		1971[a]		1972[a]		1973[a]		1974[a]	
£Nm	%	£Nm	%	£Nm	%	£Nm	%	£Nm	%	£Nm	%
112.8[b]	*47.3*[b]	*229.4*	*50.5*	338.4	36.9	249.2	35.3	227.2	37.4	277.7	20.5
6.0	*2.5*	*8.3*	*1.8*	10.2	2.1	14.7	2.1	15.6	2.6	47.4	3.5
11.1	*4.6*	*12.2*	*2.7*	15.7	3.4	23.1	3.3	26.2	4.3	37.2	2.7
108.7	*45.6*	*204.7*	*45.0*	264.2	57.5	419.2	59.4	337.6	55.7	993.1	73.3
238.6	*100.0*	*454.6*	*100.0*	628.5	100.0	706.2	100.0	606.6	100.0	1355.4	100.0

[a]In 1970 the procedure for the classification of expenditures on general administration and internal security was changed. Although figures for 1969 were revised to conform to the new procedure, I retained the original figures, as more comparable to the other war years.

[b]From 1969 through 1974, the first two categories are lumped together. Central Bank of Nigeria, *Annual Report and Statement of Accounts for the Year ended 31st December, 1969* (Lagos, 1970), p. 64. Assume that, from 1968 through 1970, the current expenditure on general administration remains constant in real terms. And suppose that the current factor cost of keeping this the same is the figure for 1968 times 1.02^n where n is the year minus 1968. (For this computation, the GDP price deflator at factor cost is assumed to be 1.02 in both 1969 and 1970. See table 5.2, which is, however, based on the fiscal year, not the calendar year.) Given these assumptions, current expenditure on defense and internal security would be £N94.3 million in 1969 (or £N112.8 million - £N18.5 million), and £N210.6 million in 1970 (or £N229.4 million - £N18.8 million).

TABLE 5.5
Capital Expenditure, 1964-74 (in £N millions and percentages)

Functions	1964		1965		1966		*1967*		*1968*	
	£Nm	%	£Nm	%	£Nm	%	£Nm	%	£Nm	%
Defense & internal security	7.6	11.0	6.3	16.2	5.6	10.8	*3.9*	*7.5*	*3.2*	*9.1*
General administration	7.4	10.7	4.5	11.5	3.9	7.5	*2.4*	*4.7*	*0.7*	*2.0*
Social & community serv.	12.4	18.0	4.7	12.1	4.8	9.2	*1.9*	*3.7*	*1.1*	*3.1*
Economic services	35.4	51.1	21.8	55.8	22.4	43.1	*24.6*	*47.6*	*23.1*	*66.0*
Transfers	6.4	9.2	1.7	4.4	15.3	29.4	*18.9*	*36.5*	*6.9*	*19.8*
Total	69.2	100.0	39.0	100.0	52.0	100.0	*51.7*	*100.0*	*35.0*	*100.0*

Sources: Central Bank of Nigeria, *Annual Report and Statement of Accounts for the Year Ended 31st December, 1966* (Lagos, 1967), p. 71, Central Bank, *Annual Report for the Year Ended 31st December, 1967* (Lagos, 1968), p. 52, Central Bank, *Annual Report for the Year Ended 31st December, 1968* (Lagos, 1969), p. 61, Central Bank, *Annual Report, 1969*, p. 65, Central Bank, *Annual Report, 1972*, p. 74, and Central Bank, *Annual Report, 1974*, p. 72.

TABLE 5.5 (continued)

1969		*1970*[a]		1971[a]		1972[a]		1973[a]		1974[a]	
£Nm	%	£Nm	%	£Nm	%	£Nm	%	£Nm	%	£Nm	%
4.2[b]	*12.1*[b]	*72.5*	*65.6*	31.6	36.4	54.4	24.1	66.9	23.7	134.2	17.3
0.9	*2.5*	*1.6*	*1.4*	6.6	7.6	21.0	9.3	20.2	7.1	179.0	23.1
13.6	*38.2*	*21.7*	*19.7*	29.1	33.5	66.4	29.5	124.8	44.1	233.1	30.1
16.7	*47.0*	*14.7*	*13.3*	19.6	22.5	83.8	37.1	71.0	25.1	228.4	29.5
35.5	*100.0*	*110.5*	*100.0*	86.9	100.0	225.6	100.0	282.9	100.0	774.7	100.0

[a]See footnote a, table 5.4.

[b]From 1969 through 1974, the first two categories are lumped together. Central Bank, *Annual Report, 1969* (Lagos, 1970), p. 65.

TABLE 5.6
Current Revenue, 1964-74 (£N millions)

Sources of current revenue	1964	1965	1966	*1967*	*1968*	*1969*	*1970*	1971	1972	1973	1974
Import duties	75.6	84.6	58.4	*54.8*	*54.5*	*75.8*	*107.8*	142.4	137.2	153.9	164.1
Export duties	14.7	15.8	14.3	*14.0*	*14.5*	*18.8*	*20.6*	18.9	13.4	6.2	2.8
Excise duties	12.1	16.6	33.8	*30.1*	*24.5*	*36.0*	*56.3*	84.3	89.9	98.0	82.2
Direct taxes	27.6	10.7	13.1	*18.2*	*21.5*	*22.0*[a]	*72.2*[a]	225.6[a]	312.2[a]	426.4[a]	1516.0[a]
Petroleum & other mining (royalties, fees, rents, etc.)	8.9	12.8	10.3	*27.8*	*10.6*	*11.8*	*34.4*	63.5	111.9	123.4	427.1
Interests and repayments	7.0	7.3	8.9	*12.0*	*10.9*	*10.6*	*13.2*	18.3	22.4	24.9	63.6
Post & telegraph	5.1	6.6	2.6	--	--	--	--	--	--	--	--
Miscellaneous	17.1	6.0	11.6	*6.6*	*5.9*	*13.9*	*12.1*	31.5	15.4	14.8	12.7
Total	168.1	160.4	153.2	*163.5*	*142.4*	*188.9*	*316.6*	584.5	702.4	847.6	2268.5

[a]Petroleum profits taxes, listed separately for the first time in 1969, were £N4.9 million in 1969, £N48.8 million in 1970, £N191.6 million in 1971, £N270.2 million in 1972, £N384.6 million in 1973, and £N1,436.2 million in 1974.

Sources: Central Bank, *Annual Report, 1966*, p. 68, Central Bank, *Annual Report, 1967*, p. 48, Central Bank, *Annual Report, 1968*, p. 56, Central Bank, *Annual Report, 1969*, p. 70, Central Bank, *Annual Report, 1972*, p. 72, and Central Bank, *Annual Report, 1974*, p. 67.

TABLE 5.7
Summary of Federal Fiscal Operations, 1964-74 (£N millions)

	1964	1965	1966	*1967*	*1968*	*1969*	*1970*[a]	1971[a]	1972[a]	1973[a]	1974[a]
Current revenue	168.1	160.4	153.2	*163.5*	*142.4*	*188.9*	*316.6*	584.5	702.4	847.6	2268.5
Current expenditure	143.1	145.4	149.5	*153.8*	*208.9*	*238.6*	*453.0*	411.8	706.2[b]	606.6[b]	1355.4[b]
Current balance	+ 25.0	+ 15.0	+ 3.7	*+ 9.7*	*- 66.5*	*- 49.7*	*-136.4*	+172.7	- 3.8	+241.0	+913.1
Capital expenditure	69.2	39.0	52.0	*51.7*	*35.0*	*35.5*	*110.5*	86.9	225.6	282.9	774.7
Overall balance	- 44.2	- 24.0	- 48.3	*- 42.0*	*-141.7*	*- 85.2*	*-246.9*	+ 85.8	-229.4	- 41.9	+138.4

[a]See footnote a, Table 5.4.

[b]Includes transfer to Development Fund, which consisted of £N200.0 million in 1972, £N124.8 million in 1973, and £N596.9 million in 1974.

Sources: Central Bank, *Annual Report, 1966*, pp. 68, 70-1; Central Bank, *Annual Report, 1967*, pp. 48, 51, 52; Central Bank, *Annual Report, 1968*, p. 55, Central Bank, *Annual Report, 1969*, p. 59, Central Bank, *Annual Report, 1972*, p. 72, and Central Bank, *Annual Report, 1974*, pp. 66, 71-2.

increment in Central Bank credit operations, largely to the government, stimulated the economy. But commercial bank credit grew only slightly during 1967-68, as most of the increased lending to the government was at the expense of the private sector. Nonbank holdings of treasury bills and development stock had little impact on aggregate demand, as these holdings were mostly in lieu of commercial paper.[22]

During the war, the federal government had neither resources for the substantial capital requirements to establish the new states nor the time to devise a formula to distribute federal revenue to them. The share of federal revenue to the regions/states decreased from £N65,372,000 in 1965 and £N60,654,000 in 1966 to £N42,861,000 in 1967 and £N38,546,000 in 1968, while revenue raised by the regions/states went from £31,641,000 in 1965 and £N28,933,000 in 1966 to £N16,079,000 in 1967 and £N17,348,000 in 1968. In 1968/69, the overall expenditure of Kwara state was £N5.4 million, compared with current revenue of only £N2.5 million, as it tried to set up new administrative and political machinery, and pay the high recurrent cost of programs inherited from the former Northern Region.

By 1969, the state had to reduce essential services, limit capital expenditures to £N29,000 (compared with £N21,237,000 for the twelve states), and obtain emergency assistance from the federal government. Ironically, Kwara, the Northern state with the most manpower for providing competent services was least able to do so for lack of finances. On the other hand, Kano state had a surplus largely because it lacked the manpower to staff services.[23]

THE BALANCE OF PAYMENTS

Nigeria's balance-of-payments and foreign-exchange position deteriorated substantially during the war. The value of the country's external assets was slashed from £N84.4 million at the end of 1966 to £N38.9 million at the end of 1967 (table 5.8). By the middle of 1968 foreign reserves had been drawn below a point that international bankers often considered the critical minimum--an equivalent of the value of imports for four months. An external liquidity crisis was averted only by stringent trade barriers and exchange controls.

A major cause of the deteriorating external economic position was military expenditures abroad, whose primary cost was estimated by A. Akene Ayida, permanent secretary in the Federal Ministry of Economic Development, to be £N38 million per annum, or equal to about one-fifth the value of merchandise exports in 1968 (table 5.9). If secondary or indirect costs are included, the foreign-exchange cost of the war was estimated at £N63 million per annum, of which only about 10 percent constitutes "normal peacetime" military expenditure.[24]

In addition, the value of exports dropped 14 percent in 1967, and 13 percent more in 1968, from disruptions in production, transportation bottlenecks, and loss of exports from war areas. As a result of Eastern secession and the federal embargo, the value of crude-petroleum exports decreased from £N91.1 million in 1966 to £N72.0 million in 1967 to £N37.0 million in 1968, while the net

TABLE 5.8
External Assets, 1959-81

End of year	Total external assets[a] (£N million)
1959	233.0
1960	195.6
1961	174.3
1962	142.9
1963	98.0
1964	81.3
1965	93.2
1966	84.4
1967	*38.9*
1968	*49.1*
1969	*54.5*
1970	*88.4*
1971	151.6
1972	135.3
1973	219.2
1974	1770.4
1975	1848.2
1976	1741.2
1977	1517.0
1978	693.6
1979	1625.4
1980	2824.1
1981	1293.0

[a]Defined as the holdings of gold and foreign exchange by the Central Bank, by the federal, regional and state governments, by semi-official agencies (such as marketing boards); the Special Drawing Rights holdings and International Monetary Fund gold tranche position of the Central Bank; and the net holdings of foreign exchange by commercial banks, at the end of the year.

Sources: Nigerian Institute of Social and Economic Research, "Economic and Social Survey," Conference on National Reconstruction and Development in Nigeria, University of Ibadan, 24-29 March 1969, p. 8; Nigeria, Central Planning Office, Ministry of Economic Development and Reconstruction, *Economic and Statistical Review, 1972* (Lagos, n.d.), p. 19, and Central Bank of Nigeria, *Annual Report and Statements of Accounts* (Lagos).

positive contribution of crude oil to the balance of payments dropped from £N43.4 million and £N48.7 million in 1966 and 1967, respectively, to £N28.8 million in 1968 (see table 5.9).

The increase in repatriation of earnings in 1966-67, and the drop in foreign official aid and private capital inflows except for oil during 1966-67 and 1969 contributed to the balance-of-payments

TABLE 5.9
Nigeria: Balance of Payments, 1965-80 (£N million)

Items	1965			1966			*1967*			*1968*		
	Oil	Non-oil	Total	Oil	Non-oil	Total	Oil	Non-oil	Total	Oil	Non-oil	Total
Merchandise exports (inc. re-exports) f.o.b.	68.1	197.2	265.3	91.9	187.1	279.0	*72.0*	*166.8*	*238.8*	*37.0*	*171.4*	*208.4*
Merchandise imports (c.i.f.)	13.5	254.6	268.1	19.5	228.5	248.0	*17.5*	*200.9*	*218.4*	*9.9*	*181.2*	*191.1*
Balance on visible trade	+54.6	-57.4	-2.8	+72.4	-41.4	+31.0	*+54.5*	*-34.1*	*+20.4*	*+27.1*	*-9.8*	*+17.3*
Balance on invisible trade	-36.4	-27.2	-63.6	-57.9	-34.0	-91.9	*-51.3*	*-59.8*	*-111.1*	*-28.2*	*-90.4*	*-118.6*
Balance on unrequited transfers	-	+2.7	+2.7	-	+1.7	+1.7	-	*+7.7*	*+7.7*	-	*+17.2*	*+17.2*
Balance on current account	+18.2	-81.9	-63.7	+14.5	-73.7	-59.2	*+3.2*	*-86.2*	*-83.0*	*-1.1*	*-83.0*	*-84.1*
Balance on capital account[a]	+17.4	+48.6	+66.0	+28.9	+19.5	+48.4	*+45.5*	*+15.9*	*+61.4*	*+29.9*	*+50.1*	*+80.0*
Balance on current and capital account	+35.6	-33.3	+2.3	+43.4	-54.2	-10.8	*+48.7*	*-70.3*	*-21.6*	*+28.8*	*-32.9*	*-4.1*
Net errors and omissions			+9.6			+2.0			*-12.1*			*+7.1*
Net capital movements of the monetary sector[b]			+11.9			-8.8			*-33.7*			*+3.0*

Items	1973			1974			1975			1976		
	Oil	Non-oil	Total	Oil	Non-oil	Total	Oil	Non-oil	Total	Oil	Non-oil	Total
Merchandise exports (incl. re-exports) f.o.b.	1003.0	181.8	1184.8	2835.4	217.5	3052.9	2383.2	174.9	2558.1	2958.9	212.8	3171.7
Merchandise imports (c.i.f.)	20.5	580.8	601.3	26.2	807.0	833.2	59.0	1755.5	1814.5	45.0	2479.5	2524.5
Balance on visible trade	+982.5	-399.0	+583.5	+2809.2	-589.5	+2219.7	+2324.2	-1580.6	+743.6	+2913.9	-2266.7	+647.2
Balance on invisible trade	-313.1	-226.3	-539.4	-280.6	-376.8	-657.4	-289.6	-394.2	-683.8	-273.7	-453.8	-727.5
Balance on unrequited transfers	-	-17.7	-17.7	-	-31.0	-31.0	-	-38.4	-38.4	-	-48.9	-48.9
Balance on current account	+669.4	-643.0	+26.4	+2528.6	-997.3	+1531.3	+2034.6	-2013.2	+21.4	+2640.2	-2769.4	-129.2
Balance on capital account[a]	+32.2	+40.2	+72.4	+67.9	-70.8	-2.9	+60.7	+9.8	+70.5	-21.0	-4.3	-25.3
Balance on current and capital account	+701.6	-602.8	+98.8	+2596.5	-1068.1	+1528.4	+2095.3	-2003.4	+91.9	+2619.2	-2773.7	-154.5
Net errors and omissions			-11.6			+22.8			-13.1			-15.0
Net capital movements of the monetary sector[b]			+87.2			+1551.2			+78.8			-169.5

Note: "Non-oil" refers to all other sectors of the economy except the oil prospecting and mining companies.

Sources: Central Bank, *Annual Report, 1967*, p. 58; *Annual Report, 1968*, p. 65; *Annual Report, 1969*, p. 69; *Annual Report, 1970*, p. 78; *Annual Report, 1971*, p. 76; *Annual Report, 1972*, p. 76; *Annual Report, 1973*, p. 88; *Annual Report, 1975*, pp. 82-3; *Annual Report, 1977*, pp. 72-4; *Annual Report, 1978*, p. 72; *Annual Report, 1979*, pp. 68-9; and *Annual Report, 1980*, p. 86.

TABLE 5.9 (continued)

1969			1970			1971			1972		
Oil	Non-oil	Total	Oil	Non-oil	Total	Oil	Non-oil	Total	Oil	Non-oil	Total
130.8	181.5	312.3	258.6	187.1	445.7	490.2	182.0	672.2	593.2	125.4	718.6
12.7	216.2	228.9	26.2	333.0	359.2	25.3	504.4	529.7	22.6	457.2	479.8
+118.1	-34.7	+83.4	+232.4	-145.9	+86.5	+464.9	-322.5	+142.5	+570.6	-331.8	+238.8
-48.1	-100.0	-148.1	-40.6	-93.4	-134.0	-164.6	-93.5	-258.1	-264.5	-128.5	-393.0
-	+10.4	+10.4	-	+22.5	+22.5	-	+0.9	+0.9	-	-7.2	-7.2
+10.0	-124.3	-54.3	+191.8	-216.8	-25.0	+300.3	-415.0	-114.7	+306.1	-467.5	-161.4
-16.7	+57.0	+40.3	+17.5	+46.8	+64.3	+2.0	+144.7	+146.7	+97.9	+36.7	+134.6
+53.3	-67.3	-14.0	+209.3	-170.0	+39.3	+302.3	-270.3	+32.0	+404.0	-403.8	-26.8
		+21.6			+47.4			+27.7			+1.8
		+7.6			+86.7			+59.7			-25.0

1977			1978			1979			1980		
Oil	Non-oil	Total	Oil	Non-oil	Total	Oil	Non-oil	Total	Oil	Non-oil	Total
3726.8	261.5	3988.3	3002.4	313.8	3316.2	4718.4	335.0	5053.4	6123.4	277.0	6400.4
51.1	3415.7	3466.8	55.0	3936.0	3991.0	115.0	3454.7	3569.7	120.8	4237.4	4358.2
3675.7	-3154.2	+ 521.5	+2947.4	-3622.2	- 674.8	4603.4	-3119.7	1483.7	6002.6	-3960.4	2042.2
- 503.5	- 286.9	- 790.4	- 212.6	-217.6	- 430.2	- 107.9	- 754.2	- 862.1	- 156.2	- 931.9	-1088.2
-	- 59.4	- 59.4	-	- 85.3	- 85.3	- 1.5	- 115.3	- 116.8	- 2.6	- 155.0	- 157.6
+3172.2	-3500.5	- 328.2	+2734.8	-3925.1	-1190.3	+4494.0	-3989.2	+ 504.8	5843.5	-5047.3	+796.2
+ 73.8	+ 43.4	+ 117.2	+ 46.0	+ 461.8	+ 507.8	- 2.2	+ 408.8	+ 406.6	- 15.0	+402.3	+387.3
+3246.0	-3457.1	- 211.1	+2780.8	-3463.3	- 682.5	+4491.8	-3580.4	+ 911.4	+5828.5	-4645.0	+1183.5
		- 12.4			- 8.7			+ 23.1			+ 17.5
		- 223.5			- 691.2			+ 943.5			+1201.0

[a]Capital account includes net capital movements of the non-monetary (i.e., private and government) sectors, but not net capital movements of the monetary sector (defined in footnote b).

[b]The monetary sector refers to federal monetary institutions and commercial banks. The allocation of SDRs (Special Drawing Rights) is included in the monetary sector.

deficit.[25] These developments stemmed primarily from growing anxieties about Nigeria's political instability and how that influenced her domestic and international economic position. The outflow of investment income, for example, was induced and the inflow of private capital hampered in 1966-67 by increased restrictions in the remission of profits and dividends, and fear of further controls, while official foreign capital inflows were curtailed partly as a result of difficulties in implementing viable projects in the government sector during political upheavals. Finally, Nigeria experienced speculative capital outflows and declining foreign-exchange holdings by £N8.3 million as a result of the devaluation of British sterling in November 1967.[26]

Nigeria, however, decided not to devalue its currency. Although devaluation might have relieved some of the pressure borne by trade and exchange regulations, it probably would not have improved the balance of trade. The sums of the elasticities of demand for exports, consisting mainly of primary products, and the demand for imports, limited mostly to necessities as a result of trade and payments restrictions, appeared too low.

Several measures, in addition to restrictive domestic financial policies, were undertaken to improve the country's balance-of-payments position. During Biafran secession, Nigeria required prior official permission for all foreign payments--a measure that also hampered the international use of Nigerian currency by the Biafrans. Import duties were increased, a surcharge on imports of many consumers goods was levied, some bans on imported consumer goods were instituted, bank credit for imports was curtailed, the basic travel allowance for Nigerian citizens was decreased, and personal remittances by resident foreign nationals were limited.[27] In January 1968, to prevent Biafra from using Nigerian money to obtain foreign exchange, the banking system issued new currency notes to replace those in circulation. The Biafran government, taken by surprise, is estimated to have lost £N30 million altogether.[28]

In 1968, after previous changes proved inadequate, more severe controls were placed on international trade and payments. Transfers of dividends, profits, and other capital abroad were suspended. An embargo was placed on payments for certain invisible trade items, such as management agency fees, royalties, commissions, and expenses due from Nigerian firms to their agents and representatives in other countries. Transfers for directors' fees for companies in Nigeria and personal remittances by foreign nationals were further limited. Even so, in 1968-69, the Nigerian government was able to prevent an international payments crisis only by delaying the release of several approved foreign exchange payments--totalling £N60 million by the end of the war.[29] Finally, in May 1969, the federal government required importers to obtain specific licenses on virtually all goods purchased from abroad.

The restrictions, together with the loss of import demand from the East, decreased imports 12 percent in 1967, and another 12 percent in 1968--a reduction concentrated primarily in consumer goods. In 1969, the balance-of-trade surplus increased by £N67.1 million, largely from expanded petroleum exports, up £N93.8 million to £N130.8 million, the highest total up to then. The expansion stemmed primarily from resumption of oil production in areas regained in the fighting in 1968.

Although some industrialists gained from the opportunities for import substitution, businessmen in general were dissatisfied with the increased restrictions on trade and payments. Foreign firms were prevented from repatriating earnings and, in some cases, lacked foreign exchange for routine expenditure in offices overseas. Several factories were forced to cut back substantially on production and employment, or even close down, as a result of delays and rejections in obtaining the import licences needed for equipment, inventories, repairs, raw materials, or other essential items. The customs office lacked the skilled administrators necessary to process the heavy volume of requests for licenses.

COSTS AND BENEFITS OF THE WAR

Official figures suggest that the cost of the war, as one would expect, was substantial. If the 1958/59-1965/66 real growth rate in gross domestic product of 6.0 percent per annum had continued without interruption, GDP would have been £N1,943.7 million in the fiscal year, 1969/70 (in 1962/63 prices) rather than £N1,513.8 million (table 5.1).

The gap between the actual GDP and the hypothetical GDP with the prewar rate of growth, would have been £N267.5 million in 1967/68, £N358.5 million in 1968/69, and £N429.9 million in 1969/70, for a total of £N1,055.9 million (all in 1962/63 prices) in the fiscal years, 1967/68-1969/70. If average or total real net domestic product (where capital consumption and destruction are subtracted) or real consumption of civilian goods were used, the gap would have been wider (see below, this chapter).

High growth rates in GDP in the postwar period--33.6 percent in 1969/70-1970/71, 57.6 percent in 1970/71-1971/72, and 9.6 percent in 1971/72-1972/73 (in 1962/63 prices)--may have helped compensate for a small portion of the growth foregone during the war. A substantial portion of postwar growth in GDP can be attributed to the postwar oil boom, and replacing destroyed capital not subtracted from GDP during the war years. If the real GDP originating in the mining and building and construction sectors were assumed to remain constant after 1969/70, growth in 1969/70-1970/71 would be 22.9 percent, in 1970/71-1971/72 11.5 percent, 1971/72-1972/73 7.2 percent, and 1969/70-1972/73 13.7 percent per annum (in 1962/63 prices).

Because of the limited reliability of statistics on GDP, other approaches to the cost of the conflict may be useful. Figures based on estimates in early 1969 by Ayida, then permanent secretary, Federal Ministry of Economic Development, and data on defense spending from the Central Bank indicate a total direct military expenditure by the Nigerian government during the war between 1 June 1967 and 15 January 1970, of £N501 million, a cost of £N448 million above the "normal peacetime" level and equal to almost one-tenth of GDP for that period; £N116 million of the total was primary foreign exchange expenditure. In addition, secondary and indirect foreign exchange commitments resulting from the war are estimated at £N77 million during the same period. Finally, for the remainder of 1970, 16 January-31 December, direct military expenditures are estimated at £N300 million.[30] Crude estimates indicate that Nigerian spent about five to ten times more foreign currency, and more real local resources on the war than Biafra.

The replacement figure of physical assets damaged and destroyed by the end of the second year of the conflict was estimated to be £N250 million. The major losses involved buildings, roads, bridges, vehicles, transport equipment, and public utilities and services. Other costs of the war included decreased foreign exchange from losses in export earnings, the drop in government revenue from the loss of civilian production, postponement of human and physical capital investment, and projects in the First Development Plan not started.

The socioeconomic loss from deaths to persons was incalculable. UNICEF estimated that at least two million died of starvation alone from the beginning of the war to early 1969. And by the end of the war, numerous family units were broken up and several million persons were displaced--primarily in the East.[31]

Nigerian economists listed several benefits resulting from the war. Resources that otherwise would have been idle were used. The damage to assets provided an opportunity for replacement with more modern and productive capital equipment. Centralizing the government and mobilizing the population during the war led to instigating fundamental long-term economic reforms and structural changes that would not have otherwise been undertaken.

The necessity for long-term preparedness forced the country to do more planning for the future. A new spirit of national consciousness and commitment to development increased the willingness of Nigerians to unitedly sacrifice to increase resources for national development. Under military rule, 1967-70, favoritism, nepotism, and corruption were less pervasive, and the governing elite accepted more public responsibility. Finally the military government, by creating new states, broke up the dominance of the federation by the Northern political oligarchy and eliminated the unstable power struggle among the three largest ethnic communities.[32]

Upon closer examination, however, the benefits appear meager compared to the costs. Although the war decreased unemployment, the old forces of sectionalism probably increased postwar unemployment, due to the increased geographical segmentation of the labor market. Replacing old capital equipment could have been done without the wide destruction. The war may have decreased the opposition to some needed reforms and changes but most of them could have been done by a military government without war. In fact, some resources used for war precluded undertaking reforms. For example, the fiscal problems resulting from the war prevented the federal government from allocating the funds needed to set up the administrative machinery of the new states.

With regard to planning, the political crisis disrupted the implementation of the last three years of the 1962-68 National Development Plan, and postponed the Second Development Plan for more than two years. Examples of the lack of national consciousness and development commitment were the tax disturbances and riots in the Western state in 1968-69, in which approximately 160 persons were killed[33] (see chapter 6).

In addition, any increased national unity among the peoples of the federation was countered by the deeper bitterness and ill-feeling among Biafran loyalists. Furthermore, there were widespread reports of communalism, nepotism, and favoritism in the military government, especially during the postwar period. Finally the concentrated regional and ethnic political power in the country probably was greatly diminished by creation of new states, which probably made the civil war inevitable. Nevertheless, the period of the second republic beginning in 1979 indicated that regional and communal politics were alive again.

SUMMARY

Real net domestic product per person probably declined substantially during the Nigerian-Biafran war, 1967/68 through 1969/70. Consumer prices in federal Nigeria during the war were relatively stable, especially in 1967-68, when food supplies were diverted from the blockaded Eastern Region to other parts of the country. Yet real wages for workers declined, as money wages paid by the leading employer, the government, remained constant from 1964 to 1970.

Nigeria's external assets decreased from £N84.8 million at the end of 1966 to £N54.5 million at the end of 1969. In addition to increased military expenditure abroad, a major reason for the deteriorating foreign-exchange position was the drop in the value of crude-petroleum exports in 1967 and 1968.

Two Nigerian economists, Ayida and Aboyade listed these benefits from the war: higher employment rates, replacement of obsolete capital, centralization of government, mobilization of the population, increased planning, and increased spirit of national consciousness. These benefits, some of which do not stand close examination, are insignificant compared to the costs of the war, whether measured by foregone growth of output, increased foreign-exchange expenditures, destruction of physical assets, or deaths and misery of millions, regardless of their loyalty.

NOTES

1. P.N.C. Okigbo, *Nigerian National Accounts, 1950-57* (Enugu, Federal Ministry of Economic Development, 1962), pp. 35-98; Nigeria, Office of Statistics, *Gross Domestic Product of Nigeria, 1958/59-1966/67* (Lagos, 1968), pp. 3-24; and Nigeria, Ministry of Information, *Second National Development Plan, 1970-74* (Lagos, 1971), pp. 20 and 43-5. Wolfgang F. Stolper, head of the Economic Planning Unit in preparing the First National Development Plan, 1962-68, characterized plan formulation with Nigeria's aggregate economic statistics as *Planning Without Facts: Lessons in Resource Allocation from Nigeria's Development* (Cambridge, Mass.: Harvard University Press, 1966), pp. 6, 41, and 91-137.

2. O. Aboyade, chief planning officer of the Ministry of Economic Development, and A.A. Ayida, then permanent secretary of the same Ministry, indicate that "The correct story of [gross product originating in the secessionist areas during the war] may

never be fully told." "The War Economy in Perspective," *The Nigerian Journal of Economic and Social Studies*, XIII, No. 1 (March 1971), 28.

3. The Nigerian pound, exchanged for £1 or $2.80 before November 1967, and about £1.17 or $3.04 from 1968 through the end of the war.

The widely discussed inadequacies of international comparisons from national income data suggest that the product per capita of less developed economies (including Nigeria) is understated relative to developed economies. However, these inadequacies do not distort short-term time series in a given country, such as Nigeria, so much. Everett E. Hagen, *The Economics of Development* (Homewood, Ill.: Richard D. Irwin, 1975), pp. 9-17; Surendra J. Patel, "The Economic Distance between Nations: Its Origins, Measurement and Outlook," *Economic Journal*, LIV (March 1964), 122-9; and Simon Kuznets, "Levels and Variability of Growth Rates," *Economic Development and Cultural Change*, V, No. 1 (October 1956), 5-9.

4. As a result of the quadrupling of world oil prices between October 1973 and April 1974, the rates of real growth depend heavily on the choice of the base year. The share of GDP originating in the mining sector is far greater when GDP is computed at constant 1974/75 prices (as in the Third Plan) than at constant 1962/63 prices (as in the Second Plan). Nigeria, Central Planning Office, Ministry of Economic Development, *Third National Development Plan, 1975-80*, I (Lagos, 1975), 21, and Nigeria, Central Planning Office, Ministry of Economic Development and Reconstruction, *Second National Development Plan, 1970-74: Second Progress Report* (Lagos, 1974), p. 12. Pre-1973/74 prices are more appropriate when discussing the civil war and the three years after it.

5. Nigeria, Ministry of Information, *Second National Development Plan, 1970-74; Programme of Post-War Reconstruction and Development* (Lagos, 1970), p. 77; Ifagun I.U. Eke, "Population of Nigeria, 1952-1965," *Nigerian Journal of Economic and Social Studies*, VIII, 3 (November 1968), 308-9; and T.M. Yesufu, "Comments on Professor Ogunsheye's paper," in *Reconstruction and Development in Nigeria*, A.A. Ayida and H.M.A. Onitiri, eds. (Ibadan: Oxford University Press, 1971), p. 680.

6. I use the term "capital exhaustion" for the total of these two aggregates, as I found no other term in the literature.

7. Simon S. Kuznets, *National Product in Wartime* (New York: National Bureau of Economic Research, 1945), pp. 6, 20.

8. A.A. Ayida, "Development Objectives," in *Reconstruction and Development in Nigeria*, Ayida and Onitiri, eds., pp. 14-5. See also chapter 8, below.

9. Estimated fixed capital formation at constant 1962/63 prices declined from £N233.3 million in 1966/67 to £N223.5 million in 1967/68 to £N213.9 million in 1968/69, but increased slightly in 1969/70 to £N220.2 million. Aboyade and Ayida, *Nigerian Journal*, XIII, No. 1, 30.

A series, which is more accurate but not comparable to the previous one, indicates a decrease in foreign private investment from £N63.0 million in 1964 to £N55.2 million in 1965, £N49.4

million in 1966, £N47.6 million in 1967, and £N36.7 million in 1968, returning to about the prewar level in 1969, with £N59.4 million. Foreign investment in mining and quarrying dropped sharply from £N47.8 million in 1966 to £N20.0 million in 1967, and even further to £N18.3 million in 1968. Overseas capital formation in manufacturing and processing declined precipitously from £N24.8 million in 1967 to £N2.7 million in 1968, largely as a result of restrictions on repatriation of earnings, and increased to £N14.8 million in 1969, with some relaxation of restriction on international payments. World Bank, *Nigeria: Options for Long-term Development* (Baltimore: Johns Hopkins University Press, 1974), p. 220.

10. Cf. Morris E. Zukerman, "Nigerian Crisis: Economic Impact on the North," *The Journal of Modern African Studies*, VIII, No. 1 (April 1970), 44-5.

11. Central Bank of Nigeria, *Annual Report and Statement of Accounts for the Year ended 31st December, 1966* (Lagos, 1967), pp. 36, 38.

12. S.A. Aluko, "Prices, Wages and Costs," in *Reconstruction and Development in Nigeria*, Ayida and Onitiri, eds., pp. 420-1; and Central Bank of Nigeria, *Annual Report and Statement of Accounts for the Year ended 31st December, 1967* (Lagos, 1968), p. 24.

13. Central Bank of Nigeria, *Annual Report and Statement of Accounts for the Year ended 31st December, 1970* (Lagos, 1971), pp. 37, 39.

14. Robin Cohen, *Labour and Politics in Nigeria, 1945-71* (London: Heinemann Educational Books, 1974), pp. 225-7; and John F. Weeks, "The Impact of Economic Conditions and Institutional Forces on Urban Wages in Nigeria" *Nigerian Journal of Economic and Social Studies*, XIII, No. 3 (November 1971), 331-7.

15. S.U. Ugoh, "Presidential Address," *Nigerian Journal of Economic and Social Studies*, XIII, No. 1 (March 1971), 6-8.

16. Cohen, *Labour and Politics*, pp. 133-7; Adedotun O. Phillips, "The Economic Implication," *Quarterly Journal of Administration*, VI, No. 2 (January 1972), 104-6; and Richard Sandbrook and Robin Cohen, eds., *The Development of an African Working Class: Studies in Class Formation and Action* (London: Longman, 1975), p. 202.

17. See Nigeria, Ministry of Economic Development, *National Development Plan, 1962-68* (Lagos, n.d.), p. 4.

18. Archibald Callaway, "Creating Employment for Nigeria's School Leavers," *Quarterly Journal of Administration*, III, No. 1 (October 1968), 1.

19. J.H. Smith, "The Impact of the Creation of States upon the Public Service of Northern Nigeria," on file at Rhodes House Library, Oxford, ca. 1969.

20. Central Bank, *Annual Report, 1967*, p. 24; Central Bank of Nigeria, *Annual Report and Statement of Accounts for the Year ended 31st December, 1968* (Lagos, 1969), p. 27; Yesufu, "Manpower and Educational Objectives for Nigeria's Reconstruction and Development," Reconstruction and Development Conference, March 1969, pp. 8, 15-18; Central Bank of Nigeria, *Annual Report and Statement of Accounts for the Year ended 31st December, 1969*

(Lagos, 1970), p. 19; Central Bank, *Annual Report, 1971*, p. 33; Central Bank, *Annual Report, 1972*, pp. 31-32; Central Bank, *Annual Report, 1973*, pp. 35, 38; Central Bank, *Annual Report, 1974*, pp. 36-37; Central Bank, *Annual Report, 1975*, pp. 43-4; Central Bank, *Annual Report, 1976*, pp. 27-9; Central Bank, *Annual Report, 1977*, pp. 27-8; and Robin Luckham, *The Nigerian Miltary: A Sociological Analysis of Authority and Revolt, 1960-67* (Cambridge: Cambridge University Press, 1971), p. 90.

21. Chief Obafemi Awolowo, then federal commissioner for finance, implied that published figures of expenditures by the Ministry of Defence and Vital Supplies tended to understate actual expenditures. "Nigeria's Post-War Prospects," *West Africa*, (26 April 1970), p. 45.

22. Central Bank, *Annual Report, 1967*, pp. 27-37, Central Bank, *Annual Report, 1968*, pp. 12, 14, 30-41, and Central Bank, *Annual Report, 1969*, pp. 33-67.

23. Central Bank of Nigeria, *Economic and Financial Review*, IX, No. 1 (June 1971), 117-25, 147; and Smith, "The Impact of the Creation of States."

24. Ayida, "Development Objectives," in *Reconstruction and Development in Nigeria*, Ayida and Onitiri, eds., p. 14.

25. The net balance on capital account (which encompasses net official and private inflows) dropped from £N83.3 million in 1964 and £N66.0 million in 1965, to £N48.4 million in 1966, £N61.4 million in 1967, and £N40.3 million in 1969 (see table 5.9). The net *negative* contribution of investment income (an "invisible" trade transaction) to the balance of payments was £N27.7 million in 1964, £N32.8 million in 1965, £N41.1 million in 1966, £N40.4 million in 1967, and £N22.7 million in 1968. H.M.A. Onitiri, "Nigeria's External Trade, Balance of Payments and Capital Movements, 1959-68," in *Reconstruction and Development in Nigeria*, Ayida and Onitiri, eds., pp. 276-7.

26. Central Bank, *Annual Report, 1967*, p. 63.

27. Central Bank, *Annual Report, 1968*, p. 70.

28. A mere nineteen days were given for the currency exchange, which had been kept a closely guarded secret. The Biafran government mounted an operation to sell Nigerian money on the international currency centers. Stories abounded of mysterious men carrying suitcases bulging with Nigerian currency, fanning out to the world's exchange markets. But even at concessionary rates for the Nigerian pound, only a small proportion of Biafra's holdings of Nigerian money was converted to other international currency. John de St. Jorre, *The Nigerian Civil War* (London: Hodder & Stoughton, 1972), p. 187.

29. Central Bank, *Annual Report*, 1968, pp. 70-1; and "Nigeria," *Standard Bank Review* (March 1970), p. 18.

30. The first assumption made is that the monthly local current military expenditures in any year are in direct proportion to the current expenditures for defense and internal security of that year--£N32.0 million in 1967, £N75.0 million in 1968, £N94.3 million in 1969, and £N210.6 million in 1970 (see table 5.4 with figures in 1969 and 1970 based on the assumption in footnote a). On the basis of that assumption, the local currency expenditure of £N48 million from 1 September 1967 through 31 May 1968 estimated by

Obafemi Awolowo, then federal commissioner for finance, can be divided into £N12.23 million from 1 September through 31 December 1967, and £N35.77 million from 1 January through 31 May 1968. Local currency military expenditures for other periods between 1967 and 1970 follow from the assumption. Since the federal commissioner for finance implied that official figures underestimate military expenditures, I adjusted the figures with a multiplier of 1.71, the same one used by Ayida.

Monthly primary foreign exchange military expenditures, and monthly secondary and indirect foreign exchange military expenditures in any year are also assumed to be in the same ratio as current expenditures for defense and internal security for that year. Ayida's estimates of £N60 million primary foreign exchange expenditures and £N40 million secondary and indirect foreign exchange expenditures from 1 September 1967 through 31 March 1969 are the basis for estimates of these expenditures in other periods. Since it is less likely that these figures are underestimations, no multiplier is used. Ayida, "Development Objectives," in *Reconstruction and Development in Nigeria*, Ayida and Onitiri, eds., p. 14; Obafemi Awolowo, *The People's Republic* (Ibadan: Oxford University Press, 1968), p. 325; and Obafemi Awolowo, "Nigeria's Post-War Prospects," *West Africa* (25 April 1970), p. 45.

31. Ayida, "Development Objectives," in *Reconstruction and Development in Nigeria*, Ayida and Onitiri, eds., pp. 14-15; O. Aboyade, "The Development Process," ibid., pp. 51-5; U. Asika, "Rehabilitation and Resettlement," ibid., pp. 635-43; and "Nigeria: West Tax Probe Opens," *West Africa* (11 January 1969), p. 53.

32. Ayida, "Development Objectives," in *Reconstruction and Development in Nigeria*, Ayida and Onitiri, eds., pp. 15-18; and O. Aboyade, "The Development Process," ibid., pp. 52-5, 66-7.

33. Western State of Nigeria, *Report of the Commission of Inquiry into the Civil Disturbances which occurred in certain parts of the Western State of Nigeria in the month of December 1968, and other matters incidental thereto or connected therewith* (Ayoola Commission Report), (Ibadan, 31 March 1969).

6
Industry and Agriculture

Chapter 5 analyzed the impact of the war on aggregate economic variables. This chapter discusses the impact of the conflict on major sectors of the economy--oil, manufacturing, transportation, domestic trade, and agriculture.

OIL

The dominant structural change in the Nigerian economy in the prewar decade was the phenomenal increase in crude-oil output centered largely in the East. Although in 1958/59, less than one-tenth of 1 percent of Nigeria's gross domestic product (GDP) originated in the oil sector, by 1966/67 more than 4 percent came from oil.[1]

GDP originating in the oil sector grew by 69.2 percent per annum in constant (1962/63) prices, and by 80.6 percent per annum in current prices from fiscal years, 1958/59 to 1966/67.[2] The value of crude-oil output grew 77.8 percent per annum between 1958 and 1966 to £N100 million per year, or 415,000 barrels per day.[3]

In July 1967, after Nigeria increased the blockade to include oil tankers and Shell-B.P. halted its production in the East, Biafra's crude-oil output, produced only for local requirements, dropped to 5,000 barrels per day--slightly more than 1 percent of prewar output--before ceasing in subsequent months because of the war. In Nigeria, crude-petroleum production, curtailed to the offshore wells in the Mid-West, decreased 86.7 percent from the first half to the second half of 1967 (table 6.1).

Although crude-oil output in the first seven months of 1967 averaged more than half a million barrels a day and was 41.4 percent higher than in the corresponding period in 1966, output the last five months of 1967 averaged only 55,000 barrels a day--about 11 percent of the corresponding months of 1966. Annual oil production in Nigeria dropped by nearly 25 percent, from 415,000 barrels per day in 1966 to 317,000 barrels per day in 1967,[4] while the value of petroleum exports as a percentage of total export value was reduced from 32.5 percent in 1966 to 29.8 percent in 1967 (table 6.2).

Crude-oil output fell another 56 percent in 1968 to 142,000 barrels per day, while the value of crude petroleum exports as a percentage of total exports declined more than 12 percentage points to 17.5 percent. On a quarterly basis, production roughly leveled off in the first quarter of 1968, swung upward in mid year, then increased abruptly in the final quarter to nearly six times as high as the same period in 1967.

The sharp rise resulted from resumed limited production by onshore wells in the Rivers and Mid-Western states in October 1968. Restoration of output lagged about six to twelve months behind regaining the territory because it was necessary to repair and replace pumping and transport facilities damaged in the fighting.[5]

In the first half of 1969 the rate of crude petroleum output increased 67 percent over the final 1968 quarter. After a series of attacks by Biafra on Nigerian oil installations, crude-oil production increased less than 3 percent in the second half of 1969. Although production in 1969 exceeded the previous peak year, 1966, by 29 percent, the output reached in the second quarter of 1967 was not surpassed until the fourth quarter of 1969, when a steady increase in production began and continued for at least five years.

From 1969 to 1974, crude-oil output increased 33.1 percent per annum. Altogether, despite the interruption of an upward trend for more than two years during the civil war, the growth rate from 1963 to 1974 was 36.0 percent annually.

Table 6.3 shows that the steady increase in the percentage of GDP contributed by the mining sector, consisting primarily of petroleum, was interrupted by declining from more than 7 percent in 1966/67 to 3-5 percent in the three fiscal years of the war. Estimates made in the 1970s, though not comparable with the previous figures, suggest that the mining sector reached its prewar share of GDP the first year after the war, and increased its relative size thereafter.

Nigeria's only oil refinery, six miles east of Port Harcourt, Eastern Nigeria, came into service in October 1965, with a processing capacity of 45,000 barrels a day. In June and July 1967, Biafra produced 5,000 barrels of refined petroleum a day, decreasing production within a few months for lack of qualified technicians and spare parts, and disruptions from air and ground attacks. After the federal army occupied Port Harcourt and the nearby oil refinery in May 1968, Biafran scientists and engineers developed grain alcohol and palm oil lubricants, and designed make-shift refineries that provided fuel for essential vehicles.[6] But fuel and lubricant production was only a fraction of prewar levels.

In 1967 only 50 percent of Nigeria's refined petroleum products was produced domestically, compared with 90 percent in 1966. And that whole demand was increasing to supply military machinery like jets and armored cars. Thus, imports of mineral fuels, lubricants, and related materials increased substantially during the war--from £N3.8 million in 1967 to more than £N14 million per annum in 1968 and 1969.[7] Despite regaining Port Harcourt in early 1968, the Nigerians found that the severe damage to the refinery, by retreating Biafrans, and lack of qualified personnel delayed resumption of production until May 1970.

MANUFACTURING

The rate of growth in manufacturing output decreased from 16.2 percent per annum in 1964-65 to 14.5 percent in 1966, to 4.4 percent in 1967, and 0.6 percent in 1968, but reverted to 22.6 percent in 1969 (table 6.1). The deceleration in growth began in the last half of 1966, as a result of lower profit expectations and reduced investment ensuing from the political crisis of 1965, loss of skilled labor from population movements, and increased cost of distribution from disruptions in the trade and transport sectors. Manufacturing output rapidly picked up between the last quarter of 1966 and the first quarter of 1967. Then after Biafra's secession and its blockade in the middle of 1967, all Nigerian manufacturing decreased 35.8 percent between the second and third quarters of 1967. Manufacturing output in the East, which had accounted for about 30 percent of the national total before the war, was virtually at a standstill. Output in the federation decreased because of further disruption of established trading networks and the loss of Eastern markets.

The position improved fairly steadily from the third quarter of 1967 until the beginning of 1969, with production in the fourth quarter in 1968, 31.6 percent higher than the corresponding quarter in 1967. In part, the increase reflected the growth of import substitution in response to tightening trade restrictions. The sluggishness of growth for most of 1969 resulted partially from production bottlenecks caused by delays and rejections in obtaining inputs from abroad.

Except for the dip in manufacturing output the second quarter of 1969, output from the fourth quarter of 1968 to the third quarter of 1969 slightly exceeded the prewar production peak in the first quarter of 1967. By the first quarter of 1969, manufacturing or processing of vegetable oil products, food products, metal containers, paints, varnishes, lacquer, paper packaging, tires, vehicle assembly, plastics, natural rubber, footwear, cotton textiles, soft drinks, and beer and stout had surpassed peak prewar production--in some instances as a result of higher protection from imports or increased demand by the military. The output of cement, with a major plant in Nkalagu, and of soap, with plants in Umuahia, Aba, Uyo, and Ikot Ekpene, still remained substantially below prewar rates.[8]

Few Eastern factories resumed operating in 1968 and 1969 after they were captured by the federal forces. Even though physical installations were largely intact, production was not possible because of storage-facility looting, dispersal of skilled manpower, lack of finance, disruption of normal trade flows, the state of machinery disrepair (due to lack of spare parts), and the small size of the Eastern market. Still because of the slow rate of overall growth during the war and replacement of imports by domestic manufacturers, the relative contribution of the manufacturing and crafts sector to GDP increased more rapidly during the war than the prewar trend would have suggested (table 6.3).

TABLE 6.1
Indices of Nigerian Crude Petroleum and Manufacturing Production, 1964-81 (1963 = 100)

Year or quarter	Crude petroleum index	Manufacturing index
1964	157.6	123.7
1965	358.4	143.7
1966	546.0	164.5
1967	*417.2*	*171.8*
1st quarter	725.6	202.0
2nd quarter	756.3	200.7
3rd quarter	*111.9*	*128.8*
4th quarter	*74.9*	*155.8*
1968	*181.6*	*172.8*
1st quarter	*65.2*	*161.0*
2nd quarter	*108.9*	*161.2*
3rd quarter	*139.2*	*164.7*
4th quarter	*415.0*	*205.1*
1969	*706.5*	*211.9*
1st quarter	*694.2*	*204.2*
2nd quarter	*698.7*	*200.3*
3rd quarter	*625.5*	*212.4*
4th quarter	*807.6*	*230.6*
1970	*1,394.7*	*236.2*
1st quarter	*1,032.4*	*216.3*
2nd quarter	1,237.7	223.5
3rd quarter	1,550.3	247.5
4th quarter	1,759.3	252.2
1971	2,037.8	249.6
1972	2,374.7	265.4
1973	2,678.7	326.4
1974	2,939.9	317.2
1975	2,329.6	392.0
1976	2,704.8	483.6
1977	2,733.3	516.2
1978	2,446.0	587.4
1979	2,886.3	598.5
1980	2,608.9	664.0
1981	1,802.3	701.6

Sources: Central Bank, *Annual Report, 1970*, pp. 27, 29; *Annual Report, 1974*, pp. 26, 29; *Annual Report, 1977*, pp. 12, 17; *Annual Report, 1978*, pp. 15, 19; *Annual Report, 1979* (Lagos, 1980), pp. 15, 17; *Annual Report, 1980*, pp. 18, 21; and *Standard Chartered Review* (March 1982), p. 38.

Note: Production figures from the secessionist areas are excluded from the third quarter of 1967 until the last quarter of 1969; however, crude petroleum production and manufacturing production were virtually at a standstill then.

TRANSPORTATION

The disruption of road, rail, water, and air traffic by the political disturbances and civil war adversely affected domestic trade and exports, and created shortages and price increases in parts of Nigeria. The first major bottlenecks came in railways, lorry transport, airlines, and maintenance when experienced Ibos and other southerners fled to their regions of origin in late 1966.[9] The Northern Region was especially hurt by loss of transport labor, as its economy depended on the railways to bring petrol from the south and to take groundnuts and groundnut oil to the coast.

In 1967-68, transport problems were exacerbated by the loss of locomotives and rolling stock to Biafra, civil transport diverted for military use, closing of the eastern route to the port of Port Harcourt, the embargo on Eastern and (in 1967) Mid-Western ports, destruction of strategic roads and bridges in the Biafran retreat, the shortage of coal after the Enugu mines were closed, the cutback in import of transport vehicles and parts, and the severe cut in funds for road maintenance.

Passengers and tonnage of goods carried by the railways declined 31.0 and 40.0 percent, respectively, in the fiscal year 1967/68, after both had decreased 13.8 percent in the 1966/67 fiscal year (table 6.4). Although passenger traffic revived in 1969, goods carried continued to decline until a rail link was opened between Port Harcourt and the hinterland in September 1970.[10]

The disruption in domestic transportation was one factor causing the total cargo handled at Nigerian ports to decline from 22.5 million tons in 1966 to 8 million tons in 1967 (64.4 percent), and a further 37.5 percent decline to 5 million tons in 1968. Shipping activity exceeded its prewar rate in 1969, but that rise, with the regulations on import license and decreased use of Mid-Western ports following Biafran attacks, congested the wharves in Lagos. By early 1970, the average wait for ships at the wharves was 20 days--a situation under which shipping firms threatened to levy a 20 percent surcharge on freight destined for Nigerian ports.

The surcharge was avoided by appointing a "military commander" of Lagos port 1 May 1970 who decreased the backlog appreciably within two months. But the volume of crude petroleum exports and merchandise imports increased sharply after the war (table 5.9) so ship delays were reduced only temporarily, despite reactivation of Port Harcourt and Calabar ports in early 1971.[11]

DOMESTIC TRADE

Cutbacks in transport, combined with political uncertainty, restraints on imported consumer goods, departure of traders to their regions of origin, and restrictive policies toward the private sector created depressed conditions in internal trade the last part of 1966, which continued until the war's end.

TABLE 6.2
Changes in the Structure of Exports, 1959, 1962, 1965-80
(in £N million and percentage)

	1959		1962		1965		1966	
	£Nm	%	£Nm	%	£Nm	%	£Nm	%
Cocoa	38.3	23.9	33.3	20.3	42.5	15.8	28.2	10.0
Palm kernels	26.0	16.2	16.9	10.3	26.5	9.9	22.4	7.9
Palm oil	13.8	8.4	8.9	5.5	13.6	5.1	11.0	3.9
Groundnuts	27.5	17.1	32.4	19.8	38.0	14.2	40.7	14.4
Groundnut oil & cake	6.3	3.9	8.6	5.3	15.1	5.6	14.4	5.1
Petroleum	2.7	1.7	16.7	10.3	68.1	25.4	97.9	32.5
Rubber	11.6	7.2	11.4	6.9	10.9	4.1	11.3	4.0
Raw cotton	7.3	4.5	5.9	3.6	3.3	1.2	3.3	1.2
Total other	27.0	16.8	29.8	18.0	45.3	16.9	54.5	19.3
Total domestic exports	160.5	99.7[b]	164.0	100.0	263.3	48.3	277.7	98.1
Re-exports	a	a	a	a	5.1	1.9	5.4	1.9
Total export[b]					268.4	100.0	283.1	100.2

	1972		1973		1974		1975	
	£Nm	%	£Nm	%	£Nm	%	£Nm	%
Cocoa	50.6	7.0	56.2	4.9	79.5	2.7	90.5	3.7
Palm kernels	7.8	1.1	9.4	0.8	21.8	0.7	9.2	0.4
Palm oil	0.1	c	c	c	c	c	0.6	c
Groundnuts	9.6	1.3	22.8	2.0	3.4	0.1	-	-
Groundnut oil & cake	8.4	1.2	20.8	1.8	8.1	0.3	0.4	c
Petroleum	588.1	82.0	946.8	83.1	2682.8	92.6	2281.6	92.7
Rubber	3.7	0.5	9.7	0.9	16.6	0.6	7.6	0.3
Raw cotton	0.3	0.1	2.4	0.2	-	-	-	-
Total other	42.3	5.9	66.6	5.9	79.8	2.8	70.2	2.8
Total domestic exports	710.9	99.1	1134.7	99.6	2892.0	99.8	2460.1	99.9
Re-exports	6.2	0.9	4.5	0.4	5.4	0.2	2.7	0.1
Total export[b]	717.1	100.0	1139.2	100.0	2897.4	100.0	2462.8	100.0

Sources: H.M.A. Onitiri, "Nigeria's External Trade, Balance of Payments and Capital Movements 1959-1968," in *Reconstruction and Development in Nigeria*, p. 256; Central Bank, *Annual Report, 1967*, p. 61; Central Bank, *Annual Report, 1968*, p. 68; Central Bank, *Annual Report, 1971*, p. 80; Central Bank, *Annual Report, 1972*, p. 80; Central Bank, *Annual Report, 1974*, p. 86; Central Bank, *Annual Report, 1975*, p. 99; Central Bank, *Annual Report, 1976*, p. 75; Central Bank, *Annual Report, 1977*, p. 71; Central Bank, *Annual Report, 1978*, p. 75; Central Bank, *Annual Report, 1979*, p. 73; and Central Bank, *Annual Report, 1980*, p. 89.

TABLE 6.2 (continued)

1967		1968		1969		1970		1971	
£Nm	%	£Nm	%	£Nm	%	£Nm	%	£Nm	%
54.5	*22.5*	*51.7*	*24.5*	*52.6*	*16.5*	*66.5*	*15.0*	71.6	11.1
7.8	*3.2*	*10.2*	*4.8*	*9.9*	*3.1*	*10.9*	*2.5*	12.9	2.0
3.9	*1.3*	*0.1*	--	*0.4*	*0.1*	*0.6*	*0.1*	1.7	0.3
35.6	*14.7*	*38.0*	*18.0*	*35.8*	*11.3*	*21.8*	*4.9*	12.2	1.9
9.9	*4.1*	*14.4*	*6.8*	*15.6*	*4.9*	*17.1*	*3.9*	9.7	1.5
72.0	*29.8*	*37.0*	*17.5*	*130.8*	*41.1*	*258.6*	*58.4*	490.2	75.8
6.3	*2.6*	*6.3*	*3.0*	*9.6*	*3.0*	*8.7*	*2.0*	6.2	1.0
4.1	*1.7*	*3.3*	*1.6*	*3.3*	*1.0*	*6.6*	*1.5*	5.5	0.9
46.6	*19.3*	*45.5*	*21.6*	*56.7*	*17.8*	*47.7*	*10.8*	30.4	4.7
238.1	*98.4*	*206.5*	*97.8*	*314.7*	*98.8*	*438.5*	*99.1*	640.4	99.2
3.7	*1.5*	*4.6*	*2.2*	*3.5*	*1.1*	*4.2*	*0.9*	6.3	1.0
241.8	*99.9*	*211.1*	*100.0*	*318.2*	*99.9*	*442.7*	*100.0*	646.7	100.2

1976		1977		1978		1979		1980	
£Nm	%	£Nm	%	£Nm	%	£Nm	%	£Nm	%
109.4	3.3	155.6	4.1	189.0	6.2	216.1	4.1	155.9	2.2
13.5	0.4	16.3	0.4	6.4	0.2	5.9	0.1	5.8	0.1
0.2	c	-	-	-	-	-	-	-	-
0.1	c	c	c	c	c	c	c	-	-
1.7	0.1	1.0	c	-	-	-	-	-	-
3160.8	93.7	3536.4	92.7	2700.8	89.1	5083.4	93.8	6761.5	96.1
7.2	0.2	11.1	0.1	6.3	0.1	6.5	0.1	5.8	0.1
-	-	10.1	0.1	2.1	0.1	c	c	1.3	c
78.9	2.2	80.3	2.5	121.3	4.1	98.4	1.7	94.8	1.3
3371.8	99.9	3810.8	99.9	3025.9	99.8	5410.3	99.8	7025.1	99.8
3.8	0.1	4.6	0.1	6.3	0.2	8.1	0.2	13.4	0.2
3375.6	100.0	3815.4	100.0	3032.2	100.0	5418.4	100.0	7038.5	100.0

[a]Does not include figures for re-exports.

[b]May not add to 100 percent because of rounding.

TABLE 6.3
Percentage of All-Nigerian Gross Domestic Product at Constant Factor Cost, 1962/63-72/73

Sector	1962/3	1963/4	1964/5	1965/6	1966/7	*1967/8*	*1968/9*	*1969/70*	*1969/70*	1970/1	1971/2	1972/3
Agriculture, livestock, forestry, & fishing	61.18	61.08	59.23	56.44	54.92	*55.89*	*54.62*	*52.97*	*48.76*	43.66	43.67	41.54
Mining	2.04	2.20	3.25	5.34	7.23	*3.52*	*3.77*	*4.52*	*8.28*	12.06	13.76	14.84
Manufacturing & crafts	5.77	5.39	5.38	5.94	5.88	*7.45*	*8.56*	*9.43*	*8.42*	7.60	7.24	7.59
Transport & communication	4.51	4.78	4.59	5.60	4.20	*3.96*	*3.90*	*3.86*	*3.43*	3.31	2.94	2.81
Construction, services, distribution, other sectors	26.50	26.55	27.55	26.68	27.77	*29.18*	*29.15*	*29.22*	*31.11*	33.37	32.39	33.22
Total	100	100	100	100	100	*100*	*100*	*100*	*100*	100	100	100

Source: Table 5.1. These fiscal years begin 1 April; figures in italics cover the 1967-70 war period. Figures left and right of double lines are not comparable.

TABLE 6.4
Passengers and Goods Carried by the Nigerian Railway Corporation, 1965/66-1967/68

	1965/66	1966/67	1967/68[a]
Passengers carried (millions)	11.6	10.0	6.9
Goods carried (millions of tons)	2.9	2.5	1.5

[a]Eastern Line disrupted.

Source: Tillo E. Kuhn, "Transport and Communication Systems Planning for Reconstruction and Development," in *Reconstruction and Development in Nigeria*, p. 502.

Shortages of food and higher food prices resulted from the exodus of traders from their usual markets during the riots and political disturbances the last part of 1965 and in 1966. But the demand for food decreased more than the supply of food the first 15 to 18 months of the war, so prices decreased as food was diverted from the East, a food-importing area, to the rest of the federation, previously a food-exporting area. In spite of the prewar self-sufficiency in food in most of the areas regained from Biafra in 1968-69, the demand for food increased more than its supply in Nigeria as requirements were increased for an enlarged army, and fighting disrupted planting and destroyed crops in the recovered areas. Consequently, food prices increased 18.9 percent in 1969.

In each of the first two years after the war, 1970 and 1971, food prices increased more than 20 percent (table 5.3), from destruction of crops in 1969-70, the war ending after the season when bush clearing for farming had virtually passed, from lack of seeds, seedlings, and implements in the East in 1970,[12] and resumed demand for food in the federation from the Ibo heartland, a food-deficit area.

After 1966, a year of substantial gains in farm production, the index of output of agricultural export commodities declined 16 percent in 1967, leveled off in 1968, but decreased another 16 percent in 1969. Although movements in agricultural export output can be expected to be volatile and irregular, even the use of a five-year moving average to smooth out irregular fluctuations indicated a steady decline during the civil war and beyond (table 6.5).

Several effects of the political upheavals can be mentioned. First, investment in agriculture declined in 1966-70, as a result, among other things, of growing uncertainties about the Nigerian economy during the political crises, and of wartime controls, which limited the import of agricultural machinery.[13] Second, in the 1970s, farmers shifted from export crops to domestic food after sharp increases in its prices (table 5.3) primarily from war-related causes. Third, after 1970, international buyers made a

TABLE 6.5
Aggregate Index of Output of Nigerian Agricultural Export Commodities, 1961-78 (1960 = 100)

Year	Index (on annual basis)	Index (five-year moving average)
1961	104.5	
1962	112.6	
1963	110.7	112.7
1964	127.3	116.8
1965	108.2	115.1
1966	125.0	114.0
1967	*104.5*	*113.5*
1968	*104.9*	*104.7*
1969	*88.0*	*99.8*
1970	*100.9*	*91.8*
1971	80.9	84.3
1972	84.2	80.5
1973	67.6	74.7
1974	69.1	72.0
1975	71.6	65.6
1976	67.6	62.6
1977	52.3	
1978	52.6	

Source: Central Bank, *Annual Report, 1969*, p. 17; Central Bank, *Annual Report, 1971*, p. 61; Central Bank, *Annual Report, 1973*, p. 19; Central Bank, *Annual Report, 1974*, p. 18; Central Bank, *Annual Report, 1975*, p. 24; Central Bank, *Annual Report, 1976*, p. 11; Central Bank, *Annual Report, 1977*, p. 9; and Central Bank, *Annual Report, 1978*, p. 13.

long run shift to substitute vegetable oils and oil seeds for palm oil, whose primary source of supply, Eastern Nigeria, was cut off during the conflict. Finally, the embargo on exports in rebel territory, the destruction and disruption of war, and the loss of manpower to the military all reduced crop production.

The output of yams, cocoyams, rubber, palm oil, and palm kernels, major crops in the East, dropped during the hostilities. The highest annual tonnage of yams produced in 1966/67-1968/69 was less than the lowest annual level from 1961/62-1965/66. Also, the volume of cocoyams, grown mainly in the East, declined from an average of 1,556,000 long tons per annum in 1962/63-1965/66 to an average of 1,516,000 per year in 1966/67-1969/70.

A major reason for the low output of these two leading staples in the East was the drop in average yield as a result of war damage. Every annual rate of output of rubber, produced in the war-affected areas of the Benin lowlands, the lower Niger valley, the Niger delta, and the Cross River basin, from 1966/67 to 1969/70 was below the lowest yearly production of 1963/64-1965/66. No annual output of palm oil or palm kernels in 1967-70 exceeded the lowest production of the commodity from 1960 through 1966.[14]

The decreases in crop production in the East and Mid-West were instrumental in the general decline in the index of agricultural export commodities from 1966 through 1969. No annual values of exports of palm kernels, palm oil, or rubber in 1967-70 exceeded either of the yearly values for the same crop in 1965-66. Some of the disruption even extended to areas outside the East and the Mid-West. For example, an unusually large percentage of groundnuts, a major Northern export crop, was spoiled in 1966-67 before it could be evacuated to the ports because of transport tie-ups primarily from the flight of Eastern drivers with their lorries.[15]

Not all decrements in farm output during the war can be blamed on the hostilities. The volume (though not necessarily the value) of groundnut exports declined each of the three years between 1968 and 1970. But the major reason was smuggling of groundnuts into neighboring countries, because the price paid by the Northern Nigerian marketing board to farmers was far below the world price. However, some crops, like cocoa, grown in the West, were virtually unaffected by the war. In fact, the annual export value of cocoa in each year, 1966-69, exceeded that of 1965, a year of unfavorable weather and black-pod diseases.[16]

REVOLTS AMONG FARMERS

A tax rebellion primarily of independent small holders in Ibadan, Egba, and southern Osun divisions took place in September-December 1968 and (after the release of the Ayoola Report commissioned by the Western state government on the riots) July-October 1969. Beer estimates the rebellion caused approximately 160 deaths. During the riots, palaces were burned; property was destroyed; tax officials conducted raids; citizens without tax receipts were jailed; District Council officials, *obas*, chiefs, and village heads were murdered; farmers organized military units to ambush officials; and mobs resisted tax assessment and fought soldiers and police.

The revolt arose from development of a specifically rural political consciousness in which farmers emphasized that those who participated were "real farmers" (*agbe gidi*), whose labor and resources were being expropriated by corrupt officials and produce buyers. Discontent had grown in response to the crisis faced by cocoa farmers in areas of poor harvest from heavy rains in 1967/68. They were squeezed by lower produce prices and higher input prices than during crop years 1962/63-64/65, and by continued contributions to marketing board surpluses.

Direct taxes in the West also were higher (with a flat-rate tax for all persons whose cash income was below £N50 per annum) and more regressive (increasing as a percentage of income below £N300 per annum) than before the war. Even as unrest was exacerbated when the Western state increased the number of persons on income tax rolls through legislation (such as an amendment 1 April 1968 to include self-employed women whose incomes exceeded £N100 per annum) and wider enforcement, farmers were aggrieved by the continued widespread tax evasion and avoidance by many high-income professionals, businessmen, and traders.

As late as 1965/66, only 89,000 persons from a population of 9.5 million in the West were assessed income taxes in excess of the flat-rate for lowest income earners. In addition, the new series of levies, including the compulsory contribution of 5 percent of annual income (with a minimum of 10 shillings) toward the purchase of National Reconstruction Savings Bonds, lacked prior discussion at the local level, and was not understood by most rural people, who felt that the urban elite was not sacrificing during the war.

In rural Western Nigeria, taxes often were associated with collectors, inspectors, and petty council officials who embezzled money, extracted bribes for nonimplementation of incomprehensible regulations, arrested tax defaulters, raided defaulters' property, harassed and tormented those with tax receipts, demanded lump-sum payments in 30 days without considering timing of farm harvests and sales, increased water rates and tax assessments, and denied promised benefits and amenities. Former leaders of the Nigerian National Democratic Party, who were underrepresented in the Western government after the coups, and who were instrumental in agitating for an Oyo state they could expect to dominate, gave impetus to the revolt. But beginning 15 October 1969, after the government made concessions on tax rates and fees, the method of collecting taxes, and representation on the farmers' union, order was restored for more than two years among Western farmers.[17]

SUMMARY

Oil, whose production was centered in the Eastern region, was the main economic sector disrupted by the civil war. Crude-petroleum output the second quarter of 1967, just before the civil war, was not surpassed until the fourth quarter of 1969.

Although the growth rate of manufacturing output decelerated, especially the first year of the war, the absolute level of manufacturing output grew each year during the war. The Ibo exodus the year or so before secession of the Eastern Region seriously disrupted transportation and internal trade. The decline of agricultural exports, which began before the conflict, continued during the war and persisted after it.

NOTES

1. Nigeria, Office of Statistics, *Gross Domestic Product of Nigeria, 1958/59-1966/67* (Lagos, August 1968), p. 25.

2. The growth rate of 34.8 percent per annum in current prices, and 35.3 percent per annum in constant prices, in the mining sector, the fastest rate of any sector from 1958/59-1966/67, resulted almost entirely from the rapid increase in crude-oil production.

3. *Gross Domestic Product of Nigeria, 1958/59-1966/67*, pp. 25, 30; *Petroleum Press Service*, January 1968, p. 7; Scott R. Pearson, "Nigerian Petroleum: Implications for Medium-term Planning," in *Growth and Development of the Nigerian Economy*, Carl K. Eicher and Carl Liedholm, eds., (East Lansing, Mich.: Michigan

State University Press, 1970), p. 357; and Nigerian Institute of Social and Economic Research, "Economic and Social Survey 1958 to 1968," Reconstruction and Development Conference, 1969, p. 46.

See chapter 4 for further background on the oil sector, including problems involved in assessing the export value of oil.

4. *Petroleum Press Service*, April 1968, pp. 148-9, and August 1968, pp. 289-90; Central Bank, *Annual Report, 1967*, p. 16; and Pearson, "Nigerian Petroleum: Implications for Medium-term Planning," in *Growth and Development*, Eicher and Leidholm, eds., p. 46.

5. The Biafran army, however, did not deliberately destroy oil installations or blow up oil fields when it retreated from the Port Harcourt vicinity in May 1968. Apparently Biafra, like Nigeria, did not perceive severe damage to these vital economic assets to be in its interest.

6. Central Bank, *Annual Report, 1967*, p. 19; and N.U. Akpan, *The Struggle for Secession, 1966-1970: A Personal Account of the Nigerian Civil War* (London: Frank Cass, 1976), p. 109.

7. Central Bank, *Annual Report, 1967*, p. 19; and *Standard Bank Review*, February 1970, p. 17.

8. Central Bank, *Annual Report, 1969*, p. 22; and P.C. Asiodu, "Planning for Further Development in Nigeria," in *Reconstruction and Development in Nigeria*, A.A. Ayida and H.M.A Onitiri, eds. (Ibadan: Oxford University Press, 1971), pp. 188-9.

9. Central Bank, *Annual Report, 1966*, pp. 32-3.

10. Central Bank, *Annual Report, 1969*, p. 26; and Central Bank, *Annual Report, 1970*, p. 34.

11. Central Bank, *Annual Report, 1968*, pp. 26-27; Central Bank, *Annual Report, 1969*, p. 29; Central Bank, *Annual Report, 1970*, pp. 34, 35; Central Bank, *Annual Report, 1971*, pp. 31-2; "Nigeria," *Standard Bank Review* (February 1970), p. 22; "Commercial News," *West Africa* (9 May 1970), p. 525; and "Giving the Harbour its Due," *West Africa* (6 June 1970), p. 603.

12. Central Bank, *Annual Report, 1970*, p. 20.

13. Standard Bank Group, *Annual Economic Review--Nigeria* (July 1969), p. 6.

14. World Bank, *Nigeria: Options for Long-term Development* (Baltimore: Johns Hopkins University Press, 1974), pp. 237-9.

15. Central Bank, *Annual Report, 1967*, pp. 15, 62.

16. Central Bank, *Annual Report, 1969*, p. 17; and Central Bank, *Annual Report, 1970*, p. 21.

17. Gavin Williams, "Political Consciousness among the Ibadan Poor," in *Sociology and Development*, Emanuel de Kadt and Gavin Williams, eds. (London: Tavistock Publications, 1974), pp. 126-36; Western State of Nigeria, *Report of the Inquiry into the Civil Disturbances which occurred in certain parts of the Western State of Nigeria in the month of December 1968, and other matters incidental thereto or connected therewith* (Ayoola Commission Report), (Ibadan, 31 March 1969); and Christopher E.F. Beer, *The Politics of Peasant Groups in Western Nigeria* (Ibadan: Ibadan University Press, 1976), pp. 160-206.

7
The Biafran Economy

> All things abound in Biafra,
> All things abound in our land,
> All things abound in Biafra,
>
> And Death, Death,
> Death that is universal,
> And Death! Death! Death!
>
> An Ibo saying during the Nigerian civil war. Elechi Amadi, *Sunset in Biafra: A Civil War Diary*, 1973.

> With hunger and starvation in the land,
> farming had become a battle-cry.
>
> Andre Aletta, "A Villager in Agony," in Chinua Achebe, Arthur Nwankwo, Samuel Ifejika, Flora Nwapa, et al., *The Insider Stories of War and Peace from Nigeria*, 1971.

> Biafra fought in the belief that it was the only way to protect themselves from possible extermination. We believed that we were fighting to ensure our very survival.
>
> . . . One finds it difficult to determine who indeed was rebelling against the Nigerian Government. Could it be Biafrans . . . or was it Gowon?
>
> Alexander A. Madiebo, *The Nigerian Revolution and the Biafran War*, 1980.

In the previous two chapters, I alluded to the economy of Biafra, and even included its territory in the rough estimates of Nigerian domestic product. A disproportional number of Nigeria's economists and statisticians cast their lot with the Biafran side. Among them were Biafra's chief economic planner, Dr. Pius Okigbo, author of the major study of Nigeria's national accounts,[1] ambassador to the European Economic Community, 1963-65, and permanent secretary of the Ministry of Finance and chief economic advisor to the Ironsi government in 1966. Yet understandably, in the fight for the survival of Biafra, the development of accurate statistical data by its Ministry of Economic Planning was accorded very low priority. And important economic documents were destroyed by the Biafran government before its defeat. Still, scattered information from the Biafran period can help paint a broad picture of the economy.

OUTPUT AND PRICES

The average level of material well-being apparently declined more in Biafra than in Nigeria, and the decline affected all segments of the Biafran population. Much higher proportions of the population and capital stock were used in direct military activity than on the Nigerian side. For example, the Biafran army used land rovers, taxis, "mammy wagons," Bedford lorries, and push carts for transport during the August 1967 Mid-West invasion. The economy was geared almost entirely to mobilizing for the war and producing basic necessities. The few civilian goods Biafra received from abroad were primarily food, medicine, and other essentials from relief organizations, and desperately needed capital goods. Nevertheless, the upper classes, especially in the military and civil service, spent more than the general population. In addition, as in the Confederate States of America in 1861-65, the military and civil service classes had access to restricted goods, including the few imported luxury goods.

Real output per capita per annum decreased substantially in Biafra during the war, more than on the federal side. Estimates in the Second National Development Plan, 1970-74, indicated that in 1967/68 only 10 percent of gross domestic product originated in the East compared with its "normal" 20 percent,[2] and an apparent estimate of 31.6 percent for 1965/66 by the Biafran Economic Planning Commission.

Biafra's food scarcity in the final eighteen months of the conflict, which approached famine conditions in some areas, resulted from war damage and lack of trade with the outside world. In the East, just before the war, a farm laborer earned 6 shillings, 8 pence (£N1/3) per day,[3] and a lower clerk £N240 per year (or about £N1 per day). Despite wages remaining relatively constant and rationing being used to repress demand, prices of basic items of food, clothing, and tools increased substantially between May 1967 (two months before Nigeria's blockade) and May 1969.

According to a report by agricultural consultants to the International Red Cross, gari, a staple food item made from cassava, rose to 3 to 6 shillings per cup, 18-36 times its May 1967 price. (Nigerian coins were the only ones available.) In "normal" times, one person would eat about 1½ cups per meal. Four bananas increased by 40 times to 10 shillings in the same period; 2-3 mangos rose in price by 110 times to 5 shillings; one chicken increased 12 fold to £B4; a pound of salt rose over 1,000 times to £B14-16; a pair of rubber shoes 6 times to £B1½; and a hoe 15-20 fold to £B3-4. In 1969, a bottle of beer sold for £B10 and a gallon of motor oil for £B80.[4]

Data from Red Cross consultants indicate that general prices increased by 20-30 times in the 24 months after May 1967. In comparison, during the U.S. civil war, the general price index of the eastern section of the Confederacy increased by 12 times between April 1861 (two months before the Northern blockade) and April 1863, and 8 times between April 1863 and April 1865, somewhat less than the Biafran raises.[5]

Despite the economic sacrifice, the Biafran government had substantial popular support in Ibo areas. A psychological state of siege was continually abetted by propaganda about attempted genocide by Nigeria, reinforced by frequent indiscriminate air bombings of large Biafran civilian population centers (markets, churches, schools, hospitals, and refugee camps), which created the climate for even risky innovations to flourish. Chemists and electrical engineers built guns, rockets, hand grenades, and the well publicized, anti-personnel device, *ogbunigwe* (mass destroyer). After Port Harcourt fell in May 1968, a Biafran research institute, Research and Production, designed make-shift refineries to produce fuel. The refineries, established in village compounds, kept the Biafran government's fleet of vehicles on the road. Scientists and engineers improvised substitutes for such import items as engine oil, brake fluid, alcoholic drinks, drugs, toilet soap, and machetes.[6]

ECONOMIC POLICY ORGANIZATION

At the beginning of the war, Biafra established several economic policy institutions, usually headed by people outside the civil service, and separate from the ministries, so many, as a result, functioned only nominally. The advantage of the institutions, such as the directorates, was their power to spend money or employ staff without being subject to the procedures and "red-tape" of the government service.[7] Ten economic directorates were established: food production, food supply, medical supply, housing, clothing, fuel supply, transport, manpower utilization, price control and rationing, and requisition and supply. The primary tasks of the Land Army, created in response to the Directorate of Food Production's inability to cope with food deficiencies, were organizing the distribution of farm implements, maintaining communal farms, shifting of all available space that could be cultivated to food farms, and other measures to increase food output. Research and Production, a prestigious "think-tank" where a number of leftist intellectuals were concentrated, was responsible for applied research and the production of replacements for goods cut off from abroad.

The Directorate of Food Supply procured and collated food, drinks, and tobacco from Biafra, Nigeria, and abroad, and allocated them according to military priorities. Manufacture and procurement of drugs and medicines were the responsibility of the Directorate of Medical Supply. The Housing Directorate commandeered, allocated, and maintained public-sector housing (except refugee camps). The Directorate of Clothing organized the production of uniforms and boots for the armed forces.

Petrol, diesel oil, kerosene, and other scarce fuels were stored and rationed by the Directorate of Fuel Supply. It was the first to experiment with refining crude petroleum, later handed to Research and Production, an agency with more expertise. The Directorate of Transport purchased or commandeered lorries, jeeps, automobiles, bicycles, and canoes for the public.

The Directorate of Manpower Utilisation was essentially an employment agency, matching appropriate registered labor with requesting establishments and agencies, and facilitating the draft of able-bodied men into the armed forces. Least successful of the directorates was that of Price Control and Rationing, which tried to stabilize prices in an economy facing a trade embargo and war disruption.

As a result of the abuses of the other directorates, the Directorate of Requisition and Supply was designed to contain excesses such as comandeering private property without compensation, and to centralize and coordinate economic planning. In a siege economy, this directorate, responsible for short-term planning and policy, was more powerful than, and not coordinated with, the older Economic Planning Commission, which was concerned with decisions about longer-term development. Additionally, economic decision-making was uncertain, hanging in the balance of conflicting pressures by the Bank of Biafra, the heads of directorates, and the economic committee of the executive council.

FINANCIAL POLICIES

Biafra had little scope for fiscal policy to dampen inflation or to mobilize savings. The income tax rate was not raised and the potential for personal taxation was restricted because personal income was not rising. International trade in civilian goods declining to only a trickle left little room for import or export duties, or marketing board surpluses. The opportunities for excise tax revenue receded as industrial establishments closed. Some government spending was cut, however, by eliminating certain fringe benefits for civil servants. And savings were fostered through the compulsory exchange of Nigerian currency notes for Biafran notes, an excercise that netted around £N41 million for the government.[8]

The monetary tools available to manage the economy had little more potency than the fiscal weapons. To be sure, the delay in the immediate issue of Biafran notes during the initial stages of the currency conversion slowed inflation by drying up purchasing power. But, once the initial problems of producing and distributing Biafran currency were overcome, the tight monetary controls gave way to an excessive supply of money. Illicit purchases from Nigeria and rationing dampened the inflation fires at first but pressures of shortages, bottlenecks, and dislocations eventually became so great that little could be done to stem the hyper-inflation.[9]

In January 1968, when the Central Bank of Nigeria issued new currency notes to replace those in circulation, old Nigerian coins remained in circulation. They were the only ones available in Biafra, and served as the medium of exchange (or "bullet") of the hazardous "attack trade" involving purchase of vital commodities from the Nigerian side. Eventually, Nigerian coins, which were in heavy demand, became the standard against which Biafran paper currency was measured. In Biafra, in February 1969, the median exchange rate was £B1 equals 3 shillings, six pence in Nigerian coin (a ratio of 24 to 7).[10] After Biafran currency was issued in early 1968, virtually nothing could be bought for less than a Biafran five-shilling note, the smallest denomination issued by the Bank of Biafra.[11]

By early 1969, the Biafran authorities declared the "attack trade" illegal, and both the Nigerian and the Biafran armies discouraged smuggling food into Biafra. Still, the trade continued, but at a slower rate. The declaration, to Aboyade and Ayida, was "from an objective standpoint, wrongheaded," as it worsened food shortages and increased inflationary pressures. Secessionist officials, however, feared that Biafrans might be caught by Nigerians or buy food with poisonous ingredients. Senator Goodell's pro-Biafran study mission reported that Biafran scientists and pharmacists found evidence of arsenic and cyanide in a few laboratory samples of salt and powdered and evaporated milk acquired in 1967-68.[12]

So long as Biafra's external transactions were little affected by the competitive strength of export goods, and the relative price of imports to domestic goods, and so long as Nigerian currency could be sold for international convertible currency, there was no pressure on the Bank of Biafra to relate the supply of money to the constraints of the balance of payments. During a part of the war, however, Biafra experienced some severe shortages of foreign-exchange reserves, as the next section indicates.

FOREIGN-EXCHANGE RESERVES

The few published data available suggest that Biafra had relatively substantial financial reserves when she seceded, obtained by converting funds--from revenues collected in the East on behalf of the federal and regional governments, from the reserves of the African Continental Bank, and from the money of the N.C.N.C., an Eastern-based party--to foreign exchange, which then was deposited in banks overseas before secession. Biafra was able to finance purchase of armaments and supplies from private arms dealers to fight the initial campaign in what it expected to be a short war of independence.[13]

In January 1968, the Nigerian government introduced new currency notes that rendered valueless the millions of old Nigerian pounds still in Biafran hands (chapter 5). In addition, because of the federal blockade, oil revenues did not materialize.[14] And no foreign private interests were yet willing to risk purchasing monopoly rights to exploit Biafran petroleum and other mineral resources. Thus, by April 1968 Biafra's foreign-exchange reserves were virtually exhausted. Before September 1968, foreign assistance was limited primarily to Portugal, which made available supply stations for planes flying into Biafra.[15]

However, by the end of 1968, Biafra may have obtained as much as £7-8 million of foreign exchange funds, which prevented the collapse of secession. France used its secret service fund to supply perhaps more than £2 million worth of arms and related assistance the last four months of 1968. Not only was a unified Nigeria a potential threat to France's hegemony in French-speaking West Africa but French oil interests also would have gained substantial concessions with British companies expelled after a

Biafran victory. Relief and mission organizations also spent £3.5 million and £0.8 million, respectively, in obtaining Biafran currency needed for the local costs of their programs.

Other sources of foreign currency included donations of about £750,000 from 5,000 to 6,000 Ibos overseas; £150,000 from "aid-Biafra" groups in the west; and less than £100,000 of local Nigerian currency from a few of the four million or so Ibos in Nigeria (used for salt, motor parts, textiles, and other vital civilian goods). It was estimated in 1969 that the total foreign exchange available to Biafra increased, as the government acquired additional funds from gold, jewelry (purchased from Biafra's hard-pressed citizens), and stamps sold abroad.[16]

Although Nigeria tried to make its local currency component of military costs as large as possible, it probably spent 5-10 times as much as Biafra on foreign exchange for direct defense in 1968. Although her expenditures were modest for a twentieth-century war, Biafra did not collapse for some time, as it was fighting primarily a defensive war consisting of small and irregular infantry formations. In such a campaign it was possible to rely mainly on old but usable small-arms ammunition obtained from Europe.

Lindsay estimates that the battle for the important cities of Aba and Owerri in September 1968 probably cost Biafra less than £100,000 in foreign exchange for military armaments and equipment. Except for defense expenditures, most of Biafra's foreign exchange was spent for essential equipment, intelligence requirements, supply planes, ocean shipping, overseas missions, and propaganda.[17]

FOOD AND OTHER STAPLES

The embargo on Biafran ports prevented trade with an area that was overpopulated and plagued by refugees, and which had been an importer of food (chapter 4). The availability of food was linked to military strength and international propaganda, which were in turn related to the problems of obtaining international recognition, foreign currency, and military armaments. Food shortages reached a crisis in mid 1968, when Biafra was a shrinking enclave surrounded by Nigerian territory.

Gradually, beginning in the last two months of 1967, Nigeria retook the outlying areas of the East, areas that constituted its most fertile agricultural land. Large portions of the rural economy were destroyed and disrupted. At the same time the internal transportation and distribution system became dislocated and refugees fled from areas captured by Nigeria into a contracting territory.

In the area remaining, Biafran farmers attempted to use more intensive methods of production, to expand higher-yielding starchy crops, and to increase cultivated acreage by using fallow land and school land.[18] By late 1968, Biafra, with a population of approximately 14 million at the beginning of the war, was supporting a population of 7-8 million, with one-fifth its original territory. About 3 million of the population were refugees from Eastern territory regained by the Nigerians.

After the middle of 1968, food, medical supplies, and other forms of relief were flown into Biafra by the International Red

Cross, Joint Church Aid, Oxfam, and other humanitarian organizations. To arrange relief flights not subject to attack was difficult, since both Biafra and Nigeria refused to allow entries that would cast doubt on their claims of sovereignty or interfere with their military plans. Nigeria offered relief organizations the use of an Eastern land corridor for daytime flights by aircraft inspected by federal authorities. Biafra, however, refused aircraft inspected by Nigeria, and would not allow daytime flights, because relief and arms flights could be differentiated so easily. Thus, throughout the war, relief agencies flew predominantly at night, usually without Nigerian permission.

Hunger was widespread throughout the Biafran population in 1969. Red Cross consultants estimated that about 1.5 million Biafrans died from starvation between June 1967 and May 1969.[19] The cutback of relief flights the last half of 1969 by the International Red Cross for lack of agreement with Nigeria on proposed daylight flights led to a rapidly deteriorating medical and health situation in Biafra just before the war ended. The relationship between curtailing relief efforts and the collapse of the Biafran military position seems to support the Nigerian charge that relief flights prolonged the war.

A major breakthrough for the federal army was the strategic link-up of the first and third divisions in Umuahia on Christmas Day 1969. The link-up severed the area around the temporary Biafran capital, Owerri, from the food-supplying areas of Arochukwu to the east. One reason for the sudden collapse of Biafra in the second week of January 1970 was that even soldiers, despite their high priority, were no longer receiving daily food allotments.[20]

After the end of the war, food shortages continued for several months, because indigenous resources to organize the relief arrangements were missing as the federal government insisted they be primarily Nigerian, and because Nigerian currency was not issued to holders of Biafran currency for a long time. Still, as indicated in chapter 8, reconstruction took place without the bitterness or punitive measures characteristic of so many other countries, as the United States after civil war.

CONCLUSION

The average material level of living, which declined substantially in Nigeria, dropped even more precipitously in Biafra during the war. General prices increased at least tenfold per annum in secessionist territory in marked contrast to price stability in the federation.

By late 1968, hunger was widespread in Biafra, where about half of its prewar population lived on one-fifth its prewar territory. In contrast, Nigeria encountered few major food shortages, except in 1969-70 in war-damaged areas regained from the secessionists.

Because of the embargo on the ports of Biafra, its foreign purchases were restricted to basic essentials--food, relief, vital capital goods, and military arms--during the first ten months of the war. Between April 1968, when Biafra's foreign-exchange reserves were virtually exhausted, and September 1968, when foreign assistance increased, Biafra even cut down on import of necessities. Although Nigeria, which experienced substantial deterioration in its external asset position during the war, had to use trade and payments restrictions that were stringent by "peacetime" standards, she did not curtail essential food, arms, or capital.

In Biafra crude petroleum and manufacturing production was virtually at a standstill during the war. Nigeria, in comparison, faced less disruption in these vital sectors. Its manufacturing output continued to increase during the conflict. Moreover, crude-petroleum production grew from the second quarter of 1968 until it finally surpassed its prewar peak output in the final quarter of 1969.

NOTES

1. *Nigerian National Accounts, 1950-57* (Enugu: Federal Ministry of Economic Development, 1962).

2. Federal forces had captured the cities of Nsukka, Bonny, Enugu, Calabar, and Onitsha by the end of the 1967/68 fiscal year. Apparently the authors of the Plan include both Biafra and territory captured by Nigeria as part of the East. Nigeria, Ministry of Information, *Second National Development Plan, 1970-74: Programme of Post-war Reconstruction and Development* (Lagos, n.d.), pp. 20-4.

3. 12d (pence) = 1s (shilling); 20s = £N1.

4. In February 1969, the median exchange rate was £B1 equals 3 shillings, 6 pence in Nigerian coin.

5. Nigeria, Ministry of Information, *Second National Development Plan 1970-74* (Lagos, 1970), pp. 20-1, 49; Comité International de la Croix-Rouge, "Food and Agricultural Situation in Biafra," mimeographed (Geneva, 1969), pp. 12-13; O. Aboyade and A. Ayida, "The War Economy in Perspective," *Nigerian Journal of Economic and Social Studies*, XIII, No. 1 (March 1971), 16-19, 31; and Eugene M. Lerner, "Money, Prices, and Wages in the Confederacy, 1861-65," in *The Economic Impact of the American Civil War*, Ralph Andreano, ed., (Cambridge, Mass.: Schlectman, 1962), p. 15.

6. Aboyade and Ayida, *Nigerian Journal*, XIII, No. 1, 24; John de St. Jorre, *The Nigerian Civil War* (London: Hodder and Stoughton, 1962), p. 224; Ntieyong U. Akpan, *The Struggle for Secession, 1966-1970: A Personal Account of the Nigerian Civil War* (London: Frank Cass, 1976), pp. 108-9; and C.S. Whitaker, Jr., and Barbara Callaway, "Social Conflict in Nigeria: From Competition to Enmity" (Paper presented to the American Political Science Association meetings, Chicago, September 1971), p. 38.

7. This section is based on Aboyade and Ayida, *Nigerian Journal*, XIII, No. 1, 22-5; and Akpan, *Struggle for Secession*, pp. 98, 117-18.

8. Aboyade and Ayida, *Nigerian Journal*, XIII, No. 1, 31.

9. Ibid.

10. The extremes were 1 Biafran pound for 6 Nigerian pence near the perimeter of Biafra, and 1 pound for 5 shillings in the quieter urban areas. Senator Charles E. Goodell's Biafra Study Mission, United States *Congressional Record*, Senate, 91st Congress,

First Session, V. 115, No. 33 (25 February 1969), S1985.

11. Aboyade and Ayida, *Nigerian Journal*, XIII, No. 1, 31-2.

12. Ibid., p. 32, and *Congressional Record* (25 February 1969), p. S1979.

13. In 1861, the U.S. Confederate South went to war largely financed by a $500,000 loan from the state of Alabama, and $390,000 in bullion seized from the federal mint at New Orleans. An internal loan later brought in $100 million, and after April 1863, an unpopular 10 percent tax in kind was levied on all produce. But the South relied mainly on printing money. By the end of the war, the Georgian was correct who predicted that an oak leaf would be worth as much as the promise of the Confederate treasury to pay one dollar. American Heritage, *Picture History of the Civil War* (New York: American Heritage, 1960), p. 413.

14. Analogously, because of the Northern blockade, the Confederacy's cotton exports to England were virtually severed during the American civil war. Britain did not support the South against the North, nor run the blockade. England had an oversupply of cotton in 1861 and subsequently found alternative sources, and depended upon the North Central states for wheat imports. Donald L. Kemmerer and C. Clyde Jones, *American Economic History* (New York: McGraw-Hill, 1959), p. 263.

15. Kennedy Lindsay, "How Biafra Pays for the War," *Venture*, XXI, No. 3 (March 1969), 26-7.

16. Ibid.

17. Ibid.

18. Comité International de la Croix-Rouge, pp. 5-8.

19. Ibid., p. 31.

20. de St. Jorre, *The Nigerian Civil War*, p. 395, and A.H.M. Kirk-Greene, *Crisis and Conflict in Nigeria: A Documentary Sourcebook, 1966-1970*, II (London: Oxford University Press, 1971), 141.

Part 3

Conclusion

8 Reconstruction, Reconciliation, and Reorientation in Postwar Nigeria

> The war which is coming
> Is not the first one. There were
> Other wars before it.
> When the last one came to an end
> There were conquerors and conquered.
> Among the conquered the common people
> Starved. Among the conquerors
> The common people starved too.
>
> Bertolt Brecht, *From a German Primer*, 1937.

> I need not tell you what horror, what devastation and what extreme human suffering will attend the use of force. When it is all over and the smoke and dust have lifted, and the dead are buried, we shall find as other people have found, that it has all been futile, entirely futile, in solving the problems we set out to solve.
>
> Colonel Robert Adebayo, Military Governor, Western Region, 3 May 1967 (reported in the *Daily Times*, Lagos, 5 May 1967).

The focus of this chapter is the 1970s, i.e., 13 January 1970, the Biafran surrender, through 21 September 1978, the lifting of the ban on party politics, which began a one-year transition from military to civilian rule. In the Nigerian postwar government, 1970-78, ethnic representation was broader than in the prewar civilian regime. The power of prewar elites was undermined. Their ability to use their regional bases to control the center declined with the creation of states, so political competition was more within the states. The components of the power of the Northern aristocracy were incorporated as part of local, state, and (to a lesser extent) federal government. The old Native Authority police were controlled by the federal government; the old Native Courts were state area courts; and the relationship of the traditional authorities, the emir and his council, to local elected authorities was defined by the 1976 local government reforms.[1] Under military rule, members of prewar opposition parties and politicians from minority communities replaced leaders from the prewar ruling alliance among the civilian leaders.

After 1966-67, with a military government, growing federal

revenue, and twelve (later nineteen) states, power became more centralized. Economic strength shifted from interest-groups in the regions, including merchants and medium-sized industrialists, to those at the federal level, such as civil servants and high-level personnel in the large public corporations. Public officials tended to undermine local businessmen as middlemen for the foreign seller or investor seeking access to local markets.[2]

Nevertheless, regional issues became increasingly pronounced as the 1970s proceeded and politicians anticipated the return to civilian rule. The three largest ethnic groups, Hausa-Fulani, Yoruba, and Ibo, relying on the size and relative cohesion of their potential electoral bases, especially welcomed the prospect of a return to open, competitive politics. The small ethnic groups, especially those in the Middle Belt highly represented in the army, were more reluctant to relinquish military rule.

One harbinger of possible future regional animosities was the controversy surrounding the November 1973 census. State and regional political and military leaders zealously defended their interests in planning and conducting the census, and later applying it, because future political representation and distribution of amenities depended on census results. General Yakubu Gowon announced the "very provisional and preliminary" results in May 1974, four months later than first promised.

Southern leaders alleged that in the far North, which accounted for 52.1 percent of the population in 1973 compared with 42.0 percent in 1963 (table 8.1), the civil service had helped fabricate census forms after the head count had been completed. Chief Obafemi Awolowo, the most vocal southern opponent of the results, called on the Supreme Military Council to reject the figures.

The bitter ethnic strife over the census in 1963 (chapter 1) reappeared in 1973-74 and helped influence General Gowon to announce 1 October 1974 that civilian rule would be delayed beyond 1976. Within a year, Gowon was replaced in a coup, partly for failing to maintain the 1976 deadline. The new government of General Murtala Mohammed agreed to continue to work on the basis of the 1963 figures.[3]

In early 1978, regional and religious enmities erupted, as members of the Constituent Assembly debated a draft constitution for the second republic. Violence broke out in the assembly, and nearly 90 members, predominantly Muslims from the North, walked out. The controversy focused upon the Islamic courts, the Sharia Courts of Appeals, and their relationship to the Federal Court of Appeals. Muslims who left the assembly wanted a Federal Sharia Court of Appeals separate from other federal courts, while their opponents objected to a recommendation that judges "versed in Islamic law" render judgments of Muslim legal matters at the federal appeal level.

In mid-April 1978, thousands of demonstrators in the Northern states, some carrying such banners as "No Sharia, no Muslims, no Nigeria," called for a Federal Sharia Court of Appeals to be entrenched in the constitution. A few days later, however, the 90 favoring a separate Sharia system returned to the assembly after: (1) General Olusegun Obasanjo, head of state, threatened to suspend

TABLE 8.1
Population of Nigeria by States, 1963 and 1973 Censuses (in millions)

	1963	1973	(1973)[a]
South			
Lagos	1.44	2.47	1.8
Western	9.49	8.92	11.5
Mid-Western	2.54	3.24	3.2
Rivers	1.54	2.23	1.9
East-Central	7.23	8.06	9.2
South-Eastern	3.62	3.46	4.6
Middle Belt			
Benue-Plateau	4.01	5.17	5.1
Kwara	2.40	4.64	3.0
Far North			
North-West	5.73	8.50	7.3
North-Central	4.10	6.79	5.2
Kano	5.77	10.90	7.3
North-East	7.79	15.38	9.9
	55.66	79.76	70.0

[a]Federal military government estimate of state populations in Nigeria. It served as a basis of budgetary and other allocations and was compiled independently of the 1973 census.

Source: Ian Campbell, "The Nigerian Census: An Essay in Civil-Military Relations," *Journal of Commonwealth and Comparative Politics*, XIV, No. 3 (November 1976), 247.

the program to return to civilian rule in 1979, and (2) a compromise permitted appeals from the state Sharia Courts of Appeals to three judges learned in Muslim law at the Federal Court of Appeals.[4]

In the 1967-75 military government, the Supreme Military Council--consisting of General Gowon, the military state governors, and senior military and police officers--was the highest governing authority. After Gowon was deposed in the 29 July 1975 coup, military governors were dropped from the Supreme Council to a subordinate body, the Council of States. But the Supreme Military Council rarely met, so it was the Federal Executive Council, consisting of appointed civilian heads of administrative departments, and military leaders, that exercised day-to-day authority.

In practice, decisions often were made informally by the head of state, with his closest associates and advisors--senior military officers, senior civil servants, and key permanent secretaries from the ministries--the composition depending upon the issue at hand. The heavy reliance on advice from the public service contrasts with the infrequent consultation under the prewar government.[5]

From 1965 to 1971 the armed forces expanded from 10,500 to approximately 250,000. The ratio of armed personnel to the total population, which at about 1:5,500 in 1965, was lower than the ratios in Sierra Leone (1:2,500), Tanzania (1:1,700), Ghana (1:800), or Zaïre (1:480), but by 1971 was one of the highest in Africa (1:270).

Around 1975, when expenditures on defense were 1.8 percent of gross domestic product in Canada, 2.5 percent in Brazil, 2.9 percent in West Germany, 3.1 percent in France, and 5.1 percent in South Korea, they were 7.6 percent in Nigeria.[6] That economic burden for defense, together with the potential threat of such a large force on the military government or an eventual civilian government, brought pressures for substantial demobilization.

In the last half of 1975, spokesmen for the Mohammed government stated its intention to reduce the army more than 50 percent to some 100,000 soldiers. Anxiety about the distribution of dismissals by rank, branch, and ethnic community was exacerbated by three factors: examinations to reassess officer potential, mass retirement of 216 officers in November 1975, and discontent about the January 1976 promotions.

Weakened morale and career uncertainty contributed to an atmosphere of unrest in which Plateau and southern Zaria junior and middle ranking officers conspired to overthrow the Mohammed government (resulting in the assassination 13 February 1976 of Head of State Mohammed and Military-Governor Colonel Ibrahim Taiwo of Kwara state).

After that, except for modest reductions, the military government kept its 1976 promise to the soldiers of "no outright demobilization."[7] Although the civilian government reduced armed personnel from 213,000 in September 1978 to 120,000 in October 1981, the ratio of armed personnel to the total population was still high (about 1:700). Unfortunately, a civilian government with a large military force is not likely to spend substantial sums for social services, or emphasize the needs of the underprivileged classes.[8]

RELIEF, REHABILITATION, AND RECONSTRUCTION

After mid 1968, food was scarce in several Biafran areas because of the blockade and war destruction. The food crisis continued the first year or so after the war, especially in the East-Central state for several reasons. First, the ravages of war and demands for consumption limited yam and maize seeds available for planting the first half of 1970, so the late 1970 harvest was less than in prewar years. The destruction of war and population displacement had dislocated production, transportation, and distribution. Resources for the distribution of food were limited as soldiers and vehicles could not readily be diverted from the task of maintaining law and order in the aftermath of the war. In light of the disruption and frequent change in administrative agencies, the organizational and planning machinery to distribute food and drugs and to assist the wounded and diseased was insufficient. Finally, because the elite was adequately fed throughout the civil war and early postwar period, the hungry and destitute lacked articulate spokesmen.

Reconstruction of damage was a major item in the Second National Development Plan, 1970-74. The replacement cost of physical assets damaged and destroyed by the war was estimated to exceed ₦600 million (or £N300 million).[9] [In this chapter, figures are reported in the decimal currency used since 1 January 1973, nairas (equivalent to two old Nigerian pounds), which exchanged for $1.52 in January 1973 and March 1982, despite the floating exchange rate.] The major damage was in the war-ravaged areas of the East and Mid-West, with the East-Central state bearing the brunt. Sam Ikoku, then commissioner for economic development and reconstruction in the East-Central state, who declared that ₦400 million was needed to rebuild property in the state, could budget only ₦30 million for that purpose in fiscal 1970/71.

Relief and rehabilitation require large amounts of financial resources and much manpower. Each of the 200,000 depositors of old Nigerian or Biafran currency in former rebel territory received ₦40, but not until May 1970. There were important political limits on mobilizing resources for reconstruction of war-affected areas. Despite offers of massive foreign assistance, resources were lacking in 1970-72, as the federal government, fearing economic and political dependency on developed countries, insisted that reconstruction be primarily a Nigerian effort.

In distributing reconstruction assistance, Nigerian leaders were highly sensitive to charges from loyal elements, especially in the Rivers, South-Eastern, and Mid-Western states, that a major focus on the needs of the East-Central state could be interpreted as rewarding secession. In 1970-72, the National Rehabilitation Commission distributed substantially more per capita to other Eastern states than to the East-Central state, despite devastation and malnutrition being worse there.

IBO REINTEGRATION

The difficult problem of reintegrating the Ibos and other Eastern communities into the national mainstream still was not completed in 1979, even though federal and state authorities contributed to a reconciliation between populations on both sides. Despite the decline in population during the war, the East was still overpopulated in the 1970s--especially in Ibo areas. During the political crises a number of Easterners employed in other regional or federal positions were replaced. Even where they later were rehired, they often lost ground to employees who took their places during the war. Also, much of the vacuum in trade and transport, from the exodus of self-employed Easterners to their communal homelands, was filled by other Nigerians during the war.

Since then discrimination additionally limited the return of Ibo traders and workers to areas outside of Iboland, especially to the neighboring Rivers state. To be sure, the Mohammed government announced, 3 February 1976, a policy of paying a flat compensation for rent arrears to the prewar owners of abandoned property, mostly Ibos, and requiring fair purchase prices by the Rivers and Cross River states.[10] But some Ibos displaced during the civil war were still trying to return to their homes and were having difficulty getting their rights restored in Port Harcourt, under a non-Ibo Rivers state government in late 1978.

The chairman of the Abandoned Property Implementation Panel announced in June 1977 that citizens from Imo and Anambra states (formerly the East-Central state) were to be barred from buying abandoned houses in Port Harcourt.[11] Although "administrative" reasons were given, undoubtably the chairman was influenced by local businessmen, who did not want Ibos to re-establish economic dominance.

Furthermore, an August 1970 military decree gave the federal and state governments power to dismiss civil servants who participated in the Biafran rebellion.[12] In the East-Central state, civil servants past 50 years old were retired because of the large supply from elsewhere, particularly those from the federal government who were replaced during the war, and from the old Eastern Region.

States experiencing shortages however, such as Benue-Plateau, Kano, North-Western, and South-Eastern, offered Ibos appointments as senior civil servants, or state counsels and magistrates.[13] Still because of inadequate economic opportunities for Ibos outside East-Central state, the rates of unemployment and underutilization of Ibo labor, especially educated manpower, was higher in the 1970s than in the prewar period. For many Ibos, reconciliation would never be complete until Ibo soldiers and civil servants were restored to their prewar jobs, notwithstanding Odumegwu Ojukwu's return to Nigeria 18 June 1982 after a presidential pardon.

But there was less bitter recrimination toward Ibos than toward the defeated in many other civil wars. No one "waved the bloody shirt" at the losers, as in the United States Congress during reconstruction (1865-77).

OVERALL ECONOMIC GROWTH

Crude and refined oil flows were quickly restored in the Eastern states after the war, as neither the Biafrans or Nigerians deliberately blew up oilfields, pipelines, or refineries. And Shell-B.P. survey teams and technicians, stationed in federal Nigeria in 1969, were prepared to repair and restore damaged production facilities in the East as soon as the war ended.

Nigeria experienced unprecedented economic growth during the 1970s oil boom. The official estimate of 1978/79 gross domestic product at current prices, subject to a large error, was ₦27,369.7 million (table 8.3). That divided among an estimated population of 80.7 million is ₦339.2 (or about $522) per capita. The official annual real growth in gross domestic product from 1970/71 through 1977/78 was 10.0 percent per annum (at 1974/75 factor costs),[14] compared with 4.3 percent from 1960/61 through 1965/66, and negative from 1965/66 through 1969/70 (table 5.1).

With population growth estimated at 2.5 percent per annum, real GDP per capita grew 7.3 percent per annum during the period, a

TABLE 8.2
Estimated All-Nigerian Gross Domestic Product at Constant (1973) Factor Cost, 1970-76 (₦ millions)

Sector	1970[a]	1971[a]	1972[a]	1973[a]	1974[b]	1975[c]	1976[c]
Agriculture	3262	3433	3183	3123	3331	3212	3290
Petroleum	1002	1414	1673	1899	2190	1593	1938
Other mining & quarrying	48	63	75	90	100	83	63
Manufacturing	448	434	537	591	595	797	890
Construction	296	418	515	646	746	900	1000
Electricity and water	30	36	42	52	59	55	66
Transport & communication	165	202	248	268	313	420	489
General government	361	372	334	463	547	800	900
Health & education	199	224	239	256	308	483	587
Other services	950	1011	1010	1065	1140	1300	1400
Gross domestic product at factor cost	6761	7601	7856	8453	9329	9643	10623
Growth rate of GDP at factor cost		12.4%	3.4%	7.6%	10.4%	3.4%	10.2%
Growth rate of non-oil GDP		7.4%	-.1%	6.0%	8.9%	12.8%	7.9%

[a]Federal Office of Statistics data.

[b]World Bank Mission estimates.

[c]World Bank Mission projections.

Source: World Bank, West Africa Regional Office, *Nigeria: Recent Economic Developments and Short-term Prospects*, Report No. 1690a-UNI, 23 December 1977, p. 30.

Note: See text and note 16.

high rate among developing countries.[15] Table 8.2 includes unofficial estimates of GDP 1970-76, which should be used with caution.[16]

TABLE 8.3
Estimated All-Nigerian Gross Domestic Product at Current Factor Cost, 1977/78-1978/79 (₦ millions)

Sector	1977/78	1978/79
Agriculture	3,167.7	3,292.4
Livestock	556.7	577.6
Forestry	522.1	563.9
Fishing	896.9	955.3
Crude petroleum	6,847.9	5,725.5
Other mining and quarrying	547.5	655.8
Manufacturing	1,441.8	1,750.2
Utilities	96.8	121.6
Construction	2,488.5	2,981.0
Transport	1,268.3	1,320.1
Communication	82.4	98.0
Wholesale and retail trade	5,353.6	5,482.1
Hotel and restaurant	54.8	62.3
Finance and insurance	237.4	270.6
Real estate and business services	100.6	113.6
Housing	1,020.5	1,153.2
Government services	2,075.0	2,246.5
Gross domestic product at factor cost	26,758.5	27,369.7

Source: Nigeria, Office of Statistics, *Economic and Statistical Review, 1978* (Lagos, 1979).

Note: These statistics are not comparable with those in table 8.2 in several ways: (1) The sectoral categories differ. (2) This table uses current rather than constant prices. (3) These are based on the fiscal year (beginning 1 April) rather than the calendar year.

Although reliable series are lacking, Nigeria probably had high urban unemployment and a trend toward wider income inequality in the 1970s. Statistics from the Central Bank on the number of registered unemployed indicated that the unemployment rate increased over that during the 1960s (chapter 5). Sada's series on the distribution of gross income in Nigeria shows rising concentrations of income between 1969/70 and 1971/72. Byerlee's simulation model indicates continually increasing income disparities (or a growing concentration ratio) from 1960 to 1983 (projected).[17]

Nigeria, with an estimated population of 85 million in 1980, had about five times the gross national product (GNP) of the second-ranking country in sub-Saharan black Africa (although six countries in this region had a higher GNP per capita). Nigeria's GNP, according to the World Bank, surpassed that of South Africa in 1978.[18]

INDUSTRIAL DEVELOPMENT

Manufacturing output increased more than 275 percent between 1969 and 1979, continuing the steady growth of the 1960s (table 6.1). During the 1970s, the federal military government instituted policies to reduce the relative size of the foreign industrial sector. Among the political reasons for government actions were: the mixed support of the west for the federal government during the war; the decline of civilian politicians and indigenous high-level personnel who gained from the presence of foreign capitalists; and the enhanced power of the civil servants, intelligentsia, and domestic industrialists, especially from the south, who wanted foreign investment deemphasized. The result of the Nigerian Enterprises Promotion Decrees of 1972 and 1977 was a shift in the manufacturing sector from foreign dominance in ownership in the 1960s (table 2.4) to indigenous domination in the mid and late 1970s, even though some foreigners naturalized, converted equity to debt holdings, or used other loopholes to continue ownership or control.

Schedule I of the February 1972 decree listed twenty-eight industrial and commercial ventures reserved exclusively for Nigerians, including newspaper publishing and printing, radio and television broadcasting, nondepartmental retail trading, rice milling, bottling of soft drinks, hairdressing, and road haulage. The decree indicated twenty-five activities in Schedule II that required Nigerian equity participation of no less than 40 percent. Notable among the Schedule II activities were beer brewing, soap and detergent manufacturing, paper conversion, fish and shrimp trawling and processing, and wholesale distribution. To finance indigenous acquisitions, the government established the Bank for Commerce and Industry, and directed commercial banks to allocate at least 40 percent of their loans to Nigerian businesses.[19] Ironically, an indigenization policy designed partly to reduce foreign concentration created native monopolies and oligopolies, especially among certain privileged bureaucrats, managers, and businessmen with the wealth and influence to obtain finance capital and government loans to purchase shares of foreign enterprises.

In response to indigenous concentration, the January 1977 decree set an upper limit of 5 percent of the shares of an enterprise that any Nigerian could acquire. Nigerian business interests have complained that the wide dispersion of indigenous ownership has continued foreign control of the firms.[20]

The 1977 decree expanded Schedule I (businesses to be owned wholly by Nigerians) to include most service activities, all wholesale distribution of locally manufactured goods, all retail trade (except large supermarket chains), all distribution (except motor vehicles, machinery, and spare parts), and a number of simple industries, such as bakeries and clothing manufacturers. Schedule II, requiring Nigerian equity participation of not less than 60 percent, included banking, insurance, many manufacturing industries (such as plastic products, rubber, and paints), most industries based on local raw materials, and distribution of motor vehicles, technical goods, and imported goods. Schedule III, which requires 40 percent equity participation by Nigerians, encompassed all industries not specified in Schedules I and II, including most highly sophisticated manufacturing industries. But in response to rising food imports and falling foreign reserves, the 1978/79 budget announcement transferred agricultural businesses from Schedule II to Schedule III.[21]

In 1972-76, foreign banks failed to meet the targets the government stipulated in its credit guidelines in April 1972 for loaning to indigenous businesses; Finance Commissioner Dr. A.E. Ekukinam was especially disappointed that the banks emphasized short-term, low-risk ventures such as commerce and import trade rather than agriculture and manufacturing, sectors stressed by the government. As a result, another decree required banks to have at least 60 percent Nigerian ownership and a Nigerian board chairman by late 1976.[22]

CHANGES IN TRADE PATTERNS

The decline of the colonial economic nexus, which began in the late 1950s (table 2.1), continued during military rule, as indicated by exports to the United Kingdom as a percentage of total exports; the percentages went from 69.9 in 1955 to 48.1 in 1960, to 37.7 in 1966, to 8.3 in 1977. Imports from Britain as a percentage of the total likewise decreased--from 46.7 in 1955, to 42.3 in 1960, to 19.7 in 1966, but up slightly to 21.6 percent in 1977.

Nigeria bought more imports from the United Kingdom than from any other country in 1977. But, the leading buyer of Nigeria's exports since 1973, when it first surpassed Britain, has been the United States. In 1977, 42.4 percent of Nigeria's ₦8,673.6 million exports were to the United States, which accounted for five times as much as the second-ranking country, the United Kingdom.

Crude petroleum comprised ₦3,578.2 million, or 98.9 percent, of Nigeria's exports to the United States in 1977. That was 44.9 percent of its total ₦7,969.2 million oil exports in 1977 and six times as much as the next oil buyer, the Netherlands. In that year, 17.2 percent of the U.S.'s crude-petroleum imports were from Nigeria, second only to the 20.6 percent from Saudi Arabia. Still Britain was the largest source of foreign investment in Nigeria, while the United States was the major source of government loans and other foreign aid.[23]

THE PETROLEUM BOOM

Since 1966, the crude-oil mining and prospecting sector has continued to be Nigeria's most rapidly growing sector. The volume of crude petroleum, which grew from 5,000 barrels a day in 1958 to 415,000 barrels a day in 1966, increased over 5 times to 2,256,000 barrels a day in 1974, more than 450 times the 1958 rate. By

1974/75, value added by the petroleum industry (crude oil and natural gas) accounted for 45 percent of Nigeria's gross domestic product (GDP), and 41 percent of its gross national product (i.e., GDP less factor payments made abroad).[24]

The growing strength of the Organisation for Petroleum Exporting Countries (OPEC) was another factor improving Nigeria's revenue position, as the Lagos government imposed OPEC terms on oil companies in January 1967, and became a member of OPEC in July 1971.[25] The steady increase in output, together with quadrupling international oil prices in 1973-74 and subsequent price raises, increased Nigeria's per capita income, government revenue, and import capacity (tables 6.1, 5.9, and 8.4). The federal government increased tax and royalty rates on oil in 1974, and by 1975 acquired majority equity holdings in extracting, refining, and distribution of petroleum products in Nigeria.[26] But two years later, in response to reduced profit margin per barrel for international oil companies, Nigeria granted increased tax credits, drilling allowances, and capital amortization, and reduced royalties and profit taxes.[27]

The favorable balance-of-payments impact of the crude-oil mining and prospecting sector in the 1970s was instrumental in reversing the erosion of Nigeria's external reserve position. The value of crude-oil exports increased from ₦136.2 million in 1965 to ₦261.6 million in 1969, to ₦2,006.0 million in 1973, to ₦7,453.6 million in 1977, and to ₦12,246.9 million in 1980, while the net positive contribution of crude oil to the balance of payments on current and capital account increased from ₦71.2 million in 1965 to ₦106.6 million in 1969, to ₦1,403.2 million in 1973, to ₦6,492.0 million in 1977, and to ₦11,657.0 million in 1980.[28]

Accordingly, the country's external assets grew from ₦77.8 million in 1967 to ₦109.0 million in 1969 to ₦438.4 million in 1973 (a period when restrictions on international trade and exchange were being relaxed) to more than ₦3,000 million in 1974-77 (table 5.8).

GOVERNMENT REVENUE

The rapid growth of petroleum revenue in the 1970s removed much of the severe constraint placed on federal and state budgets in the 1960s (chapter 5). Total federal revenue increased from ₦306.4 million in 1966 to ₦633.2 million in 1970 to ₦4,537.0 million in 1974 to ₦7,791.0 million in 1977, a twenty-five-fold increase in current prices in 11 years. Petroleum revenue as a percentage of the total increased from 26.3 in 1970 to more than 70 in 1974-77 (tables 5.6 and 8.3).[29]

During the civil war, the states faced a revenue crisis (chapter 5). But in the 1970s, the federal government was freed to distribute more to the states, thus strengthening federal power as well as the states' fiscal positions. Statutory appropriations from the federal government to the states/regions, only about ₦128 million in fiscal year, 1965/66, increased to ₦267.6 million in 1970, ₦330.8 million in 1971, and ₦331.0 million in 1972, then decreased to ₦307.2 million in 1973 (as immediate reconstruction needs diminished), then expanded to ₦643.0 million in 1974, and

₦1,040.0 million in 1975 with the oil boom, but dropped to ₦502.2 million in 1976, as the decline in oil revenues in the previous year became evident to Lieutenant General Olusegun Obasanjo, new head of state (see below).

The 1970-75 growth in grants to the states was less rapid than the growth of federal current revenue during the period, which increased more than eightfold from ₦633.2 million to ₦5,514.8 million (table 8.4).[30] In 1978, the federal government, compelled to cut spending for the Third Development Plan, returned much of the financial responsibility for housing and primary education to state and local governments.[31]

TABLE 8.4
Share of Petroleum in Nigeria's Total Federal Revenue: 1970-1978, 1980[a] (₦ millions)

Year	Total federal revenue	Revenue from petroleum[b]	Petroleum revenue as % of total
1969	377.8	78.6	20.8
1970	633.2	166.4	26.3
1971	1,169.0	510.2	43.6
1972	1,404.8	764.4	54.4
1973	1,695.2	1,016.4	60.0
1974	4,537.0	3,726.8	82.1
1975	5,514.8	4,271.6	77.5
1976	6,766.0	5,365.2	79.3
1977	8,042.4	6,080.6	75.6
1978	7,469.3	4,654.1	62.3
1980	15,813.1[c]	13,229.5[c]	83.7

[a]The 1979 figure is omitted, since the official figure is for the fiscal year beginning 1 April 1978, rather than the calendar year.

[b]Components are petroleum profits tax, and mining royalties, rents, fees, etc.

[c]Estimate based on figures for nine months.

Sources: Central Bank of Nigeria, *Economic and Financial Review*, XIII, No. 2 (December 1975), 81; ibid., XIV, No. 3 (December 1976), 77; ibid., XV, No. 2 (December 1977), 79; ibid., XVI, No. 2 (December 1978), 133; and ibid., XVII, No. 2 (December 1979), 88; and Central Bank of Nigeria, *Annual Report and Statement of Accounts for the Year Ended 31st December, 1980* (Lagos, 1981), p. 75.

Despite the improved finances of the states, they depended more on federal revenue in the 1970s than in the 1960s. Before the civil war, a major source of interregional contention was a formula for revenue allocation, especially oil revenue (chapter 4). In the

1960s, a major principle in the distribution of tax revenues to regions/states was derivation, in which each unit had the right to a substantial percentage of taxes levied on its output (e.g., 50 percent of mining rents and royalties, and 100 percent of agricultural exports). In 1973, the commodity export marketing boards, which had been a source of political power for the regions/states, were brought under federal control.[32] Although the federal government rejected the Revenue Allocation Review Committee (Dina) Report in 1969, which recommended a considerable reduction in the derivation principle, it promulgated Decree 13 of 1970, Decree 9 of 1971, and Decree 6 of 1975, all to decrease significantly the reliance of state revenue on that principle.

The 1970 decree achieved more fiscal equalization among the states by decreasing the share of export, import and excise duties, and mining rents and royalties distributed to the state of origin, and increasing the proportion to all states and the federal government. In 1971, the federal government strengthened its position and achieved greater equality among states when it took "all royalties, rents, and other revenues" from offshore oil production.

Decree 6 of 1975 erased all claims for revenue on the basis of derivation except 20 percent of onshore mining rents and royalties to the state of origin, reduced from 45 percent in 1970. The Mid-Western and Rivers states opposed cuts in their share of the royalties on in-state or offshore oil production. But the cuts were made by a stronger, more-centralized federal military government, which pointed to the dependence of the states on federal soldiers to expel the Biafran army during the civil war.[33] However, the Revenue Allocation Bill of February 1981, which proposed that only 2 percent of the revenue from onshore oil production be distributed on the basis of derivation, was declared unconstitutional by the Supreme Court in October 1981.[34]

THE PETROLEUM SLUMP

Despite the euphoria associated with Nigeria's substantial improvement in its international balance on current and capital account from ₦197.6 million in 1973 to ₦3,056.8 million in 1974 (table 5.9), the improvement was short-lived. From 1974 to 1975, oil production declined from 2,256,000 barrels to 1,787,000 barrels a day (table 6.1), primarily owing to weaker international demand from a recession in the industrial countries.[35]

Nigeria remained among the world's six top oil exporters from 1973 through 1980, except for 1978 when it ranked seventh. Its volume of output recovered somewhat to 2,076,000 barrels a day in 1976, and 2,097,000 barrels a day in 1977. But demand for its low-sulphur crude decreased beginning the second half of 1977, largely as a result of oil coming on tap from the North Sea, Alaska, and Mexico.

Nigeria produced only 1,908,000 barrels per day in 1978, expanding from a trough of 1,656,000 barrels a day the first half of the year to 2,160,000 barrels the last half. In 1979, output increased to 2,304,000 barrels a day. Production dropped to 2,070,000 barrels a day in 1980, and 1,430,000 in 1981, as world demand decreased and oil companies reacted to the less favorable participation terms by the Nigerian government. Still Nigeria ranked fourth among the world's oil exporters in both 1980 and 1981, partly as a result of the decline in output in Iran and Iraq during their war.[36]

The positive balances on current account in 1973-75 changed to negative balances in 1976-77, so that the overall surplus balance on current and capital account of ₦183.8 million in 1975 turned into deficits of ₦309.0 million in 1976, and ₦422.4 million in 1977, and more than ₦1 billion in 1978 (table 5.9). Crude-petroleum exports, exceeding 90 percent of exports f.o.b.[37] since 1974, replaced such traditional exports as cocoa, groundnuts, and palm kernels, each of which had exceeded the share of petroleum in exports in 1962 (table 6.2).

A negative balance prevailed during the 1970s on services, especially investment income, freight, insurance, transportation, travel, and government transactions, along with substantial increases in imports of machinery, transport equipment, electrical motors, food, beverages, tobacco, radio and television sets, cars, bicycles, and their parts,[38] for the rapidly growing economy. Consumer luxuries, such as radios, television sets, and automobiles, on which customs duties were reduced 1 April 1974, were a major part of the increased imports. At the end of 1978, external assets declined to ₦1.387.2 million, near the value of imports for two months, which is the liquidity sometimes considered the critical minimum by international bankers.[39]

The drop in oil revenues and rapid increases in the demand for consumer imports, together with Nigeria's large holdings of U.S. dollars, which depreciated against other major international currencies after mid 1977, contributed to the external economic crisis. In response, Nigeria borrowed heavily during 1978-79 from an international banking consortium, enhanced incentives for foreign investment in agricultural business, and increased tariffs, quotas, and bans on more import items, so her external asset position gradually strengthened in 1979-80.

A World Bank mission to Nigeria commented, "At present, petroleum remains a typical enclave industry whose contribution to the economy is limited largely to its contribution to government revenues and foreign exchange earnings."[40] Only about 15 to 20 percent of the petroleum industry's total expenditure on goods and services is spent on locally produced items, which do not include basic requirements of such highly complex equipment as drilling rigs, "production platforms, concrete and steel structures, offshore buoy moorings, sea-bed-completion and underwater-engineering systems, storage tanks, drill pipes and drill collars, pipeline materials and fittings, completion equipment and tubings, casing materials, and a host of other materials and equipment of advanced technology," but on such things as "electric supply, telephone and postal charges, local rents, customs duties, compensation for farm land, [and] grants and subventions."[41]

As the petroleum industry expands, there are few backward linkages generating the expansion of local equipment manufacturers, suppliers, and contractors, or forward linkages stimulating the growth of enterprises that use oil products, such as petrochemicals, as inputs. Multinational corporations have been unwilling to invest in oil-*related* activities in Nigeria and other Afro-Asian oil export countries because of (1) fear of losing their international product market to a state company, (2) apprehension about putting too many eggs into the same basket in countries considered politically uncertain, (3) such activities depending on a well-developed industrial complex, (4) the lack of a large local market for these activities, and (5) insufficient technical and managerial skills in the country.[42]

PLANNING

In March 1975, the *Third National Development Plan, 1975-80*, which envisioned a twelve-fold increase in the annual rate of public capital expenditures over the previous plan period, stated that "there will be no savings and foreign exchange constraints during the Third Plan period and beyond." The document outlined ambitious aims to expand agriculture, industry, transport, housing, water supplies, health facilities, education, rural electrification, community development, and state programs, and substantial funds for "prestige" projects, such as the Second World Festival of Black and African Arts.

Amid the euphoria of the 1974 oil boom, the Federal Ministry of Economic Development approved and added a substantial number of projects for other ministries not supported by proper appraisal of technical feasibility, costs and benefits, or the technical and administrative arrangements required to establish and operate the projects. According to Schatz, an advisor to the Federal Ministry of Transportation in preparing the plan, during 1974:

> Projects involving huge sums were added hastily, with little investigation or appraisal. Issues of project interrelation and coordination were ignored in the belief that rapid economic growth would ensure the utility of whatever was undertaken. Economic reasoning gave way before economic enthusiasm. Problems of executive capacity (the ability to carry out the Plan) were ignored.[43]

But budgetary constraints, resulting from the inflationary Udoji wage hikes after October 1974, discussed below, and the deceleration of growth soon became apparent. In June 1975, several state and local governments did not receive their monthly subventions from the federal government. In several areas, such as Ibadan, just before the 29 July 1975 coup that overthrew Gowon, government workers threatened to impair vital services unless their June wages were paid.[44]

In March 1976, in response to the overheated economy by demands for new programs and higher wages, Obasanjo, head of state, pointed out that petroleum revenue was not a cure-all. "[T]hough this country has great potential she is not yet a rich nation. . . . [O]ur resources from oil are not enough to satisfy the yearnings, aspirations and genuine needs of our people, development and social services."[45]

Many planned projects had to be postponed, scaled down, or cancelled, when projections in 1974-75 proved too optimistic. The criterion for project retention tended to be the administrative convenience or ease of plan fulfillment by the ministries, not ranking by social priority or economic productivity by the Central Planning Office or the Supreme Military Council.

Cutbacks in the plan were costly, especially in education. In the 1977-78 university academic year, the federal government dropped a program of federal loans, bursaries, and scholarships to indigent students. In April 1978 Dr. Jibril Aminu, the executive secretary of the National Universities Commission, announced that the board and lodging fees of students, which had been subsidized the 1977-78 academic year, were to be tripled for the 1978-79 academic year.

Students protesting the changes clashed with police and soldiers at several universities. Seven students and bystanders died in late April in the conflicts at Ahmadu Bello University, Zaria, and the University of Lagos.[46] Each school year, from September 1976 through September 1981, a new class of Primary I entered the universal free primary education system, which continually encountered shortfalls with the heavy demands for new classrooms and teacher training.

INFLATION

A study of twenty African countries by the Central Bank of Nigeria indicates that Nigeria moved from the most price stability, 1963-67, to the third least price stability, 1968-72.[47] World Bank data show that Nigeria, among 42 percent of thirty-six African countries with the lowest annual rate of inflation between 1960 and 1970, was among 14 percent with the highest rate between 1970 and 1978.[48]

Labor was discontented with the Adebo wage increases of 1971, and government employees were pressing for changes in gradings and increased compensation relative to the private sector (chapter 5). Rapid inflation was triggered in December 1974, when Major General Yakubu Gowon, then head of state, under pressure because of corruption among state military governors and delay in the return to civilian government, sought to accommodate high-level civil servants and military officers, by accepting the Udoji Commission recommendations for substantial salary increases for 750,000 civil servants, from 8 to more than 100 percent for government employees paid the minimum salary and high-ranking administrative servants. And the increased salaries were paid retroactive to April 1974, in a lump sum in January 1975.[49] The military also was promised comparable percentage increases, which when awarded in June 1975, made it more difficult to demobilize the armed forces. Labor unrest and work stoppages were widespread in 1975, as some public employees, especially in the middle ranks, protested changes in grading and salary differentials, while workers in the private sector tried to bargain for wage increases comparable to those of government workers.

The scramble for higher pay, together with increased prices of foreign goods, decreased domestic output of food crops,[50] acute port and road congestion, petrol shortages, an ambitious development plan, construction bottlenecks, ineffective price controls, and inadequate reserve requirements for commercial banks[51] resulted in annual double-digit consumer-price increases for both lower-income and middle-income groups in 1974-77. The increases for middle-income groups, the first 10 percent or more since independence, were 17 percent per annum in 1974, 30 percent in 1975, 17 percent in 1976, and 21 percent in 1977. For lower-income groups, the figures, 13 percent in 1974, 34 percent in 1975, 22 percent in 1976, and 22 percent in 1977, were their only double-digit rates since 1960 except for 1969-71 (table 5.3).

LABOR

With the ban on political parties and communal associations during military rule, trade unions posed one of the major potential organized threats to the government, whose decree forbidding strikes since 1969 was repeatedly defied, most notably in 1973, when the federal government gave in to demands by striking postal and telecommunications workers, about one-fifth of the federal civil service. Between 1973 and 1976, the government assumed the power to ban any trade union, prohibited trade unions from affiliating with foreign organizations or receiving foreign contributions, cancelled the registration of the existing central labor organizations, and appointed an administrator to carry out duties these organizations performed. After a 1977 report of a commission of inquiry, eleven trade unionists, including leading radicals, Michael Imoudu, S.U. Bassey, and Wahab Goodluck, were banned from all further union activity. Under terms of the Labour Amendment Decree, August 1978, the more than 1,000 previously existing unions were reorganized into 70 registered industrial unions under the Nigeria Labour Congress (NLC), the sole central labor organization.[52] Although the government consolidated and rationalized the trade union structure, it also suppressed the most effective advocates for higher wages, improved working conditions, and greater control for workers, and, of course, weakened the autonomy of union leadership. In the early 1980s, however, the government found it could no longer control the numerous shop floor bargaining units and the stronger trade unions that had previously held the workers' loyalty. In May 1981, the NLC mobilized 700,000 of 1,000,000 organized Nigerian workers for a two-day general strike, despite the opposition of a government supported faction.[53]

CONCLUSION

Nigeria, potentially the most powerful member of the Organization of African Unity (OAU) and the Economic Community of West African States (ECOWAS), and an important state in the Organisation for Petroleum Exporting Countries (OPEC), has been a prominent voice in consistently opposing both white supremacy in southern Africa and intervention by powerful industrialized nations in black Africa.[54] The country is a major power in Africa, providing military, economic, and diplomatic assistance to friendly governments or movements, and even intervening militarily into the political affairs of neighboring countries.[55] Yet despite its growing regional political power, large population, rapid economic growth, and increasing indigenous control, Nigeria still depends on foreign countries for military supplies and training, oil technology and markets, and even high-level industrial skills. Thus, there are still foreign constraints, even though lessened, on Nigeria's ability to cope with domestic political crises. Furthermore, the slower economic growth, which began in mid 1977 with Nigeria's reduced oil expansion, is likely to continue during much of the 1980s. That could make it more difficult for the government to meet the demands from increased political mobilization. Unfortunately, there are many economic limits to Nigeria's high aspirations. It is not clear whether a government with a large standing army will make the fundamental changes essential to reduce income inequality and political decay.

NOTES

1. Keith Panter-Brick, "Introduction," in *Soldiers and Oil: The Political Transformation of Nigeria*, Keith Panter-Brick, ed. (London: Frank Cass, 1978), pp. 253-6; and Abubakar Yaya Aliyu, "As Seen in Kaduna," ibid., pp. 270-87.

2. Terisa Turner, "Commercial Capitalism and the 1975 Coup," ibid., pp. 166-79.

3. Ian Campbell, "The Nigerian Census: An Essay in Civil Military Relations," *Journal of Commonwealth and Comparative Politics*, XIV, No. 3 (November 1976), 242-54, and Mohammed's charge to the military governors printed in "Nigeria: The Voice of the New Government," *Africa Report*, XX, No. 5 (September-October 1975), 13.

4. "Obasanjo Warning to Assembly Members," *West Africa* (24 April 1978), pp. 776-9, "Nigeria," *West Africa* (1 May 1978), p. 862, and Gregory M. Dennis, "Nigeria: Mohammed-Obasanjo Administration, 1975-1978" (M.Sc. Essay, London School of Economics, October 1978), pp. 21-3.

5. M.J. Dent, "Corrective Government: Military Rule in Perspective," in *Soldiers and Oil*, Panter-Brick, ed., p. 115; and Pauline H. Baker, "The Politics of Nigerian Military Rule," *African Report*, XVI, No. 2 (February 1971), 20.

6. B.J. Dudley, "The Military and Development," *Nigerian Journal of Economic and Social Studies*, XIII, No. 2 (July 1971), 163-74; and Akin Iwayemi, "The Military and the Economy," in *Nigerian Government and Politics under Military Rule, 1966-79*, Oyeleye Oyedirom, ed. (London: Macmillan, 1979), p. 62.

7. Ian Campbell, "Army Reorganisation and Military Withdrawal," in *Soldiers and Oil*, Panter-Brick, ed., pp. 58-100.

8. In May 1977, the Chief of Staff Army Brigadier General Theophilus Danjuma, who commented that more than 90 percent of the Armed Forces' budget was for salaries, noted ironically that "since the civil war the Nigerian Army has been run as a social service." Dennis, "Nigeria: Mohammed-Obasanjo Administration," p. 41.

9. A. Akene Ayida, "Development Objectives," in *Reconstruction and Development in Nigeria*, A.A. Ayida and H.M.A. Onitiri, eds.

(Ibadan: Oxford University Press, 1971), p. 14.

10. See "General Murtala's [Mohammed's] Broadcast to the Nation," *New Nigerian, Special State Issue* (3 February 1976), p. 2.

11. *West Africa,* (20 June 1977), p. 1242, and Keith Panter-Brick, "The Constitution Drafting Committee," in *Soldiers and Oil*, Panter-Brick, ed., p. 347.

12. This power was used selectively. The Nigerians had to rely on former Biafran civil servants for administration, as the Allied occupational forces relied on the defeated enemy to administer Germany and Japan after World War II, and as the United States relied on Confederate civil servants after the civil war.

In late 1974, the federal government announced the release of the last rebel soldiers held since the war. A few former Biafran officers, pardoned then by General Gowon, were integrated into the armed forces. Still the government hesitated to admit former Biafrans to sensitive positions in the armed forces and police. David J. Murray, "Nigeria: The Experience of Military Rule," *Current History*, LXVIII (May 1975), 216.

13. I.I. Ukpong, "Economic Recovery in the Eastern States of Nigeria," *Issue*, V, No. 1 (Spring 1975), 45-53.

14. The use of 1974/75 factor costs overstates the pre-1973 economic growth of Nigeria, a major oil-producing country. Those factor costs put too much weight on the rapidly growing oil sector before international oil prices quadrupled in 1973-74 (chapter 5).

The Office of Stastics' estimate for 1981 GDP at current prices was ₦43,449.0 million, which divided by an estimated population of 85.8 million is ₦506.4 (or about $770) per capita.

15. Central Bank of Nigeria, *Nigeria's Principal Economic and Financial Indicators, 1970-77* (Lagos, 1978), p. 1; Central Bank of Nigeria, *Nigeria's Principal Economic and Financial Indicators, 1970-78* (Lagos, 1979), p. 1, and table 8.2.

16. The Central Bank lacks figures on the contribution to gross domestic product by sector. In contrast, the figures in table 8.2 indicate rough trends in the growth of the relative size of sectors. The exception is petroleum, whose growth is understated after 1973, since weights largely reflect prices before international oil prices quadrupled in 1973-74. See World Bank, West Africa Regional Office, *Nigeria: Recent Economic Developments and Short-term Prospects*, Report No. 1690a-UNI, 23 December 1977, pp. 2-3.

17. See chapter 5 on the movement in the rate of unemployment in the 1960s. On trends in income distribution, see P.O. Sada, "Urbanization and Income Distribution in Nigeria" (Paper presented to a Conference on Income Distribution in Nigeria, University of Lagos, Department of Economics, January-February 1979), and Derek Byerlee, "Indirect Employment and Income Distribution Effects of Agricultural Development Strategies: A Simulation Approach Applied to Nigeria" (African Rural Employment Paper No. 9, Michigan State University, East Lansing, Mich., 1973), pp. 37-8, 71.

18. World Bank, *World Development Report, 1980* (Washington, August 1980), p. 110 and "Nigeria," *Financial Times*, London (2 November 1981).

19. Nigeria, Ministry of Economic Development, *Third National Development Plan, 1975-80*, I (Lagos, 1975), 19-20; Douglas Rimmer,

"Elements of the Political Economy," in *Soldiers and Oil*, Panter-Brick, ed., pp. 157-8; and Ono Osakwe, "Indigenisation: Probing the Irregularities," *African Development*, X, No. 4 (April 1976), 439.

20. Alan Hutchison, "Tensions between Indigenisation and Foreign Investment," *African Development*, X, No. 12 (December 1976), 1283-5.

21. "Nigeria: The Businessman's Guide," *Financial Times* (29 August 1978), p. 35; and Dennis, "Nigeria: Mohammed-Obasanjo Administration," p. 10.

22. Alan Urbach, "What Future for the New Indigenous Banks?" *African Development*, X, No. 12 (December 1976), 1295-6.

23. Central Bank of Nigeria, *Annual Report, 1977*, pp. 78-81; Central Bank of Nigeria, *Economic and Financial Review*, XIV, No. 3 (December 1976), 58; and U.S. Department of Commerce, Bureau of the Census, *U.S. General Imports: Schedule A, Commodity by Country* (Washington, March 1978), pp. 2-87-2-88.

24. Nigeria, *Third Plan*, I, 48, 58. Third Plan estimates for the percentage of value added in the petroleum industry are far in excess of 1974-75 World Bank estimates (table 8.2) based on prices before they were quadrupled in 1973-74.

25. The Nigerian Petroleum Profits Tax Ordinance of January 1967 imposed OPEC terms on oil companies operating in Nigeria. Under the terms, all companies agree to one posted price for exported oil on which profit taxes and petroleum royalties are calculated, and to treat royalties as expenses, not tax offsets, so that the Nigerian government receives additional profit taxes (amounting to 50 percent of the value of the royalties in the late 1960s). The details are in Scott R. Pearson, *Petroleum and the Nigerian Economy* (Stanford, Calif.: Stanford University Press, 1970), pp. 24-9; and L.H. Schätzl, *Petroleum in Nigeria* (Ibadan: Oxford University Press, 1969), pp. 97-8.

26. In 1969, the government had acquired majority holdings in all *new* petroleum concessions in Nigeria. S.A. Madujibeya, "Oil and Nigeria's Economic Development," *African Affairs*, LXXV (July 1976), 288.

27. Turner, "Commercial Capitalism and the 1975 Coup," in *Soldiers and Oil*, Panter-Brick, ed., pp. 179-91; Central Bank of Nigeria, *Annual Report, 1974*, p. 27; and Central Bank of Nigeria, *Annual Report, 1977*, pp. 16, 19.

28. Note that the text in this chapter uses naira, while the tables cited in previous chapters refer to Nigerian pounds.

29. In 1978, the federal government took several measures to decrease its dependence on petroleum taxation. In April 1978, the company tax rate was increased "from 45 percent to 50 percent, an excess profits tax on banks was introduced, a ports development surcharge of 5 percent of the duty on imports was imposed, the airport tax was increased, some highway tolls were introduced, and measures to speed up the payment of some taxes by firms were instituted. In addition, the termination of double taxation agreements with nine countries was announced." Lawrence A. Rupley, "Nigeria's 1979-80 Budget and 1975-79 Import Boom" (Department of Economics, University of Nairobi, Kenya, 1980).

30. Central Bank of Nigeria, *Economic and Financial Review*,

XIII, No. 2 (December 1975), 81; ibid., XV, No. 1 (June 1977), 101; and Adedotun O. Phillips, "Revenue Allocation in Nigeria, 1970-80," *Nigerian Journal of Economic and Social Studies*, XVII, No. 2 (July 1975), 8.

31. Dennis, "Nigeria: Mohammed - Obasanjo Administration," pp. 8-9.

32. Ibid., pp. 25-6.

33. S. Egite Oyovbaire, "The Politics of Revenue Allocation," in *Soldiers and Oil*, Panter-Brick ed., pp. 224-33; M.J. Dent, "Corrective Government: Military Rule in Perspective," ibid., pp. 111, 134; and Phillips, *Nigerian Journal*, XVII, No. 2, 4.

But the Constitution for the Nigerian second republic not only permits the federal legislature to enact laws based on the principle of derivation, but also establishes that principle for certain sources of revenue.

34. "Democracy Survives the Test," *West Africa* (5 January 1981), p. 7; "Opposition Puts its Case," *West Africa* (6 April 1981), p. 727; "Nigeria", ibid., p. 769; and "Revenue Act Vetoed," *Financial Times* (2 November 1981).

35. Terisa Turner, in "The Transfer of Oil Technology and the Nigerian State," *Development and Change*, VII, No. 4 (October 1976), 353-90; "Commercial Capitalism," in *Soldiers and Oil*, Panter-Brick, ed., pp. 179-91; and "Government and Oil in Nigeria: A Study of the Making and Implementation of Petroleum Policy" (Ph.D. dissertation, University of London, 1977), pp. 203-4; contends that the drop also stemmed from a policy dispute between officials of Nigeria's quasi-government oil company (the Nigerian National Oil Corporation, which held equity in oil exploration) and the Ministry of Mines and Power, over the control of oil sales, including the participation of Nigerian middlemen in bidding for government oil. However, this has not been verified by any other source.

36. E. Stanley Turner, "Revenues and Balances," *Petroleum Economist*, XLV, No. 7 (July 1978), 285; "World Oil Production," ibid., p. 311; "World Oil Production," ibid., XLVI, No. 4 (April 1979), 177; "Nigeria," ibid, XLVIII, No. 2 (February 1980), 49-51; "World Oil Production," ibid., XLVIII, No. 2 (February 1980), 88; "World Oil Production, ibid., XLIX, No. 5 (May 1982), 212; and *Standard Chartered Review* (March 1982), p. 38.

Proven reserves are about 16.7 billion barrels, thirty-two years' production at 1981 levels, and twenty years' at 1979 levels. American Petroleum Institute, *Basic Petroleum Data Book*, I, No. 2, *Petroleum Industry Statistics*, (Washington, D.C., 1981), Section II, table 3c, and Section IV, table 3c.

However, "proven" reserves, which do not represent all of Nigeria's petroleum reserves, are not satisfactory for making long run projections, as they are only reserves already located which can be recovered profitably at prevailing cost and price levels. Proven reserves are no more than an assessment of the working inventory of minerals the industry is confident are available.

37. Free on board. Transportation charges are not included.

38. The foreign exchange price of the naira is higher than equilibrium for most sectors of the economy except petroleum. Imports of food, consumer goods, and producer goods are cheaper to Nigerians, and exports to foreigners are more expensive than if the

naira were less dear. Nigeria is more likely to use such protective devices as import duties and quotas, and export subsidies, when the naira is valued highly.

39. Central Bank of Nigeria, *Annual Reports*, 1974-1978; *West Africa* (21 August 1978), p. 1627; and Rupley, "Nigeria's 1979-80 Budget and the 1975-79 Import Boom."

40. World Bank, *Nigeria: Options for Long-term Development* (Baltimore: John Hopkins University Press, 1974), p. 70.

41. S.A. Madujibeya, "Oil and Nigeria's Economic Development," *African Affairs*, LXXV (July, 1976), 291-316.

42. Ibid., and Turner, *Development and Change*, VII, No. 4, 355.

43. Sayre P. Schatz, *Nigerian Capitalism* (Berkeley, Calif.: University of California Press, 1977), p. 47.

44. Nigeria, *Third National Development Plan*, and Guy Arnold, *Modern Nigeria* (London: Longman, 1977), p. 116.

The National Electric Power Authority (NEPA) staff, which had grievances against their management, offered government an ultimatum: make reforms and remove NEPA's chairman, or the flow of electricity to Lagos, the capital, would be cut. After 24 hours of blackout, the chairman was removed. Turner, "Commercial Capitalism and the 1975 Coup," in *Soldiers and Oil*, Panter-Brick, ed., p. 186.

45. Alan Rake, "And Now the Struggle for Real Development," *African Development*, X, No. 12 (December 1976), 1263.

46. *West Africa* (28 March 1977), p. 633, (14 November 1977), p. 2291, (28 November 1977), p. 2425, (10 April 1978), p. 695, (17 April 1978), p. 766, and (1 May 1978), p. 833; and Nigeria, Cabinet Office, *Government Views on the Report of the Commission of Inquiry into the Nigerian Universities Crisis, 1978* (Lagos, 24 August 1978). The Commission of Inquiry criticized the National Universities Commission for announcing the increased fees, rather than leaving the responsibility to each vice-chancellor and his university council, and for failing to obtain the formal approval of the federal commissioner for education.

For another view, see Ladun Anise, "Confrontation Politics and Crisis Management; Nigerian University Students and Public Policy--A Social Commentary," *Issue*, IX, Nos. 1 & 2 (Spring/Summer 1979), 73-82.

47. Central Bank of Nigeria, "Origins and Development of Inflationary Trends in African Countries (Impact on Their Growth)," *Economic and Financial Review*, XII, No. 2 (December 1974), 30-1.

48. World Bank, *World Development Report, 1980* (Washington, August 1980), pp. 110-11.

49. The Gowon government implemented the pay increases, while rejecting the recommendations of the Public Service Review (Udoji) Commission concerning the introduction of increases in a phased two-year sequence, and the adoption of comprehensive administrative reform.

50. According to M.O. Ojo, "Food Supply in Nigeria, 1960-1975," in Central Bank of Nigeria, *Economic and Financial Review*, XV, No. 1 (June 1977), food production dropped by 13 percent from 1970 to 1974, while food imports increased 33 percent over the same period, and an additional 36 percent between 1974 and 1975.

51. Ian Campbell, "Army Reorganisation and Military Withdrawal," in *Soldiers and Oil*, Panter-Brick, ed., pp. 69-77; "Details of Forces Pay," *West Africa* (30 June 1975), p. 765; and Nigeria, Ministry of Information, *First Report on the Anti-Inflation Task Force* (Onitiri Report), (Lagos, October 1975).

52. Arnold, *Modern Nigeria*, pp. 117-9; M.J. Dent, "Corrective Government: Military Rule in Perspective," in *Soldiers and Oil*, Panter-Brick, ed., p. 128; Central Bank of Nigeria, *Annual Report, 1975*, p. 45; Central Bank, *Annual Report, 1976*, pp. 28-9; Central Bank, *Annual Report, 1977*, pp. 27-8; and *West Africa* (4 September 1978), p. 1762.

53. "Unions," *Financial Times* (29 September 1980), pp. xxi-xxii, and Dafe Otobo, "The Nigerian General Strike of 1981," *Review of African Political Economy* (October-December 1981), pp. 65-81.

54. General Olusegun Obasanjo, head of state, indicated in a speech 27 July 1978, "Let me at the outset reiterate Nigeria's position on the question of external intervention in the affairs of any sovereign nation. We condemn all such interventions without reservations." The speech is in "External Intervention in Africa: The View from Africa," *Survival*, XX, No. 6 (November/December 1978), 268-9.

Nigeria's forceful stance against white minority governments in southern Africa was partly influenced by those governments' support for Biafra during the civil war. Olajide Aluko, "Nigeria and the Superpowers," *Millennium*, V, No. 2 (1976), 135.

55. In the mid and late 1970s, Nigeria became increasingly active diplomatically and militarily to provide leadership for Africa, and to protect vital international interests, including support for liberation movements and black majority governments in southern Africa. During the Angolan civil war, Nigeria forcefully backed the Popular Movement for the Liberation of Angola (M.P.L.A.), while the United States was assisting the Front for the National Liberation of Angola (F.N.L.A.). General Mohammed, then head of the federal military government attacked U.S. opposition to the M.P.L.A. at an extraordinary summit of the OAU 11 January 1976. Nevertheless, Nigerian diplomats frequently provided an avenue for contact between western powers and southern African liberation movements. Moreover, in the late 1970s and early 1980s, Nigeria even threatened to reduce oil exports or deny oil drilling rights to countries that support governments in Africa dominated by a white minority.

Nigeria perceived that its security depended on minimizing conflicts within or between neighboring states. During the decade of the 1970s, Nigeria acted as a mediator between Angola and Zaïre, Ethiopia and Somalia, Uganda and Tanzania, and in the Western Sahara conflict.

Nigeria provided relief grants to states affected during the 1974 Sahelian drought, and since then small grants and interest-free loans to Benin, Niger, and Togo. The country participated in the Special Fund for African Oil Importers, the Arab-African Oil Assistance Fund, and the Islamic Development Fund, and granted an $80 million interest-free loan to the African Solidarity Fund with the African Development Bank. With other oil countries, it made substantial "oil surplus contributions" to the International Monetary Fund, World Bank, and African Development Bank. Nigeria defied OPEC restrictions to supply crude oil to other West African states at concessionary prices. It played a major role in the negotiations of the Caribbean, African and Pacific countries with the European Economic Community resulting in the Lomé Convention on January 1975. Finally, in part due to Nigerian leadership, fifteen West African states met in Lagos 28 May 1975 to sign the ECOWAS treaty, which provides for eventual free movement of population and goods within the community. Edith Penrose, "Africa and the Oil Revolution: An Introduction," *African Affairs*, LXXV (July 1976), 277-83; James Mayall, "Oil and Nigerian Foreign Policy," ibid., 317-30; Olajide Aluko, "Oil at Concessionary Prices for Africa: A Case Study in Nigerian Decision Making," *African Affairs*, LXXV (October 1976), 425-43; Arnold, *Modern Nigeria*, pp. 138-42, and Olajide Aluko, "The 'New' Nigerian Foreign Policy: Developments Since the Downfall of General Gowon," *The Round Table* (October 1976), pp. 405-14.

9 Internal Political Instability in the Third World: A Comparison with Pakistan

The political economy approach views the probability of civil war as partly a function of internal economic factors--class conflict, economic discontent, regional and communal economic rivalries, and domestic economic policy--all of which are partially influenced by transnational variables. This approach, used earlier to explain the origin of the Nigerian-Biafran war, is used here to explain the secessionist conflict in Pakistan in March-December 1971.

THE BANGLADESH SECESSION FROM PAKISTAN IN 1971

The Differential Impact of Colonialism

As discussed in chapter 1, in the decades before World War I, when Britain occupied the central position in the international capitalist system her colonies became integrated into the system as economic satellites specializing in primary products. The impact of British rule differed substantially among regions in India (which before independence in 1947 included present-day Pakistan and Bangladesh). As in southern Nigeria, British political, economic, and educational institutions intruded the coastal areas of Bengal earlier and more substantially than farther inland.

Bengal, most of which became East Pakistan in 1947, had become an important administrative and trading center after the British East Indian Company gained a foothold there in the late seventeenth century. Bengal acquired legislative institutions in 1861, and Punjab, the largest West Pakistani province, in 1897.

Like Northern Nigeria, British suzerainty was exercised in parts of West Pakistan through "indirect rule," an arrangement advantageous to both the colonial power and the native princes. Britain economized on officers and used local systems to collect taxes and maintain order, while the traditional rulers, under British hegemony, secured their positions by eliminating important sources of resistance. These rulers impeded nationalism and indigenous capitalism, and their preserving traditional systems of land tenure strengthened the concentration of land holdings among Indian zamindars, as among Nigerian emirs. Princely states that joined Pakistan maintained a semi-independent status long after 1947.

Communal and Regional Conflict

British colonial policy frequently increased differences of class, caste, and community among the people they colonized. In India, where conflict and competition between Hindu and Muslim led ultimately to partition and the creation of Pakistan, the British helped develop separate legal, political, and social institutions for different religious, caste, and ethnic communities, especially when they demonstrated loyalty to the colonial rulers.

The army was recruited among Muslims from (then) northwestern India, but it excluded Bengalis. That policy, after independence, led to a Pakistani military with a highly disproportionate representation of Westerners, who were disdainful of their Bengali countrymen.

By protecting loyal communities, such as the Muslims in India, and regional elites, such as the Northern traditional aristocracy in Nigeria, the colonial power impeded integration. In both India and Nigeria, creating new administrative units led to the evolution of new communal identities, and strengthened and politicized old ones. Migration under colonial aegis brought groups into competition with each other. Thus, Punjabis reacted adversely to Bengali officials of the colonial government, as Northern Nigerians did to the influx of Ibo workers.

Nationalism

In Pakistan, the overriding salience of Hindu-Muslim conflict overshadowed and even precluded development of other ethnic cleavages until after independence. Thus, Bengali Muslims, dominated by Hindu landlords and moneylenders, identified with the All-India Muslim League, organized to oppose control of the Indian National Congress by Hindu professionals and intellectuals.

The dominant cultural group in Pakistan--the Urdu-speaking immigrants from North India--displayed little respect for the language or culture of the majority Bengalis until political pressure compelled them to after nearly half a decade of independence. The revival of Bengali nationalism in the 1950s, 1960s, and early 1970s parallels Yoruba and Hausa-Fulani nationalisms in Nigeria (chapter 1), which were aroused in response to insufficient representation in larger nationalist movements.

Patterns and Processes of Decolonization

Former ruling powers, by the manner in which they leave, may affect the polities and economies of their colonial possessions long after they leave. Partition and federalism helped the British retain influence in their former colonies of India and Nigeria.

Partition left Pakistan, created from India's economic periphery, with few major industrial or urban economic centers. Traditional commercial patterns between the jute-growing areas of East Bengal and the major jute-processing center of Calcutta were broken. Trade with India dropped from more than 65 percent of Pakistan's total foreign trade in 1948-49 to about 3 percent in 1951, and did not rise above 6 percent any year in the 1950s.[1] A large portion of the class that had been associated with commerce and the embryonic beginnings of manufacturing was lost to India. The vacuum was filled by a new class of Muslim industrial capitalists, whose power and influence grew during succeeding years.

Federalism, both in Pakistan and Nigeria, was designed to prevent national domination by a popular majority, but in practice it facilitated regionalization of political support and ultimately domination by an elite from communities representing a minority of the population. The federal structures both countries received were extremely fragile, as changes that occurred in subsequent years demonstrated.[2]

Political organization that served as prime vehicles for nationalist movements in the 1940s, the Muslim League in Pakistan and the National Council of Nigerian Citizens (N.C.N.C.), increasingly lost ground to more regionally oriented political parties as sub-national consciousness rose in the 1950s. The League, which had secured Pakistan's independence, lost heavily in the 1954 provincial elections in the East to the newly formed Awami League. Contradictions arose when the security of one regional elite was threatened by the growing strength of another. In Pakistan, just as in Nigeria (chapter 1), the contradictions contributed heavily to political violence.

Another legacy of British rule enhanced by the methods of decolonization was an efficient and professional military establishment generally isolated from, and antagonistic toward, popular political movements. In both Nigeria and Pakistan, British commanding officers were retained well after independence. Each country experienced military intervention shortly after the British commanding officer departed.

In Pakistan, the military stepped in to forestall a threatened loss of power by the West to the East in the elections of 1958, and in 1969 to restore order after riots in both wings of Pakistan. Establishing martial law in 1958 consolidated domination of the predominantly West Pakistani industrial and commercial capitalists, civil servants, army officers, and technocrats.[3]

Though the evidence presented does not support the theory that nations as diverse as Pakistan and Nigeria were doomed from their inception, it reveals that British colonial rule has had an extensive and varied impact upon regional identities and interests, class structure, political parties, and successive governmental structures in independent Pakistan and Nigeria.

Transnational Economic Linkages after Independence

Colonial policy, which discouraged industrial growth, integrated the poor economies into the world capitalist system, and helped to support an indigenous elite oriented toward cooperating with rich capitalist countries, facilitated Pakistan's and Nigeria's dependent economic relationships after independence. Although Pakistan extricated itself from the British colonial economic nexus to a greater extent than Nigeria, instead of cutting its dependency on the west, it largely replaced British with American domination.

Pakistani political leaders negotiated a long-term military and economic aid pact with the U.S. in 1954. The continuing U.S. political, military, and economic assistance, which provided resources and support to perpetuate the West Pakistani ruling group, kept the country open to foreign investment and trade and allied with the western, capitalist world.

The ties cost the Pakistani population dearly by influencing the balance of internal political forces, affecting the shape of the class structure, making available additional means of repression against dissidents, and ultimately contributing to increased political instability. In Nigeria, British private capital, together with aid programs, cemented the pro-British sympathy of the Northern-dominated civilian government. But the Northern ruling aristocracy's supremacy exacerbated the unrest of the southern proletariat and bourgeoisie.

By the period after World War II, the international division of labor had shifted, and some underdeveloped economies began specializing in light manufactured goods in addition to primary products. In 1969/70 in Pakistan, 55.7 percent of exports and 55.0 percent of imports were secondary goods (chemicals, machinery, transport, equipment, and manufactured goods), compared with 2.7 percent of exports and 86.9 percent of imports in 1954/55. Yet most of Pakistan's secondary exports in 1969/70 involved processing raw materials or light manufactures; for example, 40.4 percent of exports were jute, cotton, or leather goods.[4] On the other hand, Nigeria still retained a colonial-type trade pattern in 1965 (see chapter 2).

After World War II, trade with the U.S. in both countries expanded at Britain's expense. Still the U.K. was Nigeria's major trading partner by far in 1965. At about the same time, the largest share of Pakistan's imports (for example, 38.6 percent in 1964/65) was from the U.S.[5]

Both Pakistan and Nigeria depended highly on patron nations for external financing; however, the chief form of the financing in Pakistan was loans, investment, and aid from the U.S. government, in contrast to private capital flows from the U.K. to Nigeria.

The United States provided 64.3 percent of the grants, and 42.7 percent of total assistance (grants and loans) to Pakistan from 1951 through 1971. An aid consortium of rich capitalist countries contributed 93 percent of total assistance to Pakistan from 1951 to 1971. In 1969/70, Pakistan received Rs. 3.100 billion in foreign grants and loans, compared with a balance-of-trade deficit of Rs. 2.690 billion (from exports of goods and services of Rs. 4.350 billion).

Debt service obligations (virtually all of which were owed to the consortium) as a percentage of foreign exchange earnings increased from 3.6 in 1960/61 to 9.9 in 1964/65 to 25.3 in 1970/71.[6]

Development plans and strategies, dependent on foreign aid for a large percentage of projects, were submitted to the consortium, which frequently insisted on changes before committing funds.[7] The U.S., for example, with a contribution of 18.6 percent of the total amount of Pakistani development projects in 1966, could control most of the projects because technical and financial assistance was distributed over many government projects.[8]

The overriding influence of the U.S. in the Pakistani economy distorted its economic development, and took away potential gains in government policy and technical project development that the indigenes could have received from the learning experience. Foreign aid gave a major impetus to the emerging industrial capitalist elite (disproportionately migrants from India at the time of partition), allied with and overlapping with large landowners, top civil servants, and army officers in the Punjab.

The severance of Pakistan from the more industrialized parts of India and the flight of the previously dominant Hindu mercantile community at the time of partition gave further impetus to the new manufacturing and commercial entrepreneurs of Pakistan. The coalition of the business classes with the older elite was maintained only with large injections of military, economic, and technical aid in the 1950s and early 1960s, and the concomitant rapid economic, especially industrial, growth.[9] The support provided enough patronage, perquisites, and resources to satisfy the various economic interests in the coalition, and gave them sufficient access to a range of sanctions and rewards to consolidate control and to prevent restiveness among the lower elites.

Foreign assistance, primarily from the U.S., then helped create a new capitalist elite who, in coalition with other conservative forces, gave little emphasis to improving the level of living of the masses. As indicated later in this chapter, Pakistan's rapid growth in the first two decades of independence was accompanied by a decline in real wages and food grains per capita.

U.S. assistance allowed the U.S. a role in shaping the forces that contributed to the rising Pakistani elite, whose interest was in harmony with U.S. economic and political hegemony in Asia. The military support, which accounted for approximately one-fourth of U.S. aid to Pakistan since its independence, let the governing elite maintain power despite their neglecting the population at large.[10]

The existence of the coalition depended on continued military and economic support from the U.S., which decreased sharply after the Indo-Pakistan War of 1965, when Pakistan's debt servicing ratio was increasing. Total U.S. assistance declined from $964.280 million in the Second Five-year Plan (1960-65) to $668.799 million in the Third Five-year Plan (1965-70), while grants decreased even more drastically.[11]

The decline in foreign help for the coalition of elites meant that some elements in the alliance had to be suppressed. Support being withdrawn by the landed elite threatened the power of the capitalist class, who then could not overcome the landowners and their military allies.[12]

Western countries, especially Britain before 1966, assumed a dominant role in Nigeria's international trade, external finance, and industrial investment. Britain's policy toward Nigeria through its political crises of the 1960s was consistent with support for an economically integrated area that would leave the federation open to foreign trade and investment. This policy favored a united

Nigeria (chapter 2) and helped prevent a peaceful division of the country. Likewise U.S. military and economic support of the ruling coalition of West Pakistanis increased the probability of civil war in Pakistan.

Class Conflict and Economic Discontent

The strength and position of broad socioeconomic groupings in society, conditioned by colonial and neo-colonial political and economic factors, constitute important background factors in considering internal war. In Pakistan, landlords, zamindars, traders, lawyers, and other professionals were formed into part of the elite in the West in the half century before independence by their leadership in the Muslim nationalist movement in India (through the Muslim League).

After independence they were joined by an emerging class of Muslim industrial and merchant capitalists, the essentially newly created civil service, army officers, and white-collar workers. Competition among elements of the landed, industrial, and bureaucratic elite for state power and for economic benefits during decelerating economic growth in the late 1960s, and the higher aspirations of those not yet a part of the elite, contributed to the subsequent disintegration of Pakistan.

In West Pakistan, where the top 0.1 percent and bottom 64.5 percent of the landowners each owned 15.0 percent of the agricultural land in 1960 (Gini index of inequality = 0.81, compared with 0.68 for the East; table 9.1), large landlords have been the dominant social group since the early British period. At least 200 of the 310 members of the 1955 interim West Pakistan assembly came from the "landed interests."

In the East, in contrast, landowners were limited to a ceiling of 33 acres each as a result of land reform legislation passed in the 1950s, which took land from Hindu rajas, who had held 75 percent of the land.[13]

At independence, when more than half of the manufacturing sector was controlled by Hindus, the government, or foreigners, barely 1 percent of national income originated in manufacturing. By 1959 when the percentage had risen to over 6, Muslims indigenous to the Indo-Pakistani sub-continent controlled two-thirds of the sector.[14] Industrial elites, with allies in the bureaucracy, used the levers of state economic policy and planning to give their enterprises privileged protection from foreign competition, ready access to licenses for foreign exchange and domestic inputs at less than market price, and subsidies or tax concessions.

In the East, the petty bourgeoisie, who constituted the top of the class hierarchy, directed their discontent against the dominant feudal and business elite in the West, who feared that a major bourgeois class allowed to establish itself in East Pakistan, with a majority of the country's population, would give it the political and economic strength to become the dominant force in national politics.

In 1956-57, with the Prime Minister H.S. Suhrawardy, founder of the Awami League, based in the East, the government awarded more import licenses to newcomers (particularly from the East),

TABLE 9.1
Distribution of Pakistani Farms by Size

Size of farms (acres)	West Pakistan, 1960		East Pakistan, 1960	
	Percentage of farms	Percentage of farm area	Percentage of farms	Percentage of farm area
Under 5	64.5	15.0	77.9	42.6
5 to under 25	28.5	31.7	21.7	52.6
25 and over	6.9	53.3	0.4	4.8
Total	99.9[a]	100.0	100.0	100.0

[a]Column may not add up to 100.0 percent because of rounding.

Sources: Pakistan, *Agricultural Census, 1960* (Islamabad, 1961), and Pakistan, *Report of the Land Reforms Commission, 1960* (Islamabad, 1960).

distributed U.S. aid for modernizing industry disproportionately to the East, gave the East parity with the West in allocating foreign exchange, and proposed to establish a public shipping corporation for coastal trade between the wings to compete with private shippers in the West.

The vehement reaction by the coalition of landed and business interests in the West encouraged President Iskander Mirza to compel Suhrawardy to resign. Then Mirza cancelled most of the measures that benefited aspiring business groups in the East.[15] From the viewpoint of major Bengali interests, the class struggle became increasingly identified as a regional struggle against the supremacy of the Western wing.

A major source of discontent in Pakistan, as in Nigeria, was younger members of the educated classes. Just after 1947 in Pakistan, as in the 1950s and 1960s in Nigeria, many top positions in the government, military, police, and universities were rapidly indigenized. But by the late 1950s there were only a few vacancies in Pakistan, because indigenization was virtually complete and those who had been only recently recruited were still relatively young.

Younger men, especially in East Pakistan (and southern Nigeria), became frustrated with the abrupt decline in openings. The substantial unrest among students, who perceived themselves as a part of a future elite and at times an alternative present elite, stemmed in part from frustration over the sharp decline in high-level employment. The military in both countries suffered frustrations.

One root of the aborted Rawalpindi conspiracy to overthrow the Pakistan civilian government in 1951 was considerable unrest among middle level officers caused by slow promotions and high expections after their predecessors' swift promotions to high ranks. A drop in openings and promotions was a prime factor for the low morale in the army before the Nigerian majors' revolt in January 1966. By the 1960s, the scramble for the few remaining posts in both countries was intense, and regional competition for them contributed to the enmity and bitterness that helped ignite the civil wars.

Labor was relatively weak and disorganized in Pakistan (as in Nigeria) between 1950 and 1971, as only a fraction of the economically active population was in wage-paid employment. In Pakistan, the nonagricultural labor force constituted 8 percent of the economically active population in 1961. In the 1950s and 1960s the labor movement in Pakistan, as in Nigeria, was fragmented into hundreds of trade unions and into several feuding, ideologically divided labor federations.[16]

Worker discontent in both Pakistan and Nigeria resulted from a growing awareness of the substantial income gap between blue-collar workers, and white-collar workers and entrepreneurs. A distinct feature of Pakistan's Planning Commission's strategy, supported by official and foreign economists, was consciously promoting income inequality, to achieve high domestic savings and economic growth.

Concentrating income and wealth in high-income groups was a key ingredient designing government policies on taxes, subsidies, licenses, and foreign exchange to redistribute resources from agriculture to industry and from East to West Pakistan. In the 15 years before 1967, when that strategy was promoted, real wages in industry declined at least 25 percent, while real per capita gross income of the country increased by 21 percent. Even in 1962/63, per capita income of the average wage-earner's family was only about 73 percent of regional per capita income in East Pakistan, and 54 percent in West Pakistan.[17]

Pakistan's political parties and independent trade unions were suppressed during the late 1950s and early 1960s, so the most politically mobilized segment of the population was the students, who formed the vanguard of the revolts. They were later joined by workers, against the rule of General Ayub Khan in the 1960s.[18] After 1966, however, Pakistani labor was mobilized in both wings as discrepancies between their static or declining real wages and the increasing wealth of the industrial and commercial elites became more obvious. The workers, by direct action, won wage increases and participated in toppling the Ayub regime.

The demands of labor in West Pakistan, directed against the Ayub government, remained essentially based on class. In East Pakistan, however, labor discontent also was channeled into supporting regional autonomy. In turn, workers entering the fray further radicalized the student activities and increased violence in the East.

Development Planning and Economic Policy

The Pakistani government pursued projects and policies primarily oriented to a "modernizing" elite--the capitalist and bureaucratic classes--and their allies among the princes and landlords. Planning and implementing were hampered in Pakistan, as in Nigeria, by the elites attempting to retain control of the benefits distributed by government.

In Nigeria the earliest national plans, between 1946 and independence, and the First National Development Plan after independence (1962-68) were drawn up primarily by foreign economists. After the lack of planning machinery thwarted Pakistan's Six-year Development Programme (1951-57), planning commissions of the next three schemes (1955-70) relied heavily on foreign advisors.[19]

Pakistan's development policies, influenced substantially by U.S. economists and government funds, emphasized dismantling controls that hamper the private sector: government investment in "pioneer" ventures with subsequent "disinvestment" in favor of private enterprise when the ventures showed prospects for profits; low tax rates at high-income levels (to encourage private investment and innovation); high financial pay-offs from directly productive investments (as opposed to investments in education, health, and social welfare); a conservative financial policy; and an economy open to trade, aid, and investment from abroad. The lack of coordination between the planning units, dominated by foreigners, and the government officials, was a dominant reason for the projects often not being implemented.[20]

Waterston indicates that the major weaknesses of Pakistani planning between independence and civil war were insufficient project analysis, excessive political intervention, lack of emphasis on the agricultural sector, inadequate attention to implementing projects, ineffectiveness and inactivity at regional and local levels, and the planning units' lack of authority relative to the ministries' authority.[21] The 1955-70 Pakistani plans, just as Nigeria's First National Plan, encountered major shortages in expenditures because feasible projects were not clearly identified and supporting government policies were not detailed. The major explanations for the ineffectiveness of planning in Pakistan are similar to those for Nigeria's planning weaknesses, discussed in chapter 3. In Pakistan, as in Nigeria, a centralized program to foster economic development among the masses would have threatened the interests of the West Pakistani ruling elite, and monopoly returns of the businessmen influential in government.

One widely held prescription for increasing the rate of economic development and modernization, and at the same time enhancing the elite's profits or patronage, has been transferring resources from the agricultural to the industrial sector. In Pakistan that transfer coincided with, and was an integral part of, a redistribution of income from the poor to the rich, and from East to West Pakistan.

Because the emerging capitalists were financially weak at independence, rapid industrialization could not be attained in a free, competitive market without massive governmental assistance. Direct controls were needed to indigenize and modernize the country through industrialization, and to ensure that industrialists took the leadership positions of the economy. Foreign exchange policy, together with the compulsory government procurement of food grains at low prices for urban areas, and the generous tax concessions to industry but not to peasant agriculture, compelled the transfer of savings from agriculture to industry, especially during the first decade of independence.

Conservative estimates based on world prices indicate that more than 24 percent of gross product originating in the agricultural sector--or about 70 percent of its savings--was transferred to the nonagricultural sector in 1964-65. Perhaps as much as 75 percent of this transfer was used to increase urban consumption. Resources were transferred from farming throughout the 15 years, 1950-1965, when real rural income per capita was declining.[22]

In Pakistan, as in Nigeria, as workers and peasants became increasingly aware of how economic policy was being used on behalf of the indigenous governing elite, discontent with the political leadership intensified.

Regional Economic Competition and Conflict

In Pakistan, Muslim nationalism helped divert attention from how the upper classes were using the state at the expense of the population as a whole. Rapid economic growth and modernization in the Punjab concealed the deteriorating economic position of the Punjabi workers and small farmers.

Even though the number of key ethnic communities and the relative distribution of political and economic advantages in Pakistan differed from those in Nigeria, in both cases competition for economic and political power became increasingly regionalized after independence.

In Pakistan, competition was frequently viewed as between the Eastern and Western wings, especially after the West consolidated into a single province in 1955. While the provincial "parity" ostensibly balanced the power of the two wings, in practice it meant that the East (with 55 percent of the population) was effectively neutralized so the Western Pakistani elite retained political and economic supremacy.

West Pakistanis owned about half the assets in large-scale manufacturing and dominated import trade in East Bengal.[23] The resentment of East Pakistan stemmed partly from its failure to share the economic fruits of independence and modernization. The hopes of Bengalis, stirred by the fall of Ayub in 1969 and the 1970 elections, were thwarted by maneuvers of Western political leaders and the military. While the grievances of the East Pakistanis arose from their poor economic position in the country, East Nigerians' discontent resulted from attempts to maintain a relatively high economic status in the Nigerian federation.[24]

In Pakistan, the average material level of living probably was higher in the West than in the East at independence, a disparity that increased over time. In 1949/50, GDP per capita, according to official sources, was 17 percent higher in the West than in the East, and it increased to 32 percent higher in 1959/60, and to 70 percent in 1969/70. For the West, this represented a real growth in GDP per capita of 0.7 percent per annum in the decade, 1949/50-1959/60, at the same time that real growth was declining in the East 0.5 percent per annum. In the next decade, 1959/60-1969/70, real GDP per capita grew 1.4 percent per annum in the East, and 4.1 percent in the West (table 9.2).[25]

TABLE 9.2
Per Capita Gross Provincial Product at 1959/60 Factor Cost in West and East Pakistan (in rupees)

Fiscal year	West	East	West/ East ratio
1949/50	342	293	1.17
1954/55	354	290	1.22
1959/60	366	278	1.32
1964/65	443	301	1.47
1969/70	546	321	1.70

Source: Kalyan Dutt, Ranajit Dasgupta, and Anil Chatterjee, *Bangladesh Economy: An Analytical Study* (New Delhi: People's Publishing House, 1973), p. 50.

East Pakistan, like Eastern Nigeria and Katanga, resented the low proportion of foreign exchange it could use in relation to what it generated. The East Pakistani demand for decentralization increased because of its strong prospective budgetary[26] and international-payments position, and its desire to shed the burden of having foreign exchange diverted to the West.

As indicated in table 9.3, between 1949/50 and 1969/70 East Pakistan's balance-of-trade position (with exports primarily of raw jute, jute goods, and tea) was stronger than that of the West, which received about 70 percent of Pakistan's foreign exchange. The rupee's being overvalued in international exchange effected a resource transfer from East to West. The East, as a price taker on its exports, received less local currency than at an equilibrium exchange rate and still bought manufactured goods at prices inflated by high tariffs.

On the other hand, the allocation of scarce import licenses meant substantial subsidies to West Pakistanis, who earned large profits, which facilitated their dominance in import trade and large-scale manufacturing in the East. In addition, throughout most of the 1960s, an export tax on raw jute and an export subsidy on jute manufacturers transferred income from Bengali small-holders of jute land to the powerful West Pakistani jute-textile capitalists.[27] Additionally, the artificially low foreign-exchange prices encouraged increases in the West's dollar imports of capital goods and industrial inputs, which exacerbated Pakistan's balance-of-payments problems.

In 1959/60, 58.6 percent of Pakistan's exports were from the East, compared with only 26.6 percent of the imports; in 1964/65, the corresponding figures were 52.7 and 31.7 percent, and even in

TABLE 9.3
Balance of Foreign Trade, East Pakistan and West Pakistan (millions of rupees)

Year	East Pakistan			West Pakistan		
	Exports[a]	Imports	Balance of Trade	Exports[a]	Imports	Balance of Trade
1959/60	1,079.6	655.3	424.3	763.1	1,805.7	-1,042.6
1964/65	1,268.1	1,701.8	-433.7	1,139.6	3,672.4	-2,532.8
1968/69	1,542.7	1,850.0	-307.3	1,762.7	3,046.6	-1,283.9
1969/70	1,670.1	1,813.1	-143.0	1,667.0	3,285.1	-1,618.1

[a]Including re-exports.

Source: *Pakistan Economic Survey, 1970-71*, pp. 90-91.

1969/70, 50.0 and 35.6 percent, respectively. These percentages were in spite of exports of raw jute declining and imports of food grains increasing in the East, while manufacturing exports increased and food-grain imports decreased in the West during the 1960s,[28] as a result in part of economic policy favoring industry and large-scale agriculture, controlled predominantly by West Pakistanis.

The West was favored when it came to development-plan expenditures, receiving 4.9 times as much per capita as the East in 1950/51-1954/55, and even 2.2 times as much in 1965/66-1969/70. During the last part of the 1960s, Eastern agriculture remained stagnant while Western agriculture encountered breakthroughs, especially in wheat. In the West, large subsidies were given for such farm inputs as water, fertilizers, seeds, plant protection service, and pesticides, while the East lacked government assistance for drainage, irrigation, flood control, extension service, and credit. One of the most striking instances of exacerbating regional (and class) differences was adopting the high-yielding grain varieties of the Green Revolution to cropland under controlled irrigation--owned primarily by rich commercial farmers in the West.[29]

A major grievance of East Pakistan was its substantial underrepresentation among the political leaders, the bureaucracy, the military, and the large bourgeoisie, even as late as the 1960s. In 1968, the East's representation in the civil service of Pakistan was only 36 percent, comparable to its representation in other government services.

Only in the last part of the 1960s were a few Bengalis appointed to posts as high as secretary in the central government. None, however, was secretary or minister in the crucial ministries of Defense, Home, and (except for a four-day portfolio) Finance.

In the army, East Pakistanis constituted no more than 5

percent of the officers in 1963, with little change the rest of the 1960s. West Indian business communities, Memons, Khojas, and Bohras, which comprised only ½ of 1 percent of the Muslim population in Pakistan, accounted for 43 percent of industrial investment by Muslims; Bengalis, with 50 percent of the Muslim population, comprised only 4 percent of industrial investment in Pakistan between 1947 and 1958.[30]

The rise in political discontent in the East was dampened in the 1950s while a facade of democracy was maintained, and the East's representation in the legislature was at least on a par with the West. But after the coup of 1958, with the legislature dissolved, the Bengali upper and middle classes felt politically impotent, with only limited representation in the army and civil service and none in higher political circles. Their feeling of political ineffectiveness, together with the growing economic disparity between the Western and Eastern wings, contributed to the increased political violence by Bengalis against the military government of Ayub Khan in the 1960s.

Regional economic factors played a major role in fanning discontent in Eastern Nigeria and East Pakistan. The latter, poorer than West Pakistan at independence, became more disadvantaged over time relative to the West. Additionally, East Pakistan was making little progress in obtaining high-level positions in the economy and polity. Easterners grew more restive as they grew more aware of the role of the coalition of Western landlords, industrialists, and army officers using state levers to increase regional income disparities.

Easterners' increasing aspirations and politicization, together with subsequent frustration with Western tactics to nullify any advantages of the electoral majority of their dominant political party, exacerbated their bitterness and discontent. Eastern Nigeria, in contrast, was by no means a disadvantaged region, but more comparable to the Punjab in terms of relative economic position. Discontent in Eastern Nigeria was partially linked to the possible decline in its relatively high economic status and the benefits from oil that formed a basis for the East's affluence.

SUMMARY: THE POLITICAL ECONOMY OF INTERNAL WAR IN PAKISTAN AND NIGERIA

In this brief summary, I generalize on the economic roots of the internal wars in Nigeria and Pakistan. In addition to the colonial legacy, I focus on the three major explanatory variables of the study: (1) transnational economic linkages, (2) class conflict and economic discontent, and (3) regional and communal competition and conflict.

Nigeria and India, as British colonies, were integrated into the international economy as satellites specializing in products instrumental for British industrial development. Britain encouraged tropical export crops and discouraged manufacturing and processing in Nigeria, West Pakistan, and East Bengal.

Colonial suzerainty was exercised in parts of Northern Nigeria and West Pakistan through "indirect rule," an arrangement that helped Britain economize on officers and funds, and supported the traditional rulers by eliminating important sources of opposition.

On the other hand, the coastal areas of southern Nigeria and East Bengal had more experience in parliamentary government, greater political consciousness, higher literacy, and more developed industrial capitalist institutions than inland regions because British intrusion there was longer and more intense. British rule in Nigeria and India brought about imbalances in mobilizing populations, created or reinforced communal identities, and exacerbated competition between classes and regional groups.

Transnational Linkages

The political and economic ties of Nigeria and Pakistan to Britain and the United States, after independence, further intensified regional and communal imbalances by strengthening the political elite in each country. Military and economic assistance, and private capital from the U.K. and the U.S. shielded the elite from peripheral groups in their own nation-state.

During the first republic, Nigeria's elite depended highly on Britain, the United States, and other western countries for trade, aid, and investment. The political and economic interests of the Nigerian elite were heavily influenced by the rewards and sanctions dispensed by foreign powers. Nigeria's dependence on foreign decisions helped create domestic political enmities and prevented it from coping with them.

In the 1950s and 1960s, Pakistan depended highly on the United States for loans, investment, and aid. Foreign economic support gave a major impetus to the emerging capitalist elite, large landowners, top civil servants, and army officers. But the decline in foreign assistance after 1965 meant that some elements in the ruling alliance could no longer retain their privileges. The competition between landed, industrial, bureaucratic, and military elites for state power and economic benefits in a period of decelerating growth in the late 1960s, and the higher aspirations of those not yet a part of the elites, all contributed to Pakistan's breakup.

Class Conflict and Economic Discontent

Class antagonisms intensified political discontent and violence in Nigeria and Pakistan. Frequently, domestic upper classes depending on foreign interests contributed to domestic class conflict.

A major restive element in the three countries was the relatively deprived members of the educated classes. In the late 1950s in Pakistan, and the middle 1960s in Nigeria, vacancies declined abruptly in the civil service, armed forces, police, government corporations, and universities. Younger men, especially in southern Nigeria (with a high educational rate) and East Pakistan, became frustrated with the decline.

Labor was relatively weak and disorganized in both Nigeria and Pakistan during most of the period after 1950. Nevertheless, discontent in the 1960s stemmed from a growing sense of injustice at the wide income gap between the upper and working classes. Labor disaffection, directed against government as ruler and major employer, intensified regional enmities in both countries.

In the June 1964 Nigerian general strike, the two major southern-based parties supported the demands on the Northern-dominated federal government by the trade unions, whose strength lay primarily in the south. In the late 1960s, East Pakistan's growing proletariat channeled its discontent with declining real wages into opposing the West Pakastani governing elite and supporting regional autonomy.

Regional and Communal Competition and Conflict

Communal economic competition cuts across class conflicts. Muslim nationalism, the partition of the Indian sub-continent, and Indo-Pakistani conflict helped divert attention from class animosities in Pakistan, while regionalism and ethnicity served a similar purpose in Nigeria.

In Nigeria, policies of regional economic discrimination, used to increase employment opportunities in the region, reduced total employment. In late 1966, in a climate of increased ethnic nationalism, many Ibos and other Easterners were forced to flee from other parts of Nigeria. Closing employment and investment opportunities outside the Eastern Region substantially decreased its costs of secession. Hostility also increased between the two major communities competing for high-level employment, the Yorubas and Ibos, after a number of prominent Ibos were dismissed from leading public service positions in 1964-66.

In Pakistan, competition was increasingly viewed as between the Eastern and Western wings, especially after the West consolidated into a single province in 1955. East Pakistanis' resentment arose in part from not sharing in the economic benefits of modernization. Bengalis were substantially underrepresented among the political elite, the bureaucracy, and the large bourgeoisie, even as late as the 1960s.

The hopes of Bengalis, stirred by the fall of Ayub Khan in 1969, and the 1970 elections, were thwarted by the maneuvers of Western political leaders and the military. While the grievances of the East Pakistanis arose from their poor economic position, the discontent of the Eastern Nigerians resulted from attempts to maintain a relatively high economic status within the Nigerian federation.

The military was an example of the way discontent with communal distribution of positions exacerbated conflict in Nigeria and Pakistan. Regional quotas for Nigerian army recruitment, instituted by a Northern-dominated government, contributed to insecurity among middle-ranking Ibo and other southern officers, which helped provide a driving force for the army mutiny in January 1966. Tensions in the army in 1965-66 were exacerbated further by the disparity between the large representation of Ibos and Easterners among high-ranking officers and the majority of Northerners among the rank-and-file. Disproportional Ibo representation among officers also made Eastern secession more viable. In Pakistan, Bengalis constituted no more than a small fraction of army officers and soldiers; their underrepresentation intensified their discontent, but hampered their armed struggle. The *mukti bahini*, Bengali guerrilla freedom fighters trained and supported by the Indian army, denied control of large areas to Pakistan for almost nine months, but Bangladesh did not win independence until the Indian army invaded in December 1971.

Regional and communal conflict over the distribution of the economic pie contributed to secession and disintegration. East Pakistan was discontented because central government policies helped widen the average income gap of the West over the East. The expansion of Nigeria's crude-oil industry, based largely in the Eastern Region, intensified conflict over the distribution of gains between that region and the rest of the federation.

In particular, East Pakistan and Eastern Nigeria (like Katanga) resented the low proportion of foreign exchange they could use in relation to the amount they generated. The export of raw materials by both East Pakistan and Eastern Nigeria contributed a disproportionally favorable balance of trade to their two countries. Between 1949/50 and 1969/70, Bengal generated the bulk of Pakistan's foreign exchange earnings, with exports primarily of raw jute, jute goods, and tea, while the West used about 70 percent of Pakistan's foreign exchange. Eastern Nigeria was especially dissatisfied because only a fraction of the revenue from crude petroleum was received after 1959 by the region that produced it--in contrast to receiving all the revenue from agricultural exports. The East Pakistani demand for decentralization and the Eastern Nigerian demand for greater autonomy increased because of their strong prospective budgetary and international-payments positions, and their expectations that less foreign exchange would be diverted to other areas of the country.

The political elites in Nigeria and Pakistan used sentiments associated with ethnic, regional, and religious identities to transfer potential hostilities from class disparities within their own communities to differences with, and antagonisms toward, other communities. That tactic enabled political elites in each country to pursue and implement policies that served their economic advantage. But these policies increased interregional discrepancies in Pakistan, and threatened established regional economic interests in Nigeria.

Though patterns of perceived deprivation thus differed, Biafra and Bangladesh came to view their participation within a larger multi-ethnic state as entailing persistent costs. The precipitants of the two conflicts--the Nigerian constitutional impasse and postponing the constituent assembly in Pakistan--were only final steps on the long road to secessionist civil war.

APPROACHES TO POLITICAL INSTABILITY IN NIGERIA AND PAKISTAN

The introductory chapter discusses four other approaches to political instability: (1) the ethnic model, (2) the "Praetorian" model, (3) the "relative deprivation" model, and (4) the Marxist model. Let us examine how adequately the models explain the roots of the Nigerian and Pakistani civil wars.

The Ethnic Model

Clearly the Nigerian and Pakistani civil wars involved ethnic strife. Some of the leading ethnic communities in federal Nigeria were Hausas, Fulanis, and Yorubas, while Ibos comprised the major leadership for Biafra. In Pakistan, Punjabis and Muslim immigrants from India were the dominant ethnic communities in the West, while Bengalis comprised the overwhelming majority of East Pakistanis.

However, the issue is not whether ethnic conflict exists, but how to explain it. Most scholars who apply the ethnic model, instead of probing the origin of ethnic identity and conflict, regard ethnicity as a primordial "given." Few show any cognizance of how ethnic identities are created, manifested, combined, and reconstituted in struggles to share benefits from modernization, economic growth, and self-government. And there is little or no emphasis on why the political leaders consider ethnic differences more salient for political mobilization than class or occupation.

The all-absorbing focus on ethnic community clouds class divisions, economic differences, and power inequities. Scholars who use the ethnic model usually fail to mention several factors contributing to political conflicts in Nigeria and Pakistan: strikes by workers, grievances by farmers over prices, and discontent by educated classes and middle ranking officers over the decline in openings and promotions.

Most of those who explain internal political violence in terms of ethnic conflict fail to analyze how ethnicity is influenced by transnational linkages, either during the colonial period or after independence. Even those, like Young, who consider these linkages, do not examine the effects of foreign investment, economic aid, and military support upon class and ethnic community.[31]

The "Praetorian" Model

For Huntington political instability results from high levels of popular mobilization and mass participation in politics relative to institutional capacity to absorb new participants. He thinks political institutions can be more effectively built under such regimes as Ayub Khan's in Pakistan, where concentration of power, with eventual tempered expansion of power, could be more systematic and better planned because "social forces are not fully articulated."[32]

I indicated above that repressing political and economic participation, and concentrating economic control in East Pakistan in the hands of the governments of Ayub Khan and Yahya Khan contributed to the Bangladesh secessionist conflict in 1971. There are, however, other problems with the Praetorian approach, especially when applied to Pakistan and Nigeria.

Huntington's analysis of political decay is primarily within a closed system, the nation-state, after independence. In Nigeria and Pakistan, weaknesses that contributed to Praetorianism, such as communal conflict, uneven regional development, constitutional flaws, and the lack of political, bureaucratic, and business leadership, were partly a product of institutions and policies in the colonial period.

For example, Huntington's statement that the Fulani-Hausa "organize[d] themselves . . . successfully for modern political life . . . to the point of dominating nearly all of Nigeria"[33] neglects to mention the support by the British colonial government in the 1950s for a Northern Region, dominated by the Fulani-Hausa traditional elite, intact with a majority of representatives in the federal legislature. And major southern parties did not dissent, not wanting to delay home rule. In the period after independence in 1960, Britain used its economic and political power to support a federal arrangement with the Fulani-Hausa upper classes dominating. In Pakistan, the United States used economic and military assistance to support a conservative elite who placed little emphasis on improving the economic welfare of the poorest half of the population. The Praetorian approach does not discuss such transnational relationships.

Moreover, Huntington neglects class conflict in developing countries like Nigeria and Pakistan, e.g., between workers and government, in roles as employer or as representative of the ruling classes. For Huntington, "the industrial worker, in most modernizing countries, is almost a member of the elite." In addition, unlike the west in the nineteenth century, labor organizations and benefits in developing countries result from the initiative of the political elite, rather than from demands and industrial action by workers.[34]

The analysis above indicates the fallacy of these statements, at least in Nigeria and Pakistan, where workers have average or below-average incomes, and have continued to struggle for greater benefits and control, even though the form the clashes took was not the same as that of western workers. Nigerian workers in 1964 and their Pakistani counterparts after 1966 used protests and strikes to demonstrate the weaknesses of the existing governments; and their actions widened the internal political conflict.

Although for Huntington, the state, as manager of the conflict and target of political violence, is above clashes by various special and parochial interests within society, the control of the state may be the object of conflict, as when Nigerian regional parties contended for political hegemony in 1960-65. Also, the state, which disproportionally represents the economic interests of various ruling elites, as party to the conflict may be engaged in such politically destabilizing activities as attempting to destroy the opposition party. Suspension of the Western Nigerian government in 1962-63 and the massacre of thousands of East Bengali people by the Pakistani army in March 1971 are examples.

Finally, for Huntington political repression of rising and dissenting classes does not result in political decay and instability. Thus, for a government interested in maintaining political stability, "the appropriate response to middle-class radicalism is repression, not reform."[35]

I argue, however, that elites using the power of the state frequently contribute more to political violence than would reform.

In Nigeria in the early 1960s, the elites used state power to rig elections, to prevent nominations by challengers, to eliminate rivals politically, to have the army and police quell dissent, to deny protection to other ethnic communities, to break strikes and prevent wage increases, to undertake economic sanctions against opponents, to deny employment opportunities to those from other regions and communities, and to provide patronage for supporters. These factors contributed to the coups and the civil war.

Another example of state repression contributing to political disorder was President Yahya Khan using the Pakistani army 25-26 March 1971 to attack East Pakistan and quell demands by the Awami League for greater autonomy as the majority party in the election to the National Assembly three months previously.

The "Relative Deprivation" Model

For Gurr, relative deprivation is the perceived discrepancy between what people think they will get and what they believe they are entitled to. This concept helps explain some of the social discontent and political violence in Nigeria and Pakistan. A major restive element in Nigeria and Pakistan in the 1960s was the relatively deprived members of the educated classes, frustrated by the abrupt decline in good positions and rapid promotions in government, the military, the police, and the universities.

Before the January 1966 coup in Nigeria and the 1951 aborted Rawalpindi conspiracy in Pakistan, unrest among middle level officers was caused partly by a sharp drop in openings and promotions. Labor discontent in the two countries arose from a growing sense of injustice at the wide gap between the wages of white-collar and blue-collar workers.

Finally, Western Nigerian cocoa farmers and East Pakistani small farmers experienced relative deprivation as a result of government policies that held agricultural commodity prices substantially below world prices.

The concept of relative deprivation carries two major difficulties: (1) how to measure it and (2) how to demonstrate its causal relationship to political conflict.

Gurr states that economic values are likely to be most salient for the majority of people in determining deprivation. In a study using cross-sectional analyses of data collected for 114 polities, he examines how economic variables affect political violence. His indicator of economic deprivation, derived from a weighted average of measures of international trade, price stability, and growth rates, correlates with the magnitude of civil strife.

Later Gurr and Duvall estimate the structural parameters essential for specifying interdependencies among eleven variables for eighty-six countries in their simultaneous-equation model. They find that economic discrimination, economic dependence, national product, and (indirectly) relative export decline are some of the determinants of the magnitude of manifest political conflict.[36]

Gurr and Duvall's research design, while enhancing the precision of parameter estimation and the generality of findings, has several specific problems.

First the composite indicator is inadequate for expressing the concept. Economic dependence, a partial contributor to the magnitude of political conflict, is limited to composite measures of factor payments abroad and export concentration by the largest receiving country. It thus omits such measures, used in this study, as the extent of specialization in primary and secondary goods, the export concentration by commodity, the structure of imports, the foreign exchange position, debt service relationships, the relative size of the foreign sector, technological transfer and dependence, and military and economic assistance.

Second is the problem of validly measuring such variables as political discrimination, conflict tradition, religious cleavage, and the magnitude of civil conflict.

Third is the difficulty of understanding causal relationships among composite indicators. As the authors suggest, a high level of economic development, with more to fight about, might contribute to economic and political stress. But the causality appears theoretically less interesting when it merely means that a higher national product results in a higher export value, a lower ratio of defense expenditures to gross national product, and fewer government sanctions and restrictions.

Fourth is the primary focus of the social-science data banks used as sources on static variables aggregated at the national level. Sub-national categories of region, community, class, occupation, and sector lack the cross-national commensurability usually essential for comparison by a standard measure. (For example, as noted in chapter 4, data on interregional trade flows are difficult to compare between two countries, especially with different numbers of regions.) Gurr and Duvall's research design precludes certain measures of the level and change of economic deprivation, such as the average income of workers compared with incomes in the country as a whole, the real wages of workers, the regional and communal differentials in both educational levels and representation in the army and civil service, and interregional revenue allocation compared to the origin of the revenue. So detailed case studies, as presented here on Nigeria and Pakistan, can provide some insights into the economic origins of civil conflict that Gurr and Duvall's quantitative cross-national analysis cannot.

The Marxist Model

Although both the political economy and Marxist approaches emphasize class conflict, they differ widely on two perspectives. First my political economy approach is not limited to conflicts between owners of capital and the working class. I also examine the unrest of classes and economic groups who are not contending over the ownership, or even control, of capital.

Second, unlike the contemporary Marxist approach, I include economic conflict between regional and communal elites in my analysis of domestic political violence. Power is transferred from one elite to another in an internal war, rather than from the advantaged classes to the dispossessed masses. Even most of the Soviet (and many of the Chinese) revolutionary leaders were part of an educated elite. This, however, does not deny that the elite, by transferring hostilities from class discrepancies in its own communities to the rulers and subjects of others, use communal sentiments and identification to further its own special interest.

CONCLUSION

Thus, each of the ethnic model, the "Praetorian" model, the "relative deprivation" model, and the Marxist model is inadequate in explaining the origins of civil wars such as those in Nigeria and Pakistan. The ethnic approach neglects transnational economic ties and class conflict, as well as the economic roots of ethnic conflict. Praetorian approaches do not consider transnational and class variables, and class interests served by state power. Scholars with the "relative deprivation" approach lack the detailed evidence and clear causal relationships needed when using aggregate economic data to show the relationship between economic deprivation and domestic political conflict. The Marxist model fails to analyze regional and communal economic conflict.

In contrast, the political economy approach uses three crucial variables to explain internal political violence: (1) transnational economic linkages, (2) class conflict and economic discontent, and (3) communal and regional economic conflict. This approach also provides some of the economic data and analyses that the economist can contribute to internal political instability.

Much additional work is needed for the political economy approach used to examine the Nigerian and Pakistani conflicts to be used as a general model to explain conflicts in other third-world countries. Further specification of the detailed relationships within a political economy approach is essential. Also, additional testing is required, either by compiling more case studies, or developing indicators with cross-national values that can be used in a simultaneous-equation model.

Thus, research is needed to test the generality of the political economy approach, to integrate its insights with the existing literature, and to find implications for policies to reduce political instability in developing countries.

NOTES

1. Arthur MacEwan, "Contradictions in Capitalist Development: The Case of Pakistan," *Review of Radical Political Economics* (*RRPE*), III, No. 1 (Spring 1971), 42-51.

2. In 1955, Punjabi control was solidified by merging several provinces of West Pakistan into a single unit, which was given equal representation with the more populous East. In 1970, popular discontent in both East Pakistan and the non-Punjabi regions of the West forced a return to four West Pakistani provinces, and representation based on population. In Nigeria, in 1966, the Ironsi government decreed that a unitary state and unified civil services were to replace the four-region federation. The Gowon regime, however, reverted in August 1966 to a federal structure, which by 27 May 1967 included twelves states.

3. Theodore P. Wright notes these groups' replacement of the earlier, predominantly immigrant, elite of lawyers, professionals, and landlords, in his "Indian Muslim Muhajirin in the Politics of Pakistan" (Paper presented to the Annual Meeting of the American

Political Science Association, New Orleans, 1973), pp. 13-15.

4. Pakistan, Ministry of Finance, *Pakistan Economic Survey, 1970-71* (Islamabad, 1971), and *Pakistan Economic Survey, 1971-72* (Islamabad, 1972).

5. *Pakistan Economic Survey, 1971-72*, appendices pp. 71-77.

6. Ibid., pp. 79-81, and Naved Hamid, "A Critical Appraisal of Foreign Aid Strategy," *Punjab University Economist*, VIII, No. 2 (December 1970), 132-3, 146.

7. Hamid, *Punjabi University Economist*, VIII, No. 2, 132-3, 146.

8. Hamza Alavi and Amir Khusro, "Pakistan: The Burden of U.S. Aid," in *Imperialism and Underdevelopment: A Reader*, Robert I. Rhodes, ed. (New York: Monthly Review Press, 1970), pp. 64-6.

9. MacEwan, *RRPE*, III, No. 1, 48.

10. Alavi and Khusro, "Pakistan: The Burden of U.S. Aid," in *Imperialism and Underdevelopment*, Rhodes, ed., pp. 64-6.

11. *Pakistan Economic Survey, 1971-72*, appendix p. 89.

12. MacEwan, *RRPE*, III, No. 1, 48.

13. Talukder Maniruzzaman, "Group Interests in Pakistani Politics, 1947-1958," *Pacific Affairs*, XXXIX, Nos. 1 & 2 (Spring-Summer 1966), pp. 84-6. Samuel P. Huntington, *Political Order in Changing Societies* (New Haven, Conn.: Yale University Press, 1968), p. 382, indicates that the Gini index for the West is substantially higher than for East Pakistan.

14. Gustav F. Papanek, "The Development of Entrepreneurship," *American Economic Review*, LII, No. 2 (May 1962), 49.

15. Ibid., pp. 83-92, and Tariq Ali, *Pakistan: Military Rule or People's Power* (New York: William Morrow and Company, 1970), p. 61.

16. Maniruzzaman, *Pacific Affairs*, XXXIX, Nos. 1 & 2, 94.

17. Keith Griffin and Azizur Rahman Khan, eds., *Growth and Inequality in Pakistan* (London: Macmillan, 1972), pp. 199-206; Azizur Rahman Khan, "What Has Been Happening to Real Wages in Pakistan?" ibid., pp. 242-3, and *Pakistan Economic Survey, 1971-72*, appendices pp. 2-3.

18. Ali, *Pakistan*.

19. Albert Waterston, *Planning in Pakistan: Organization and Implementation* (Baltimore: The Johns Hopkins Press, 1963), pp. 13-129.

20. Agha M. Ghouse, "Profitability in Public Enterprise with Special Reference to WPIDC," in *Pakistan in the Development Decade: Problems and Performance*, A. Ghouse, ed. (Lahore: Economic Development Seminar, 1968), pp. 177-80; Anwar Iqbal Qureshi, "A Decade of Economic Development in Pakistan (1958-68)," ibid., p. 108; M.S. Jillani, "Social Welfare and Economic Development," ibid., p. 362; and Pyarali G. Allan, "Tax and Fiscal Policy and its Impact on Private Enterprise," ibid., pp. 219-21.

21. Waterston, *Planning in Pakistan*.

22. Griffin and Khan, eds., *Growth and Inequality*, pp. 26, 30, 134-6; Keith Griffin, "Financing Development Plans in Pakistan," *Pakistan Development Review*, V, No. 4 (Winter 1965), pp. 37, 44-5; and A.H.M. Nuruddin Chowdhury, "The Implications of Intermediation by Income Redistribution from Rural to Urban as a Result of the Direct Controls on Pakistan's Foreign Trade," *Pakistan Economic*

Journal, XIX, No. 1 (1968-69), 75-6.

23. Azizur Rahman Khan, *The Economy of Bangladesh* (London: Macmillan, 1972), pp. 65-6.

24. To use the terminology of Ted Robert Gurr, *Why Men Rebel* (Princeton, N.J.: Princeton University Press, 1968), pp. 46-52, the East Pakistanis suffered aspirational deprivation while the Eastern Nigerians underwent decremental deprivation.

25. Kalyan Dutt, Ranajit Dasgupta, and Anil Chatterjee, *Bangladesh Economy: An Analytical Study* (New Delhi: People's Publishing House, 1973), p. 50.

26. Khan, *The Economy of Bangladesh*. 99-100.

27. Ibid., pp. 66, 89-93.

28. *Pakistan Economic Survey, 1970-71*, pp. 90-1.

29. Griffin and Khan, eds., *Growth and Inequality*, p. 29; Swadesh R. Bose, "East-West Contrast in Pakistan's Agricultural Development," ibid., pp. 69-93; and Harry M. Cleaver, Jr., "The Contradictions of the Green Revolution," *American Economic Review*, LXII, No. 2 (May 1972), 181.

30. Mohammed Ayoob, "Pakistan's Political Development, 1947 to 1970; Bird's Eye View," *Economic and Political Weekly*, VI, Nos. 3, 4, & 5 (January 1971), 202; and Papanek, *American Economic Review*, LII, No. 2, 54.

31. Crawford Young, *The Politics of Cultural Pluralism* (Madison, Wis.: University of Wisconsin Press, 1976).

32. Huntington, *Political Order*, pp. 251-5,261.

33. Ibid., p. 176.

34. Ibid., pp. 138, 287.

35. Ibid., p. 373.

36. Gurr, *Why Men Rebel*, p. 69, and "A Causal Model of Civil Strife: A Comparative Analysis Using New Indices," *The American Political Science Review*, LXII (December 1968), 1104-24; and Gurr and Raymond Duvall, "Civil Conflict in the 1960s: A Reciprocal Theoretical System with Parameter Estimates," *Comparative Political Studies*, VI, No. 2 (July 1973), 135-69.

Appendix: Dramatis Personae

Major General J.T. Aguiyi-Ironsi: Ibo. Head of state, January-July 1966. Killed in the July 1966 counter coup.

Chief Samuel L. Akintola: Yoruba. Premier of the Western Region, 1959-66. Killed in the 15 January 1966 mutiny.

Chief Obafemi Awolowo: Yoruba. A nationalist in the 1940s and 1950s. Premier of the Western Region, 1954-59. Leader of the federal opposition, 1960-62. Imprisoned for treason, 1963-66. Federal commissioner for finance and vice-president of the Federal Executive Council, 1967-71. Defeated candidate for president, 1979.

Dr. Nnamdi Azikiwe: Ibo. A leading Nigerian nationalist in the late 1930s, 1940s, and 1950s. Premier of the Eastern Region, 1954-59. Governor-general of Nigeria, 1960-63. President of Nigeria, 1963-66. Defeated candidate for president, 1979.

Sir Abubakar Tafawa Balewa: Gerawa. Federal prime minister, 1956-66. Killed in the January 1966 military mutiny.

Sir Ahmadu Bello: Fulani. Sarduana of Sakoto. Premier of the Northern Region, 1954-66. Leader of the Northern Peoples' Congress, 1954-66. Considered Nigeria's most powerful politician during civilian rule, 1960-66. Killed in the January 1966 mutiny.

Lieutenant Colonel Yakubu Gowon: Angas (small Northern ethnic community). Head of state, August 1966-July 1975.

Lieutenant Colonel Murtala Mohammed: Hausa. Gowon's successor. Head of state, July 1975-February 1976. Assassinated February 1976.

Majors C.K. Nzeogwu, E.A. Ifeajuna, and D.O. Okafor: all Ibo. Leading conspirators in the January 1966 mutiny.

Major Olusegun Obasanjo: Yoruba. Head of state, February 1976-September 1979.

Lieutenant Colonel Odumegwu Ojukwu: Ibo. Military governor of the Eastern Region, January 1966-May 1967. Biafra's head of state, May 1967-January 1970. Lived in exile, 1970-82. Pardoned by Shagari, 18 May 1982.

Dr. Michael I. Okpara: Ibo. Premier of the Eastern Region, 1960-66. Political adviser to Biafra's head of state, Ojukwu, 1967-70.

Alhaji Shehu Shagari: Fulani. Federal minister of pensions and establishments, 1960-62. Federal minister of internal affairs and communications, 1962-65. Federal minister of works, 1965-66. Federal commissioner for economic development, 1970-71. Federal commissioner for finance, 1971-75. President (head of state and government), beginning 1 October 1979. Renominated by the National Party of Nigeria as presidential candidate for 1983.

Bibliography

BOOKS AND MONOGRAPHS

Adedeji, Adebayo *Nigerian Federal Finance: Its Development, Problems, and Prospects*. London: Hutchinson, 1969.

Akpan, Ntieyong U. *The Struggle for Secession, 1966-1970: A Personal Account of the Nigerian Civil War*. London: Frank Cass, 1976.

Ali, Tariq. *Pakistan: Military Rule or People's Power*. New York: William Morrow, 1970.

Aluko, Samuel A. *Fiscal Incentives for Industrial Development in Nigeria*. New York: United Nations Department of Economics and Social Affairs, 1967.

Amandi, Elechi. *Sunset in Biafra: A Civil War Diary*. London: Heineman, 1973.

American Petroleum Institute. *Basic Petroleum Data Book*. Vol. I. Washington, D.C., 1981.

Ananaba, Wogu. *The Trade Union Movement in Nigeria*. New York: Africana, 1969.

Anderson, Charles W.; von der Mehden. Fred R.; and Young, Crawford. *Issues of Political Development*. Englewood Cliffs, N.J.: Prentice-Hall, 1974.

Andreano, Ralph, ed. *The Economic Impact of the American Civil War*. Cambridge, Mass.: Schlectman, 1962.

Arendt, Hannah. *On Violence*. New York: Harcourt, Brace & World, 1969.

Arnold, Guy. *Modern Nigeria*. London: Longman, 1977.

Awolowo, Obafemi. *Path to Nigerian Freedom*. London: Faber, 1947.

Awolowo, Obafemi. *The People's Republic*. Ibadan: Oxford University Press, 1968.

Ayida, A. Akene, and Onitiri, H.M.A., eds. *Reconstruction and Development in Nigeria--Proceedings of a National Conference*. Ibadan: Oxford University Press, 1971.

Bain, Joe S. *International Differences in Industrial Structure: Eight Nations in the 1950's*. New Haven, Conn.: Yale University Press, 1966.

Baran, Paul A. *The Political Economy of Growth*. New York: Monthly Review Press, 1957.

Bauer, Peter T. *West African Trade: A Study of Competition, Oligopoly and Monopoly in a Changing Economy*. Cambridge:

Cambridge University Press, 1954.
Beckett, Paul, and O'Connell, James. *Education and Power in Nigeria*. New York: Africana, 1978.
Beer, Christopher E.F. *The Politics of Peasant Groups in Western Nigeria*. Ibadan: Ibadan University Press, 1976.
Bretton, Harry L. *The Rise and Fall of Kwame Nkrumah: A Study of Personal Rule in Africa*. New York: Praeger, 1966.
Burton, J.W. *Systems, States, Diplomacy and Rules*. Cambridge: Cambridge University Press, 1966.
Chenery, Hollis; Ahluwalia, Montek S.; Bell, C.L.G.; Duloy, John H.; and Jolly, Richard. *Redistribution with Growth*. Oxford: Oxford University Press, 1974.
Cohen, Robin. *Labour and Politics in Nigeria*. New York: Africana, 1974.
Coleman, James S. *Nigeria: Background to Nationalism*. Berkeley and Los Angeles: University of California Press, 1958.
Crowder, Michael. *The Story of Nigeria*. London: Faber and Faber, 1962.
Crowder, Michael. *West Africa under Colonial Rule*. London: Hutchinson, 1968.
Dahl, Robert A. *Who Governs? Democracy and Power in an American City*. New Haven, Conn.: Yale University Press, 1961.
de St. Jorre, John. *The Nigerian Civil War*. London: Hodder and Stoughton, 1972.
de Tocqueville, Alexis. *Democracy in America*. 2 vols. Translated by Harry Reeve. New York: P.G. Collier & Son, 1900.
Deutsch, Karl W. *Nationalism and Social Communication: An Inquiry into the Foundation of Nationality*. New York: Wiley, 1953.
Diamond, Stanley. *Nigeria: Model of a Colonial Failure*. New York: American Committee on Africa, 1966.
Dudley, B.J. *Instability and Political Order: Politics and Crisis in Nigeria*. Ibadan: Ibadan University Press, 1973.
Dudley, B.J. *Parties and Politics in Northern Nigeria*. London: Frank Cass, 1968.
Dutt, Kalyan; Dasgupta, Ranajit; and Chatterjee, Anil. *Bangladesh Economy: An Analytical Study*. (New Delhi: People's Publishing House, 1973).
Fage, J.D. *A History of West Africa: An Introductory Survey*. Cambridge: Cambridge University Press, 1969.
Fanon, Frantz. *The Wretched of the Earth*. New York: Grove Press, 1963.
Foltz, William J. *From French West Africa to the Mali Federation*. New Haven, Conn.: Yale University Press, 1965.
Free, Lloyd A. *The Attitudes, Hopes and Fears of Nigerians*. Princeton: N.J.: Princeton University Institute for International Social Research, 1964.
Ghouse, Agha M., ed. *Pakistan in the Development Decade: Problems and Performance*. Lahore: Economic Development Seminar, 1968.
Glazer, Nathan, and Moynihan, Daniel Patrick. *Beyond the Melting Pot: The Negroes, Puerto Ricans, Jews, Italians, and Irish of New York City*. Cambridge, Mass.: The M.I.T. Press, 1963.
Glazer, Nathan, and Moynihan, Daniel Partick, eds. *Ethnicity: Theory and Experience*. Cambridge, Mass.: Harvard University Press, 1975.

Griffin, Keith, and Khan, Azizur Rahman, eds. *Growth and Inequality in Pakistan.* London: Macmillan, 1972.

Gurr, Ted Robert, ed. *Handbook of Political Conflict.* London: Free Press, 1980.

Gurr, Ted Robert. *Why Men Rebel.* Princeton, N.J.: Princeton University Press, 1970.

Gutteridge, W.F. *The Military in African Politics.* London: Methuen, 1969.

Hagen, Everett E. *The Economics of Development.* Homewood, Ill.: Irwin, 1968.

Hay, Alan M., and Smith, Robert H.T. *Interregional Trade and Money Flows in Nigeria, 1964.* Ibadan: Oxford University Press, 1970.

Helleiner, Gerald K. *Peasant Agriculture, Government and Economic Growth in Nigeria.* Homewood, Ill.: Irwin, 1966.

Henissart, Paul. *Wolves in the City: The Death of French Algeria.* New York: Simon & Schuster, 1970.

Hibbs, Douglas A., Jr. *Mass Political Violence: A Cross-national Causal Analysis.* New York: Wiley, 1973.

Hill, Polly. *Population, Prosperity and Poverty: Rural Kano, 1900 and 1970.* Cambridge: Cambridge University Press, 1977.

Hill, Polly. *Rural Hausa: A Village and a Setting.* Cambridge: Cambridge University Press, 1972.

Hopkins, A.G. *An Economic History of West Africa.* London: Longman, 1973.

Huntington, Samuel P. *Political Order in Changing Societies.* New Haven, Conn.: Yale University Press, 1968.

Idang, Gordon J. *Nigeria: Internal Politics and Foreign Policy, 1960-1966.* Ibadan: Ibadan University Press, 1973.

Jacob, Philip E., and Toscano, James V., eds. *The Integration of Political Communities.* Philadelphia: J. B. Lippincott, 1964.

Jain, Shail. *Size Distribution of Income: A Compilation of Data.* Washington: World Bank, 1975.

Khan, Azizur Rahman. *The Economy of Bangladesh.* London: Macmillan, 1972.

Kilby, Peter. *Development of Small Industries in Eastern Nigeria.* Enugu: Eastern Ministry of Information, 1963.

Kilby, Peter. *Industrialization in an Open Economy: Nigeria, 1945-1966.* Cambridge: Cambridge University Press, 1969.

Kirk-Greene, Anthony H.M. *Crisis and Conflict in Nigeria: A Documentary Sourcebook, 1966-70.* 2 vols. London: Oxford University Press, 1971.

Kirk-Greene, Anthony H.M. *The Genesis of the Nigerian Civil War and the Theory of Fear.* Uppsala: The Scandinavian Institute of African Studies, 1975.

Kirk-Greene, Anthony H.M., and Rimmer, Douglas. *Nigeria since 1970: A Political and Economic Outline.* London: Hodder & Stoughton, 1981.

Kuznets, Simon S. *National Product in Wartine.* New York: National Bureau of Economic Research, 1945.

LeVine, Robert A., and others. *Dreams and Deeds: Achievement Motivation in Nigeria.* Chicago: University of Chicago Press, 1966.

Lewis, W. Arthur. *Reflections on Nigeria's Economic Growth.*

Paris: Organisation for Economic Cooperation and Development, 1967.

Lloyd, P.C. *Africa in Social Change*. Harmondsworth, Eng.: Penguin, 1967.

Lloyd, P.C. *The New Elites of Tropical Africa*. Oxford: Oxford University Press, 1966.

Lloyd, P.C. *Power and Independence: Urban Africans' Perception of Social Inequality*. London: Routledge & Kegan Paul, 1974.

Lloyd, P.C.; Mabogunje, A.L.; and Awe; B., eds. *The City of Ibadan*. Cambridge: Cambridge University Press, 1967.

Luckham, Robin. *The Nigerian Military--A Sociological Analysis of Authority and Revolt, 1960-67*. Cambridge: Cambridge University Press, 1971.

Lugard, F.O. *The Dual Mandate in British Tropical Africa*. London: William Blackwood, 1929.

Luxemburg, Rosa. *The National Question: Selected Writings*. New York: Monthly Review Press, 1976.

Mackintosh, John P. *Nigerian Government and Politics*. Evanston, Ill.: Northwestern University Press, 1966.

Madiebo, Alexander A. *The Nigerian Revolution and the Biafran War*. Enugu: Fourth Dimension, 1980.

Melson, Robert, and Wolpe, Howard, eds. *Nigeria: Modernization and Politics of Communalism*. East Lansing, Mich.: Michigan State University Press, 1971.

Miners, N.J. *The Nigerian Army, 1956-1966*. London: Methuen, 1971.

Moore, Barrington. *Social Origins of Dictatorship and Democracy*. Boston: Beacon Press, 1966.

Nafziger, E. Wayne. *African Capitalism: A Case Study in Nigerian Entrepreneurship*. Stanford, Calif.: Hoover Institution Press, 1977.

Nicolson, I.F. *The Administration of Nigeria, 1900-1960: Men, Methods and Myths*. Oxford: Clarendon Press, 1969.

Niven, Rex. *The War of Nigerian Unity, 1967-1970*. London: Evans Brothers, 1970.

Nkrumah, Kwame. *Class Struggle in Africa*. New York: International Publishers, 1970.

Nordlinger, Eric A. *Conflict Regulation in Divided Societies*. Occasional Papers in International Affairs, No. 29. Cambridge, Mass.: Harvard University, Center for International Affairs, 1972.

Nye, Joseph S., Jr. *Pan-Africanism and East African Integration*. Cambridge, Mass.: Harvard University Press, 1965.

Obasanjo, Olusegun. *My Command: An Account of the Nigerian Civil War, 1967-1970*. London: Heinemann, 1980.

Okigbo, Pius N.C. *Nigerian National Accounts, 1950-57*. Enugu: Federal Ministry of Economic Development, 1961.

Okpaku, Joseph, ed. *Nigeria: Dilemma of Nationhood--An African Analysis of the Biafran Conflict*. Westport, Conn.: Greenwood, 1972.

Oyediran, Oyeleye, ed. *Nigerian Government and Politics under Military Rule, 1966-79*. London: Macmillan, 1979.

Panter-Brick, S. Keith, ed. *Nigerian Politics and Military Rule: Prelude to the Civil War*. London: Athlone Press, 1970.

Panter-Brick, S. Keith, ed. *Soldiers and Oil: The Political Transformation of Nigeria.* London: Frank Cass, 1978.

Pareto, Vilfredo. *The Mind and Society: A Treatise on General Sociology.* Translated by Andrew Bongiorno and Arthur Livingston. New York: Harcourt, Brace & Co., 1935.

Peace, Adrian J. *Choice, Class and Conflict: A Study of Southern Nigerian Factory Workers.* Atlantic Highlands, N.J.: Humanities Press, 1979.

Pearson, Scott R. *Petroleum and the Nigerian Economy.* Stanford, Calif.: Stanford University Press, 1970.

Perham, Margery. *Native Administration in Nigeria.* London: Oxford University Press, 1962.

Pfefferman, Guy. *Industrial Labour in Senegal.* New York: Praeger, 1968.

Post, Kenneth W.J. *The Nigerian Federal Election of 1959--Politics and Administration in a Developing Political System.* London: Oxford University Press, 1963.

Post, Kenneth W.J., and Jenkins, George D. *The Price of Liberty: Personality and Politics in Colonial Nigeria.* Cambridge: Cambridge University Press, 1973.

Post, Kenneth W.J., and Vickers, Michael. *Structure and Conflict in Nigeria, 1960-1966.* Madison, Wis.: University of Wisconsin Press, 1973.

Rabushka, Alvin, and Shepsle, Kenneth A. *Politics in Plural Societies: A Theory of Democratic Instability.* Columbus, Ohio: Charles E. Merrill, 1972.

Sandbrook, Richard, and Cohen, Robin, eds. *The Development of an African Working Class: Studies in Class Formation and Action.* London: Longman, 1975.

Schatz, Sayre P. *Nigerian Capitalism.* Berkeley, Calif.: University of California Press, 1977.

Schätzl, L.H. *Petroleum and the Nigerian Economy.* Stanford, Calif.: Stanford University Press, 1969.

Scott, James C. *Comparative Political Corruption.* Englewood Cliffs, N.J.: Prentice-Hall, 1972.

Sklar, Richard L. *Nigerian Political Parties: Power in an Emergent African Nation.* Princeton, N.J.: Princeton University Press, 1963.

Stolper, Wolfgang F. *Planning without Facts: Lessons in Resource Allocation from Nigeria's Development.* Cambridge, Mass.: Harvard University Press, 1966.

Stremlau, John J. *The International Politics of the Nigerian Civil War, 1967-1970.* Princeton, N.J.: Princeton University Press, 1977.

Suleiman, Michael W. *Political Parties in Lebanon: The Challenge of a Fragmented Political Culture.* Ithaca, N.Y.: Cornell University Press, 1967.

Taylor, Charles Lewis, and Hudson, Michael C. *World Handbook of Political and Social Indicators.* New Haven, Conn.: Yale University Press, 1972.

Tilly, Charles, *From Mobilization to Revolution.* Reading, Mass.: Addison-Wesley, 1978.

Trimingham, J. Spencer. *Islam in West Africa.* Oxford: Oxford University Press, 1959.

Udo, Reuben K. *Geographical Regions of Nigeria.* Berkeley and Los Angeles: University of California Press, 1970.

Waterston, Albert. *Planning in Pakistan: Organization and Implementation.* Baltimore: Johns Hopkins Press, 1963.

Whitaker, C.S., Jr. *The Politics of Tradition: Continuity and Change in Northern Nigeria, 1946-1966.* Princeton, N.J.: Princeton University Press, 1970.

Wolpe, Howard. *Urban Politics in Nigeria: A Study of Port Harcourt.* Berkeley and Los Angeles: University of California Press, 1974.

World Bank. *Nigeria: Options for Long-term Development.* Baltimore: The Johns Hopkins University Press, 1974.

World Bank. *World Development Report, 1980.* Washington, D.C., 1980.

World Bank. West Africa Regional Office. *Nigeria: Recent Economic Developments and Short-term Prospects.* Report No. 1690a - UNI, 23 December 1977.

Wraith, Ronald, and Simpkins, Edgar. *Corruption in Developing Countries.* London: George Allen & Unwin. 1963.

Young, Crawford. *The Politics of Cultural Pluralism.* Madison, Wis.: The University of Wisconsin Press, 1976.

ARTICLES

Aboyade, O. "Problems in Plan Revision." *Nigerian Journal of Economic and Social Studies*, VII, No. 2 (July 1965), 121-30.

Aboyade, O., and Ayida, A. Akene. "The War Economy in Perspective." *Nigerian Journal of Economic and Social Studies*, XIII, No. 1 (March 1971), 13-37.

Alavi, Hamza, and Khusro, Amir. "Pakistan: The Burden of U.S. Aid." In *Imperialism and Underdevelopment: A Reader*, edited by Robert I. Rhodes. New York: Monthly Review Press, 1970.

Aletta, Andre. "A Villager in Agony." In *The Insider Stories of War and Peace from Nigeria*, edited by Chinua Achebe, Arthur Nwanko, Samuel Ifejika, Flora Nwapa, et al. Enugu: Nwanko, Ifejika, & Co., 1971.

Aluko, Olajide. "The Civil War and Nigerian Foreign Policy." *Political Quarterly*, XLII, No. 2 (April-June 1970), 177-90.

Aluko, Olajide. "The 'New' Nigerian Foreign Policy: Developments Since the Downfall of General Gowon." *Round Table: The Commonwealth Quarterly*, October 1976, pp. 405-14.

Aluko, Olajide. "Nigeria and the Superpowers." *Millennium*, V, No. 2 (1976), 127-41.

Aluko, Olajide. "Oil at Concessionary Prices for Africa: A Case Study in Nigerian Decision Making." *African Affairs*, LXXV (October 1976), 425-43.

Aluko, Samuel A. "Resource Allocation and Overall Strategy." *Quarterly Journal of Administration*, V, No. 3 (April 1971), 267-83.

Anglin, Douglas G. "Nigeria: Political Non-alignment and Economic Alignment." *Journal of Modern African Studies*, II, No. 2 (1964), 247-63.

Anise, Ladun. "Confrontation Politics and Crisis Management: Nigerian University Students and Public Policy--A Social

Commentary." *Issue*, IX, Nos. 1 & 2 (Spring/Summer 1979), 73-82.

Ayoob, Mohammed. "Pakistan's Political Development, 1947 to 1970: Bird's Eye View." *Economic and Political Weekly*, VI, Nos. 3, 4, & 5 (January 1971), 199-204.

Baker, Pauline H. "The Politics of Nigerian Military Rule." *Africa Report*, XVI, No. 2 (February 1971), 18-21.

Baker, Pauline H. "Seeds of Radicalism among an Aspirant Elite." In *Social Change and Economic Development in Nigeria*, edited by Ukandi G. Damachi and Hans Dieter Seibel. New York: Praeger, 1973.

Baran, Paul A. "On the Political Economy of Backwardness." *Manchester School*, XX (January 1952), 66-84.

Callaway, Archibald. "Creating Employment for Nigeria's School Leavers." *Quarterly Journal of Administration*, III, No. 1 (October 1969), 1-11.

Callaway, Barbara. "The Political Economy of Nigeria." In *The Political Economy of Africa*, edited by Richard Harris. Cambridge, Mass.: Schenkman, 1975.

Campbell, Ian. "The Nigerian Census: An Essay in Civil-Military Relations." *Journal of Commonwealth Politics*, XIV, No. 3 (November 1976), 242-54.

Chowdhury, A.H.M. Nuruddin. "The Implications of Intermediation by Income Redistribution from Rural to Urban as a Result of the Direct Controls on Pakistan's Foreign Trade." *Pakistan Economic Journal*, XIX, No. 1 (1968-69), 72-84.

Cleaver, Harry M., Jr. "The Contradictions of the Green Revolution." *American Economic Review*, LXII, No. 2 (May 1972), 177-186.

Dudley, B.J. "The Military and Development." *Nigerian Journal of Economic and Social Studies*, XIII, No. 2 (July 1971), 161-77.

Dudley, B.J. "The Politics of Abedo." *Quarterly Journal of Administration*, VI, No. 3 (January 1972), 131-70.

Eckstein, Harry. "On the Etiology of Internal War." *History and Theory*, IV, No. 2 (1965), 133-63.

Eke, Ifagun I.U. "Population of Nigeria, 1952-65." *Nigerian Journal of Economic and Social Studies*, VIII, No. 3 (November 1968), 289-309.

Essack, A.K. "Nigeria at the Crossroads." *Economic and Political Weekly*, VI, No. 11 (13 March 1971), 612-13.

Friedland, William F. "Paradoxes of African Trade Unionism: Organizational Chaos and Political Potential." *Africa Report*, X, No. 6 (June 1965), 6-13.

Galtung, Johan. "A Structural Theory of Imperialism." *Journal of Peace Research*, VIII, No. 2 (1971), 81-118.

Green, Reginald H. "Four African Development Plans: Ghana, Kenya, Nigeria, and Tanzania." *Journal of Modern African Studies*. III, No. 2 (August 1965), 253-74.

Griffin, Keith. "Financing Development Plans in Pakistan." *Pakistan Development Review*, V, No. 4 (Winter 1965), 601-30.

Gurr, Ted Robert. "A Causal Model of Civil Strife: A Comparative Analysis Using New Indices." *American Political Science Review*, LXII (December 1968), 1104-24.

Gurr, Ted Robert. "Psychological Factors in Civil Strife." *World*

Politics, XX (January 1968), 245-78.

Gurr, Ted Robert, and Duvall, Raymond. "Civil Conflict in the 1960s: A Reciprocal Theoretical System with Parameter Estimates." *Comparative Political Studies*, VI, No. 2 (July 1973), 135-69.

Hakam, A.N. "The Motivation to Invest and the Locational Pattern of Foreign Private Industrial Investments in Nigeria." *Nigerian Journal of Economic and Social Studies*, VIII, No. 7 (March 1966), 49-65.

Hamid, Naved. "A Critical Appraisal of Foreign Aid Strategy." *Punjab University Economist*, VIII, No. 2 (December 1970), 132-46.

Hill, Polly. "The Myth of the Amorphous Peasantry: A Northern Nigerian Case Study." *Nigerian Journal of Economic and Social Studies*, XIII, No. 1 (March 1971), 239-60.

Hymer, Steven. "The Efficiency (Contraditions) of Multinational Corporations." *American Economic Review*, LX, No. 2 (May 1970), 441-8.

Ijomah, B.I.C. "The Social Characteristics of Nigeria's Political Leaders Before Independence." *Conch*, V, Nos. 1 & 2 (1973), 105-28.

Ikime, Obaro. "Colonial Conquest and Resistance in Southern Nigeria." *Journal of the Historical Society of Nigeria*, VI, No. 3 (December 1972), 251-70.

Joseph, Richard A. "The Ethnic Trap: Notes on the Nigerian Campaign and Elections, 1978-79." *Issue*, XI, Nos. 1 & 2 (Spring/Summer 1981), 17-21.

Kilby, Peter. "Technical Education in Nigeria." *Bulletin of the Oxford University Institute of Economics and Statistics*, XXVI, No. 2 (May 1964), 181-9.

Kuznets, Simon S. "Levels and Variability of Growth Rates." *Economic Development and Cultural Change*, V, No. 1 (October 1956), 5-94.

Langley, Kathleen M. "Financing Development in Nigeria: An Appraisal." In *South of the Sahara: Development in African Economics*, edited by Sayre P. Schatz. Philadelphia: Temple University Press, 1972.

Lewis, Roy. "Britain and Biafra: Commonwealth Civil War." *Round Table: The Commonwealth Quarterly* (July 1970), pp. 241-8.

Lindsay, Kennedy. "How Biafra Pays for the War." *Venture*, XXI, No. 3 (March 1969), 26-8.

Mabogunje, A.L. "Inter-regional Trade and National Integration in Nigeria." *Journal of Business and Social Studies*, III, No. 1 (December 1970), 98-111.

MacEwan, Arthur. "Contradictions in Capitalist Development: The Case of Pakistan." *Review of Radical Political Economics*, III, No. 1 (Spring 1971), 40-57.

Madujibeya, S.A. "Oil and Nigeria's Economic Development." *African Affairs*, LXX (July 1976), 284-316.

Maniruzzaman, Talukder. "Group Interests in Pakistani Politics, 1947-1958." *Pacific Affairs*, XXXIX, Nos. 1 & 2 (Spring/Summer 1966), 83-98.

May, Ranald S. "Direct Overseas Investment in Nigeria, 1953-63: Some Aspects of its Constitution and Contribution to Nigeria's

Economic Development." *Scottish Journal of Political Economy*, XII (November 1965), 243-66.

Mazrui, Ali M. "Black Africa and the Arabs." *Foreign Affairs*, LIII (July 1975), 725-42.

Melson, Robert, and Wolpe, Howard. "Modernization and the Politics of Communalism: A Theoretical Perspective." *American Political Science Review*, LXIV, No. 4 (December 1970), 1112-30.

Mohammed, Murtala. "Nigeria: The Voice of the New Government." *Africa Report*, XX, No. 5 (September/October 1975), 12-13.

Müller, Ronald. "The Multinational Corporation and the Underdevelopment of the Third World." In *The Political Economy of Development and Underdevelopment*, edited by Charles K. Wilber. New York: Random House, 1973.

Murray, David J. "Nigeria: The Experience of Military Rule." *Current History*, LXVIII (May 1975), 216-30.

Nafziger, E. Wayne. "A Critique of Development Economics in the U.S." *Journal of Development Studies*, XIII, No. 1 (October 1976), 18-34.

Nafziger, E. Wayne. "The Economic Impact of the Nigerian Civil War." *Journal of Modern African Studies*, X, No. 2 (1972), 223-45.

Nafziger, E. Wayne. "Inter-regional Economic Relations in the Nigerian Footwear Industry." *Journal of Modern African Studies*, VI, No. 4 (1968), 531-42.

Nafziger, E. Wayne. "The Political Economy of Disintegration in Nigeria." *Journal of Modern African Studies*, XI, No. 4 (1973), 505-36.

Nafziger, E. Wayne, and Richter, William L. "Biafra and Bangladesh: The Political Economy of Secessionist Conflict." *Journal of Peace Research*, VIII, No. 2 (1976), 91-109.

Nardin, Terry. "Violence and the State: A Critique of Empirical Political Theory." Sage Professional Papers in Comparative Politics Series Number 01-020. Beverly Hills, Calif.: Sage Publications, 1971.

Obasanjo, Olusegun. "External Intervention in Africa: The View from Africa." *Survival*, XX, No. 6 (November/December 1978), 268-9.

Obichere, Boniface I. "Military Dependence in Historical Perspective: The Case of Nigeria." *Conch*, V, Nos. 1 & 2 (1973), 82-104.

O'Brien, Donal Cruise. "Modernization, Order, and the Erosion of a Democratic Ideal: American Political Science, 1960-1970." *Journal of Development Studies*, VIII, No. 4 (July 1972), 351-78.

O'Connell, James. "The Political Class and Economic Growth." *Nigerian Journal of Economic and Social Studies*, VIII, No. 1 (March 1966), 129-40.

O'Connell, James. "Political Integration: The Nigerian Case." In *African Integration and Disintegration: Case Studies in Economic and Political Integration*, edited by Arthur Hazlewood. London: Oxford University Press, 1967.

Ojedokun, Olasupo. "The Changing Pattern of Nigeria's International Economic Relations: The Decline of the Colonial Nexus."

Journal of Developing Areas, VI (July 1972), 535-54.

Ojo, Olatunde J.B. "Nigerian-Soviet Relations: Retrospect and Prospect." *African Studies Review*, XIX, No. 3 (December 1976), 43-63.

Oni, Ola. "Development and Features of the Nigerian Financial System--A Marxist Approach." *Nigerian Journal of Economic and Social Studies*, VIII, No. 3 (November 1966), 383-402.

Onitiri, H.M.A. "Nigeria's International Economic Relations: A Survey." *Nigerian Journal of Economic and Social Sciences*, III, No. 3 (November 1961), 13-38.

Otobo, Dafe. "The Nigerian General Strike of 1981." *Review of African Political Economy* (October-December 1981), pp. 65-81.

Ottenberg, Phoebe. "The Afikpo Ibo of Eastern Nigeria." In *Peoples of Africa*, edited by James L. Gibbs, Jr. New York: Holt, Rinehart and Winston, 1965.

Ottenberg, Simon. "Ibo Receptivity to Change." In *Continuity and Change in African Cultures*, edited by W.R. Bascom and M.J. Herskovits. Chicago: University of Chicago Press, 1958.

Oyemakinde, Wale. "The Nigerian General Strike of 1964." *Genève-Afrique*, XIII (1974), 53-71.

Packard, Philip C. "A Note on Concentration and Profit Rates within the Manufacturing Sector, 1963 and 1965." *Nigerian Journal of Economic and Social Studies*, XI, No. 3 (November 1969), 379-95.

Panter-Brick, S. Keith. "The Right to Self-Determination: Its Application to Nigeria." *International Affairs*, XLIV, No. 2 (1968), 254-66.

Papanek, Gustav F. "The Development of Entrepreneurship." *American Economic Review*, LII, No. 2 (May 1962), 46-58.

Patel, Surendra J. "The Economic Distance Between Nations: Its Origins, Measurement and Outlook." *Economic Journal*, LIV (March 1964), 122-9.

Pearson, Scott R. "Nigerian Petroleum: Implications for Medium-term Planning." In *Growth and Development of the Nigerian Economy*, edited by Carl K. Eicher and Carl Leidholm. East Lansing, Mich.: Michigan State University Press, 1970.

Penrose, Edith. "Africa and the Oil Revolution: An Introduction." *African Affairs*, LXXV (July 1976), 277-83.

Phillips, Adedotun O. "The Economic Implication." *Quarterly Journal of Administration*, VI, No. 2 (January 1972), 101-29.

Phillips, Adedotun O. "Revenue Allocation in Nigeria, 1970-80." *Nigerian Journal of Economic and Social Studies*, XVII, No. 2 (July 1975), 1-28.

Schatz, Sayre P. "Nigeria's First National Development Plan (1962-68): An Appraisal." *Nigerian Journal of Economic and Social Studies*, V, No. 2 (July 1963), 221-35.

Schatz, Sayre P. "Nigeria's Petro-political Fluctuations." *Issue*, XI, Nos. 1 & 2 (Spring/Summer 1981), 35-40.

Schwarz, Walter. "Foreign Powers and the Nigerian War." *Africa Report*, XV, No. 2 (February 1970), 12-14.

Sklar, Richard L. "Democracy for the Second Republic." *Issue*, XI, Nos. 1 & 2 (Spring/Summer 1981), 14-16.

Sklar, Richard L. "Nigerian Politics: The Ordeal of Chief Awolowo, 1960-65." In *Politics in Africa: Seven Cases*, edited by Gwendolen M. Carter. New York: Harcourt, Brace & World, 1966.

Stauffer, Robert B. "The Political Economy of a Coup: Transnational Linkages and Philippine Political Response." *Journal of Peace Research*, XI, No. 3 (1974), 161-77.

Stolper, Wolfgang F. "The Main Features of the 1962-68 National Plan." *Nigerian Journal of Economic and Social Studies*, IV, No. 2 (July 1962), 85-91.

Stremlau, John S. "The Fundamentals of Nigerian Foreign Policy." *Issue*, XI, Nos. 1 & 2 (Spring/Summer 1981), 46-50.

Teriba, O. and Phillips, Adedotun O. "Income Distribution and National Integration." *Nigerian Journal of Economic and Social Studies*, XIII, No. 1 (March 1971), 77-122.

Turner, Terisa. "The Transfer of Oil Technology and the Nigerian State." *Development and Change*, VII, No. 4 (October 1976), 353-90.

Ugoh, S.U. "Presidential Address." *Nigerian Journal of Economic and Social Studies*, XIII, No. 1 (March 1971), 3-12.

Ukpong, I.I. "Economic Recovery in the Eastern States of Nigeria." *Issue*, V, No. 1 (Spring 1975), 45-53.

Usoro, Eno J. "Foreign Oil Companies and Recent Nigerian Petroleum Oil Policies." *Nigerian Journal of Economic and Social Studies*, XIV, No.3 (November 1972), 301-14.

Waterman, Peter. "The 'Labour Aristocracy' in Africa: Introduction to a Debate." *Development and Change*, VI, No. 3 (July 1975), 57-73.

Weeks, John F. "The Impact of Economic Conditions and Institutional Forces on Urban Wages in Nigeria." *Nigerian Journal of Economic and Social Studies*, XIII, No. 1 (November 1971), 327-39.

Whitaker, C.S., Jr. "Second Beginnings: The New Political Framework." *Issue*, XI, Nos. 1 & 2 (Spring/Summer 1981), 2-13.

Williams, Gavin. "Political Consciousness Among the Ibadan Poor." In *Sociology and Development*, edited by Emmanuel de Kadt and Gavin Williams (London: Tavistock, 1974).

Williams, Gavin, and Turner, Terisa. "Nigeria." In *West African States: Promise and Reality*, edited by John Dunn. London: Cambridge University Press, 1978.

Zolberg, Aristide R. "The Structure of Political Conflict in the New States of Tropical Africa." *American Political Science Review*, LXXIII, No. 1 (March 1968), 70-87.

Zukerman, Morris E. "Nigerian Crisis: Economic Impact on the North." *Journal of Modern African Studies*, VIII, No. 1 (April 1970), 37-54.

OFFICIAL PUBLICATIONS AND DOCUMENTS (except for periodicals)

Central Bank of Nigeria. *Nigeria's Principal Economic and Financial Indicators, 1970-78*. Lagos, 1979.

Nigeria. *Report of the Coker Commission of Inquiry into the Affairs of Certain Statutory Corporations in Western Nigeria, 1962*. 4 vols. Lagos, 1962.

Nigeria. Cabinet Office. *Government Views on the Report of the Commission of Inquiry into the Nigerian Universities Crisis,*

1978. Lagos, 24 August 1978.
Nigeria. Ministry of Economic Development. *National Development Plan, 1962-68*. Lagos, n.d.
Nigeria. Ministry of Economic Development. *National Development Plan: Progress Report, 1964*. Lagos, 1965.
Nigeria. Ministry of Economic Development. *Third National Development Plan, 1975-80*. 2 vols. Lagos, 1975.
Nigeria. Ministry of Economic Development and Reconstruction. *Second National Development Plan, 1970-74: Second Progress Report*. Lagos, 1974.
Nigeria. Ministry of Information. *Background Notes on the Nigerian Crisis*. Lagos, 1967.
Nigeria. Ministry of Information. *First Report on the Anti-Inflation Task Force*. (Onitiri Report). Lagos, October 1975.
Nigeria. Ministry of Information. *Report of the Commission on the Review of Wages, Salary and Conditions of Service of the Junior Employees of the Federation and in Private Establishments, 1963-64*. Lagos, 1964.
Nigeria. Ministry of Information. *Second National Development Plan, 1970-74*. Lagos, 1971.
Nigeria. Ministry of Information. *Second National Development Plan, 1970-74: Programme of Post-War Reconstruction and Development*. Lagos, 1970.
Nigeria. Office of Statistics. *Gross Domestic Product of Nigeria, 1958/59 - 1966/67*. Lagos, 1968.
Nigeria. Office of Statistics. *Industrial Survey of Nigeria, 1964 and 1965*. Lagos, 1968.
Nigeria. Office of Statistics. *Population Census of Nigeria, 1952-53*. Lagos, 1956.
Nigeria. Office of Statistics. *Population Census of Nigeria, 1963*. 3 vols. Lagos, 1968.
Pakistan. *Report of the Land Reforms Commission, 1960*. Islamabad, 1960.
Western State of Nigeria. *Report of the Commission of Inquiry into the Civil Disturbances which occurred in certain parts of the Western State of Nigeria in the Month of December 1968, and other matters incidental thereto or connected therewith*. (Ayoola Commission Report). Ibadan, 31 March 1969.

UNPUBLISHED SOURCES

Africa Research Group. "The Other Side of Nigeria's Civil War: A Class Based Probe into the War's Origins and Implication." Cambridge, Mass., April 1970.
Byerlee, Derek. "Indirect Employment and Income Distribution Effects of Agricultural Development Strategies: A Simulation Approach Applied to Nigeria." African Rural Employment Paper No. 9, Michigan State University, East Lansing, Mich., 1973.
Cohen, Robin. "'A Greater South': or What Might Have Happened in the Nigerian Civil War." Faculty of Commerce and Social Science, University of Birmingham, Occasional Paper No. 22, February 1971.
Comité International de la Croix-Rouge. "Food and Agricultural

Situation in Biafra." Mimeographed. Geneva, 1969.
Dennis, Gregory M. "Nigeria: Mohammed-Obasanjo Administration, 1975-1978." M. Sc. Essay, London School of Economics, 1978.
Eke, I.I.U. "Unemployment in Nigeria: A Study of the Strategy of Development for Nigeria." Economic Development Institute, University of Nigeria, Enugu, 1967.
Harris, John R. "Industrial Entrepreneurship in Nigeria." Ph.D. dissertation, Northwestern University, 1967.
Melson, Robert. "Marxists in the Nigerian Labor Movement." Ph.D. dissertation, Massachusetts Institute of Technology, 1967.
Nigerian Institute of Social and Economic Research. "Nigeria: Population Models for National Regional Planning, 1952-67." University of Ibadan, Ibadan, March 1969.
Norman, David W.; Pryor, David H.; and Gibbs, Christopher J.N. "Technical Change and the Small Farmer in Hausaland, Northern Nigeria." African Rural Employment Paper No. 19, Michigan State University, East Lansing, Mich., 1979.
Omorogiuwa, P. Ada. "Personal Income Taxation and Income Distribution in Nigeria." Paper presented to a Conference on Income Distribution in Nigeria, University of Lagos, January/February 1979.
Proceedings of the Conference on Problems of Integration and Disintegration in Nigeria. Northwestern University, Evanston, Ill., 31 March - 2 April 1967.
Rimmer, Douglas. "Wage Politics." Faculty of Commerce and Social Science, University of Birmingham, Occasional Paper No. 12, February 1970.
Rupley, Lawrence A. "Nigeria's 1979-80 Budget and the 1975-79 Import Boom." Department of Economics, University of Nairobi, Kenya, 1980.
Rupley, Lawrence A. "A Survey of the Nigerian Fiscal System." Ahmadu Bello University, Zaria, April 1976.
Rural Economy Research Unit. "Farm Income Levels in the Northern States of Nigeria." Samaru Miscellaneous Paper, Institute for Agricultural Research, Ahmadu Bello University, Zaria, 1972.
Sada, P.O. "Urbanization and Income Distribution in Nigeria." Paper presented to a Conference on Income Distribution in Nigeria, University of Lagos, January/February 1979.
Smith, J.H. "The Impact of the Creation of States upon the Public Service of Northern Nigeria." Rhodes House, Oxford, ca. 1969.
Turner, Terisa. "Government and Oil in Nigeria: A Study of the Making and Implementation of Petroleum Policy." Ph.D. dissertation, University of London, 1977.
Vielrose, Egon. "Distribution of Income in Nigeria." Nigerian Institute for Social and Economic Research, University of Ibadan, Ibadan, 1975.
Wright, Theodore P. "Indian Muslim Muhajirin in the Politics of Pakistan." Paper presented to the Annual Meeting of the American Political Science Association, New Orleans, 1973.

NEWSPAPERS AND PERIODICALS

African Development.
Central Bank of Nigeria. *Annual Reports and Statements*. Lagos.

Central Bank of Nigeria. *Economic and Financial Review.*
Central Bank of Nigeria. *Monthly Report.*
Daily Times (Lagos).
Financial Times.
New Nigerian.
Nigeria, Office of Statistics. *Annual Abstract of Statistics: Nigeria.* Lagos.
Nigeria, Office of Statistics. *Digest of Statistics.* Lagos.
Nigeria. Office of Statistics. *Economic and Statistical Review.* Lagos (annual).
Pakistan, Ministry of Finance. *Pakistan Economic Survey.* Islamabad (annual).
Standard Chartered Review.
Petroleum Economist (formerly *Petroleum Press Service*).
The Times.
West Africa.
West African Pilot.

Index